London Politics, 1760–1914

Also by Matthew Cragoe

CULTURE, POLITICS AND NATIONAL IDENTITY IN WALES, 1832–1886

AN ANGLICAN ARISTOCRACY: The Moral Economy of the Crowd in Carmarthenshire, 1832–95

ANTICLERICALISM (*co-edited with Nigel Aston*)

Also by Antony Taylor

LORDS OF MISRULE: Hostility to Aristocracy in Late Nineteenth- and Early Twentieth-century Britain

DOWN WITH THE CROWN: British Anti-Monarchism and Debates about Royalty since 1790

London Politics, 1760–1914

Edited by

Matthew Cragoe
Professor of Modern British History
University of Hertfordshire

and

Antony Taylor
Senior Lecturer in History
Sheffield Hallam University

Editorial matter, selection, introduction and conclusion
© Matthew Cragoe and Antony Taylor 2005
All remaining chapters © Respective authors 2005

All rights reserved. No reproduction, copy or transmission of this publication may be made without written permission.

No paragraph of this publication may be reproduced, copied or transmitted save with written permission or in accordance with the provisions of the Copyright, Designs and Patents Act 1988, or under the terms of any licence permitting limited copying issued by the Copyright Licensing Agency, 90 Tottenham Court Road, London W1T 4LP.

Any person who does any unauthorised act in relation to this publication may be liable to criminal prosecution and civil claims for damages.

The authors have asserted their rights to be identified as the authors of this work in accordance with the Copyright, Designs and Patents Act 1988.

First published in 2005 by
PALGRAVE MACMILLAN
Houndmills, Basingstoke, Hampshire RG21 6XS and
175 Fifth Avenue, New York, N.Y. 10010
Companies and representatives throughout the world.

PALGRAVE MACMILLAN is the global academic imprint of the Palgrave Macmillan division of St. Martin's Press, LLC and of Palgrave Macmillan Ltd. Macmillan® is a registered trademark in the United States, United Kingdom and other countries. Palgrave is a registered trademark in the European Union and other countries.

ISBN 13: 978–1–4039–9000–6 hardback
ISBN 10: 1–4039–9000–X   hardback

This book is printed on paper suitable for recycling and made from fully managed and sustained forest sources.

A catalogue record for this book is available from the British Library.

Library of Congress Cataloging-in-Publication Data

   London Politics, 1760–1914 / edited by Matthew Cragoe and Antony Taylor.
     p. cm.
   Includes bibliographical references and index.
   ISBN 1–4039–9000–X (cloth)
    1. London (England) – Politics and government. 2. London (England) – History – 18th century. 3. London (England) – History – 1800–1950.
   I. Cragoe, Matthew. II. Taylor, Antony.
DA683.L85 2005
320.9421′09′034—dc22   2005049203

10 9 8 7 6 5 4 3 2 1
14 13 12 11 10 09 08 07 06 05

Printed and bound in Great Britain by
Antony Rowe Ltd, Chippenham and Eastbourne

In memory of Cissie Mendik 1916–2004

Contents

List of Illustrations   ix
List of Abbreviations   x
Acknowledgements   xi
List of Contributors   xii

Introduction   1
Matthew Cragoe and Antony Taylor

1   Metropolitan 'Radicalism' and
Electoral Independence, 1760–1820   18
Matthew McCormack

2   'Policing the Peelers': Parliament, the Public,
and the Metropolitan Police, 1829–33   38
David A. Campion

3   Metropolitan Whiggery, 1832–55   57
Ben Weinstein

4   Post-Chartism: Metropolitan Perspectives on the
Chartist Movement in Decline 1848–80   75
Antony Taylor

5   Secularism in the City: Geographies of Dissidence and
the Importance of Radical Culture in the Metropolis   97
David Nash

6   Transcending the Metropolis: London and
Provincial Popular Radicalism, c.1860–75   121
Detlev Mares

7   From 'First Constituency of the Empire' to
'Citadel of Reaction': Westminster, 1800–90   144
Marc Baer

8   Late Victorian and Edwardian 'Slum Conservatism':
How Different were the Politics of the London Poor?   166
Marc Brodie

9	'In Darkest Lambeth': Henry Morton Stanley and the Imperial Politics of London Unionism *Alex Windscheffel*	191
10	London-over-the-border: Politics in Suburban Walthamstow, 1870–1914 *Timothy Cooper*	211

Conclusion 233
Matthew Cragoe and Antony Taylor

Index 243

List of Illustrations

Table

8.1 Turnout at Westminster elections between the First and Third Reform Acts   155

Figures

1. Rioters in the Strand during the West End Riots of 1886
2. 'The Mob' in the 1880s
3. 'A Struggle for Liberty': Anarchists arrested in a scuffle at the *Club Autonomie* in 1894
4. Metropolitan Police raid on the *Club Autonomie* Anarchist Society in 1894
5. Wat Tyler killing the King's poll tax inspector in 1381 (1860s)
6. 'The Reformer' speaking in Regent's Park in the 1900s
7. The aftermath of looting during the West End Riots of 1886
8. Ducking of an unpopular speaker
9. Popular disputation at a public meeting in Holborn Town Hall during the General election of 1880
10. James Gillray's depiction of the candidates at the Westminster by-election of December 1806
11. The Hustings at Covent Garden during the Westminster election of 1865

List of Abbreviations

ACLL	Anti-Corn Law League
HLA	Health of London Association
HOTA	Health of Towns Association
IWMA	International Working Men's Association
LRL	Labour Representation League
LTRA	Land Tenure Reform Association
LWWMCA	London and Westminster Working Men's Constitutional Association
MC	*Morning Chronicle*
MSA	Metropolitan Sanitary Association
NCA	National Charter Association
NRB	National Republican Brotherhood
NSS	National Secular Society
NUWC	National Union of the Working Classes
UDC	Urban District Council
WCA	Westminster Conservative Association

Acknowledgements

This volume of essays had its origin in a conference organised at the Institute of Historical Research, London, in association with the Centre for Metropolitan History. The editors wish to begin by recording their appreciation of the efforts made by the Director, Dr Matthew Davies, and Olwen Myhill to ensure that the event was such a success.

Next, we wish to register a sincere vote of thanks to all the contributors whose essays appear in this volume. Not only did each and every one turn their essays into chapters with impressive speed, despite heavy teaching loads and many other commitments, but the level of enduring enthusiasm and support has made the project a real pleasure to be involved with from start to finish.

Colleagues at our respective institutions have contributed in various ways. At Sheffield Hallam University, thanks are due to Peter Cain, Frances Dann, Steve Earnshaw and Mary Peace for their contributions to the jointly-taught course, 'London: Literary and Historical Perspectives 1728–1914', and to the stimulating students who have taken it; many of the perspectives which inform this book originated there. Many thanks to Fergus Wilde of Chetham's Library, too, for help with the illustrations. At the University of Hertfordshire, Professor Tim Hitchcock has generously shared his boundless knowledge of, and enthusiasm for, London history, at every turn.

Finally, and closest to home, we wish to thank our respective partners, Carol and Marsha, for their love and support throughout the project.

Matthew Cragoe
Antony Taylor

List of Contributors

Marc Baer is Professor of History at Hope College, Michigan. He is the author of *Theatre and Disorder in Late Georgian London* (Oxford, 1992), and is completing a book which will be titled *Workshop of Democracy: The Rise and Fall of Radical Westminster, 1780–1890*.

Marc Brodie is Lecturer in History at Monash University. His monograph, *The Politics of the Poor: the East End of London, 1885–1914*, was published by Oxford University Press in 2004.

David Campion is Assistant Professor of History at Lewis & Clark College, Portland, Oregon. He is currently working on a book about policing and public order in colonial North India.

Timothy Cooper completed his thesis on politics in Victorian and Edwardian suburbia at Cambridge University in 2005. He is currently working on the impact of suburbanisation and consumerism on the development of twentieth-century 'waste culture' at the Centre for Environmental History at St Andrew's University.

Matthew Cragoe is Professor of Modern British History at the University of Hertfordshire. He has published widely on the history of nineteenth-century politics, including, most recently, *Culture, Politics and National Identity in Wales, 1832–1886* (Oxford, 2004).

Detlev Mares lectures at the Institute of History at the Darmstadt University of Technology. He has written widely on the history of nineteenth-century British radicalism, and is the author of *Auf der Suche nach dem 'wahren' Liberalismus. Demokratische Bewegung und Liberale Politik im Viktorianischen England* (Berlin, 2002).

Matthew McCormack is Lecturer in History at University College Northampton. His publications include an article in the *British Journal for Eighteenth-Century Studies* and his book, *The Independent Man: Citizenship and Gender Politics in Georgian England* (Manchester University Press, 2005).

David Nash is Reader in History at Oxford Brookes University. He has published widely on aspects of radicalism, the secular movement, the history of blasphemy and on the history of republicanism in

England. He is currently completing 'Blasphemy in the West' for Oxford University Press.

Antony Taylor is Senior Lecturer in History at Sheffield Hallam University. He has written and published widely on the history of mid-Victorian radicalism. His latest book, *Lords of Misrule: Hostility to Aristocracy in Late Nineteenth- and Early Twentieth-Century Britain* was published in 2004 by Palgrave.

Ben Weinstein is completing a PhD on the political culture of early Victorian London at Magdalene College, Cambridge. He hopes shortly to begin a research project on the life and work of Joshua Toulmin Smith.

Alex Windscheffel lectures in Modern British History at Royal Holloway College, University of London. This chapter builds upon his forthcoming book, *Villa Toryism: The Making of London Conservatism, 1868–1900*, which will be published in 2006.

Introduction
Matthew Cragoe and Antony Taylor

In the last ten years, the history of Victorian London has undergone a renaissance. A generation of scholars has been irresistibly drawn to the underbelly of England's great, sprawling capital, and brought a flood of illumination to bear on previously unexplored areas of the city's inner life. Sharing a common insistence that London is intelligible only in terms of new cultural readings of space and geography,[1] they offer a picture of the capital focused on its role as a centre of consumption. A giant and insatiable consumer of people as well as goods,[2] nineteenth-century London now stands before its public as the 'City of Dreadful Delight', repellent yet irresistible. Other, less glamorous, areas of historical enquiry, however, have fared less well. While certain themes have found their chroniclers, notably local government, transport and sanitation reform,[3] the political life of nineteenth-century London remains understudied. Though it was home to both parliament and the crown, and centre of a worldwide empire, yet we know very little about the political history of the capital in the nineteenth century.[4] The primary aim of this collection is to offer an initial assessment to this missing dimension of metropolitan history.

The volume also has another purpose, however. If there is a 'politics-shaped' hole in the history of London, there is also a London-shaped hole in the history of nineteenth-century politics. A second aim of the collection is to call attention to its existence – if not actually to fill it. Explaining the omission is difficult, but must stem in part from the sheer size of the capital, a factor which may have deterred historians from tackling its political structures and organisation. London may, in effect, fall between two schools: far too large for social and economic historians to explore in its entirety, it simultaneously defies explanation of the type provided by the local or area-based monographs that have revolutionised our understanding of politics in the towns of the North and the Midlands.[5] To these practical problems, however, we might add an ideological factor. Another, more fundamental, reason for the neglect of London's politics stems from the preoccupation of historians with change rather than continuity. Whilst London was the undisputed epicentre of the British political world in the period before 1800, the torch of progress passed away from the capital in the early nineteenth century. It was in the great shock towns of the industrial revolution – Manchester, Leeds, Birmingham – that nineteenth-century political history was forged, and here, consequently, that 'change' occurred.[6] The topics of greatest interest to modern historians can be analysed here in great detail: the rise of 'class', the urban challenge to the privileged rule of the aristocracy – symbolised in the great cause of Free Trade – and the Anglican Church – symbolised in the campaigns of dissenters for full civil equality. London, by contrast, possessed an old-fashioned economy, lacked much in the way of religious enthusiasm and was frankly indifferent to free trade. It is arguable that the principal reason for the neglect of London's political history, therefore, is that it simply does not fit the dominant historiographical template historians wish to impose on the Victorian period. It can be safely ignored.

The result, however, is that many of the assumptions and ideas underpinning our notion of nineteenth-century British politics have been constructed around studies with a comparatively narrow, local focus, rooted in the familiar territory of Lancashire and the West Riding of Yorkshire.[7] It is perhaps time historians asked how far the political experience of towns in which the local environment was coloured by the 'single-industry' concerns that entrenched the power of employer paternalism and monolithic trades unionism in cotton and wool, really represent the totality of British political experience in the Victorian era.

The chapters in this book, therefore, aim to challenge existing conceptions of national political culture as well as to open up fresh perspectives on the political history of the capital. We hope to reverse the prevailing historiographical trend which has relegated the politics of London to the margins and rendered the capital curiously 'weightless' in comparison with both British provincial centres and other major capital cities like New York.[8] In the remainder of this introduction, the context for political activity in nineteenth-century London is laid out, and the individual contributions introduced.

London politics 1760–1914

During the Civil War, Clarendon christened London the 'sink of all the ill-humours of the kingdom'.[9] It was a fair description for a town that was always associated with a strain of ungovernable popular politics. In 1642 Puritans expelled Charles I from the town, and in 1681 there were Whig-orchestrated attempts to exclude James II from the succession. Opposition to the state and unjust governmental exactions were also endemic. During the excise crisis in 1733 there were riots in London against excise duties on wine and tobacco, and further outbreaks against, respectively, restrictions on gin in 1743, the extension of religious toleration to the Jewish community in 1753, the fall of Minorca in 1756, and Catholic Emancipation in 1780. No less a figure than Junius recorded in the 1770s that 'The noble spirit of the metropolis is the life-blood of the nation collected at the heart'.[10] For some, the mob was its expression (see Figure 2).

The tradition of popular crowd activity spilled over easily into the world of parliamentary electoral politics.[11] Yet at the start of the period covered by this volume, London's political life worked within a remarkably circumscribed arena. Just ten MPs were returned to represent the one million people who already thronged the metropolis by 1800. Eight were returned by the three Metropolitan boroughs, the City of London claiming four, Westminster and Southwark two each. If the number of seats was comparatively small, the size of the metropolitan electorates was large. The right of voting in the City was vested in its liverymen (freemen attached to the City companies and thus entitled to vote), and the electorate here was estimated at between 8000 and 10,000 in 1818; had the right been vested in the freemen at large the total might have been ten times as great.[12] As it was, Westminster, with some 12,000 voters qualified by payment of scot and lot (in effect, rate-payers), was the largest borough in Britain, and its elections, as Roland Thorne has written, were 'the most observed' of all.[13] Southwark, by contrast, was relatively small, its electorate amounting to only 2000 or 3000 in the early nineteenth century, again qualifying through payment of scot and lot. Londoners' interests were also represented in parliament by the two county members for Middlesex. The Ossulton Hundred of Middlesex hugged the northern bank of the Thames as far east as Mile End, and, as a consequence, both Westminster and the City fell within its bounds. As Sir Robert Peel remarked during the debates on the Reform Bill in 1831, both MPs for Middlesex were 'returned under town influence'.[14] Once again, the county's electorate was large, numbering 6000 men qualified by possession of a freehold worth £40/- per annum in the period before the Great Reform Act.[15]

The sheer size of the electorates in the Metropolitan constituencies rendered them immune from the influences – either aristocratic or governmental – that shaped contests elsewhere in the country.[16] As a consequence, their elections could be interpreted as registering the free voice of the people, and as having a significance that registered far beyond the boundaries of the capital.[17] The City was kept in a state of 'quasi-permanent opposition to the government of the day' for much of the eighteenth century, according to David Kynaston; its radical electorate, composed largely of smaller merchants, shopkeepers and artisans, ensured the City remained an important platform for dissident voices even after the government's repressive legislation of the 1790s.[18] The key popular constituencies, however, were Westminster and Middlesex. These seats, free from the influence of the City's great financial interests, were frequently contested and returned men who possessed the status of so many popular tribunes.

Heading the roll call of famous radicals who occupied these seats was Charles James Fox, whose triumph at the Westminster election of 1784 is best remembered for the Duchess of Devonshire trading kisses for Foxite votes. There was a perpetual undertow of drama to contests in these constituencies, and in Chapter 1, Matthew McCormack considers the cases of two popular heroes who ranked only slightly below Fox in the pantheon of radical greatness: John Wilkes and Sir Francis Burdett. Wilkes and Burdett have both been acclaimed archetypes of the capital's great 'radical tradition'. McCormack, however, questions what he sees as an artificial historiographical consensus concerning the unproblematic unity of 'London Radicalism' in the Georgian period. 'It was', he writes, 'socially and intellectually diverse, employed a range of methods and milieux, and comprehended a wide variety of rival groups and individuals over an unwieldy geographical area.' He uses the electoral careers of Wilkes (in Middlesex) and Burdett (Middlesex and Westminster) to highlight the notion that much we now accept as rather immature manifestations of an essentially nineteenth-century 'radicalism' might more profitably be seen as classic examples of eighteenth-century electoral independence. And if this is so, he argues, it becomes debatable whether the idea of 'London Radicalism', so well-established in the literature, is really supportable at all.

Independent, Radical or Whig, London's MPs were strongly supportive of the measures of parliamentary reform introduced by the Whig government of Earl Grey in 1831. The Whigs' measure aimed to double the number of MPs from the under-represented Metropolis, a proposal strongly opposed by the Tories. Sir Robert Peel argued that 'the ancient usage of England' did not recognise any argument in relation to population: parliament represented interests that had a stake in the country and required protection, not raw numbers. London, he contended, already had eight defenders of its own, plus two from Middlesex and possibly one from the county of Surrey. In addition, he argued, the interests of London were *virtually* represented by the enormous number of MPs who resided in the capital and could thus be relied upon to take an interest in its affairs. Upwards of 100 MPs lived in the government's proposed new Marylebone constituency alone! No, said Peel, 'unless some special case were made out for the metropolitan district', additional members could not be justified. Others agreed. Stout allies such as Thomas Wood, MP for Breconshire, suggested that if additional members were to be given in light of the wealth and intelligence of the metropolis, that addition should take the form of additional county representatives for Middlesex – perhaps a new Western Division focused on Brentford and a new Eastern Division with Hackney as its centre. There was also a wider nervousness lest the Metropolis be given an undue influence in the counsels of the nation.[19] Charles Wynn, MP for Montgomeryshire reiterated another argument used by Peel, that 'it was impossible to conceal the fact, that members for such places as these were more under the control of their constituents than members for any other places'. The spokesman of the people, it was perceived, was under the thumb of the people.

In the event, all the arguments mustered by the Tories proved unavailing. The 1832 Reform Act increased the number of Metropolitan Boroughs from 3 to 7, and the number of MPs from 8 to 16.[20] The boundaries of the existing City and Westminster seats were left largely unaltered, but Southwark was extended eastwards to the river. The new constituency swallowed up the parishes of St Mary Magdalen, Bermondsey, and St Mary, Rotherhithe, an adjustment which effectively doubled the number of houses taxed at £10 within the borough. To the three existing seats were added four new, two-member constituencies. In the northwest, the parishes of Marylebone, St Pancras and Paddington, were bundled into the new borough of Marylebone. In the central northern portion, the borough of Finsbury was created, embracing the rapidly growing population of Islington. In the north-east, an enormous new seat emerged. Tower Hamlets incorporated the whole of the Tower Division of the Ossulton Hundred and the Liberty of the Tower, and thus included the largely rural parishes of St John Hackney, St Mary Stratford le Bow and St Leonards Bromley. Finally, south of the river, a fourth new borough was created, Lambeth, which extended all the way down to Streatham, and westwards out to Clapham. With the metropolitan districts of London wrapped up in new boroughs it was not felt necessary to increase the number of MPs representing Middlesex, but the

Act also created a new borough in northern Kent which was effectively metropolitan: Greenwich. Tories stoutly opposed the creation of the seat on the grounds that, since there were extensive Naval Dockyards and munitions factories in Woolwich and Deptford, the government would be able to exercise an undue influence there.[21] Once again, their protests went unheard, and the two-member seat of Greenwich came into being bolstering further the representation of London's interests in parliament.

The limited contribution of London radicals to the agitation for parliamentary reform is well known. Only during the 'days of May' in 1832, when London put apparently decisive pressure on a faltering Government, did the capital's radical tradition manifest itself.[22] One important factor dampening the effectiveness of the capital's radicals may have been the presence of the new police force created by Sir Robert Peel. As David Campion remarks in Chapter 2 of this collection, 'few developments in the history of London managed to narrow the distance between the politics of the street and the politics of Westminster to the same degree as the creation of the Metropolitan Police'. He focuses on the tactics used by the police that led parliament to establish no fewer than three investigative committees in 1833. Campion reveals that during the reform crisis itself, plain-clothes policemen infiltrated the National Union of the Working Classes (NUWC), tactics which, it was complained, 'amounted to a government-sanctioned, ratepayer-supported spy network that deprived law-abiding citizens of their most basic liberties'. In early 1833, meanwhile, the apparently heavy-handed tactics adopted by the police to disperse an outdoor political meeting held by the NUWC at Cold Bath Fields in Clerkenwell, led to fresh complaints. Looking beyond the immediate question of where the blame lay in these incidents, Campion argues that the significance of parliament's inquiries was far-reaching, helping to determine the model that urban policing would follow in London and elsewhere in Britain for the rest of the nineteenth century and into the twentieth century.

Whatever the impact of the police on radicals' ability to demonstrate their support for reform in 1831–32, the passage of the Act did nothing to temper the enthusiasm of Londoners for politicians of more advanced opinions. Miles Taylor has argued that the enduring influence in mid-nineteenth century London politics of four institutions – vestries, Inns of Court, the Common Council and City of London – lent political life in the capital 'a popular and open character' that tended to benefit the reform party.[23] In any event, London remained stony ground for aspiring Conservatives. In no election between 1832 and 1865 were more than four Conservatives returned from the seven Metropolitan Borough seats; in the elections of 1857, 1859 and 1865, there were none. Greenwich and Middlesex both returned a single Conservative MP on two occasions in the period (1835 and 1852 in the case of the former; 1837 and 1841 the latter), but in Marylebone, where the vestry was particularly active, no Tory was elected before 1874.[24] The story of London politics in the period between the first and second Reform Acts, therefore, is properly the history of a complicated coalition of advanced liberal forces. The next three chapters in the volume examine these from a variety of perspectives.

In Chapter 3, Ben Weinstein explores the place of the Whigs within this informal coalition. He sets out to challenge the dominant historiographical perception articulated in Donald Southgate's dictum that 'a connection between the Whig aristocracy and a large popular electorate was not very common'.[25] He argues that, on the contrary, the Whig party had deep roots in the capital, and that the party's experience of London politics played a crucial role in redefining the parameters of Whiggery in the early Victorian period. He highlights the extent to which Lord John Russell's social reform programme was key in building up a body of support among Metropolitan professionals associated with the Health of Towns Association and Metropolitan Sanitary Association. If the establishment of the Metropolitan Board of Works in 1855 represented something of a defeat for Whig ideas in this direction, it should not, Weinstein concludes, obscure the extent to which the political ideology and culture promoted by Russell – himself a member for the City of London – was successful in binding together both Whig parliamentarians and the metropolitan rank and file throughout the age of reform.

Alongside the Whig tradition an enduring plebeian radical tradition, typified by the strong support for Chartism, flourished in the capital. In Chapter 4, Antony Taylor argues that Chartism remained as a motivating ideological loyalty in London long after the movement had collapsed elsewhere, notably in the north. London radicalism, he argues, had always been primarily about the fight for the political freedom that was the cornerstone of the Charter's demands. Even into the 1870s, people proudly proclaimed their loyalty to the Chartist cause, and Taylor suggests there were a series of factors unique to London that influenced this. On the one hand the economic and religiously oriented politics of provincial radicalism did not suit the capital. Not only were many of London's industries of precisely the type that would be damaged by the free trade policies of Manchester radicals, but also there was not the same intensity of religious culture to underpin the moral aspects of the free trade crusade. London was notoriously secular. The consequence was that all major political parties found it very difficult to organise effectively in the capital, at least before the Second Reform Act.[26] Not only did the huge, shifting population represent every registration agent's worst nightmare, but in the absence of strong religious feeling, the parties lacked the key disciplinary focal point which effectively whipped in voters in other parts of the country.[27] All these factors, says Taylor, ensured that London possessed a unique political microclimate within the hothouse of Victorian politics, one in which an apparently old-fashioned plant such as Chartism could flourish.

Another group who found in mid-Victorian London a congenial environment provide the focal point for David Nash in his chapter on freethought and secularism. The freethought and secularist movement – of which Charles Bradlaugh was the most famous product – was viewed by contemporaries as a convivial radical sub-culture devoted to the sovereignty of ideas and characterised by an alternative lifestyle. It was associated with specific localities in the metropolis, and Nash explains that the enduring division between a local model of radical activity and the occasionally more visible national movement (epitomised by the breakthrough of Charles Bradlaugh into mainstream Liberal politics) accounts for the fact that the movement enjoyed only limited success. Yet, he argues, to judge freethought by this yardstick alone is to miss both its enduring contribution to the capital's radical tradition and the implications of the movement for a deeper understanding of mid-Victorian radicalism as a whole. Freethinkers, committed to the rational testing of theories and institutions as they were, provided a call to the serious-minded that resonated throughout the radical culture not only of London but also of the country at large. Radicalism, in short, was always more than 'populism': at its core lay a sober, committed readership attracted by ideas as much as slogans and processions.

The relationship between radicalism in its metropolitan and provincial manifestations is also explored by Detlev Mares in his innovative mapping of the geographies of British radicalism. Like Taylor, he emphasises the unique character of the capital. Nowhere was there such potential for radical activity, such concentrations of people, ideas and print, he argues, and adds that if modern historians have tended to overlook the capital mid-Victorian radicals never did. Provincial movements recognised that to achieve 'national' status it was highly desirable, if not essential, to win over London opinion. The attempt to drive forward any particular movement in harness with London-based organisers seems often to have resulted in a bumpy ride for all concerned. Distance led to delay and misunderstanding, and this was exacerbated by mutual antagonisms that could arise between 'London' and 'Provincial' activists, the former suspected of arrogance, the latter of backwardness. Nevertheless, as Mares concludes, what is important is to recognise that London occupied a crucial position in the mental map of mid-Victorian radicals: the currents of radicalism did not by-pass the metropolis in quite the way its neglect by historians might suggest.

This was certainly the case when parliamentary reform came back onto the agenda in the early 1860s as Mares's account of the co-operation between the Manchester-based Reform Union and the London-based Reform League demonstrates. London was in the van of the movement for reform that culminated in the Second Reform Act (1867) in a way that had not been true in 1832.[28] Not only was it home to the League, founded in 1864, which demanded manhood suffrage and the ballot, but it also housed George Potter's breakaway London Workingmen's Association (founded in1865) which campaigned for a lodger qualification – a vital consideration for London where, as Lord John Russell argued, 'the greater portion of artisans, artists, clerks and professional men live in lodgings and are not householders in the legal sense'.[29] As in 1832, however, London posed problems for the legislators. There was a strong case to be made for increasing its representation in the Commons. As T. Chambers, MP for Marylebone, put it: 'The port of London was the greatest in the kingdom; London was the most important money city in the world; the metropolis was the seat of the Court and of Parliament, and it was incomparably the greatest manufacturing place in the country. For ten manufactories in Leeds, there were 100 in London.'[30] Add the fact that London contained three million people and the grant of extra seats did not seem unreasonable. However, the sheer number of seats that might be created in any system of distribution which accurately reflected the capital's large population alarmed opponents of expansion. The *Times* was not alone in arguing that 'an accession of metropolitan members in proportion to the population of the metropolis would seriously damage the representative character of the House of Commons'.[31] This was all the more worrying as contemporaries continued to doubt the quality of men returned from the London Boroughs, individuals who, as Jonathan Parry has expressed it, might be 'representatives of dubious morality'.[32]

In the event, the Conservatives introduced a measure which made only the smallest concession to the burgeoning population of the capital. The greatest expansion in London's population had taken place within the boroughs established in 1832. The population of Marylebone had increased by 195,958 between 1831 and 1861, yet in 1867 the seat was further expanded to the north-west to include the whole town of Highgate, the parish of St John Hampstead, and the 'populous suburbs' of Kilburn and Kilburn Park. In Finsbury, a rise of 152,862 had been recorded; the only change here was to round out the borough's northern boundary by incorporating the part of Hornsey parish lying between the parishes of Islington and Stoke Newington and below the new Tottenham and Hampstead Railway. The Tower Hamlets division had seen population rise by a staggering 286,062 since 1831, making it the largest borough constituency in the country by the 1850s.[33] Here the boundary commissioners had no option but to divide the old seat in two, thereby creating the new seat of Hackney. South of the river, in Lambeth, the population had swelled by 140,270: the Act extended the seat westwards to include the main parish of Clapham, and southwards to include the remaining part of the parish of Lambeth not included in 1832 and most of the parish of Streatham. The populous area surrounding Chelsea, Hammersmith, Fulham and Kensington was also recognised, the new Borough of Chelsea coming into being.

Very few changes were instituted in the three oldest Metropolitan boroughs. Their population had in any case grown much less quickly. Westminster's population had expanded by a comparatively modest 48,076 and that in Southwark by 59,476 since 1831. No changes were made to the boundaries of either. The population of the City of London had actually decreased by 10,486 since 1831. Here changes were made, though with the conditions of voting rather than with the boundaries. First, and in face of fierce opposition from City representatives proud of a right stretching back over 600 years, the number of votes allowed for each voter in an election was reduced from four to three, even though the number of members returned by the City remained at its original level.[34] The aim was apparently to encourage some hope for the representation of minority groups (notably the Conservatives) in this traditionally Liberal stronghold. The new Act also repealed that part of the 1832 Act which required that people be resident within 7 miles of any city or borough in which they wished to exercise their votes, and, with respect to the City of London, expanded that limit to 25 miles, an excellent indication of the impact of the transport revolution.

The number of MPs returned by the Metropolitan boroughs thus increased to 22. The first election under the new conditions suggested that things might continue much as they had before. Just two Conservatives found seats in the capital as an ungrateful public turned its back on Disraeli and returned Gladstone's Liberal Party to power. Yet for all the disappointments of 1868, the second half of Victoria's reign was to prove much happier for the Conservative Party than the first. As Trevor Lloyd has remarked, 'The City, Westminster, and the Home Counties were dominated by people prominent in finance and "society" and it was generally accepted that these interests would be hostile to the Liberals.'[35] Although Southwark, Finsbury and Hackney remained – for the time being – immune to Conservative blandishments, elsewhere in the Metropolis, the tide began to run against the Liberals. Constituencies such as Westminster and Middlesex, having each returned one Tory in 1868, were routinely turning two by 1880, as was Greenwich. The City, meanwhile, returned three Conservatives in both 1874 and 1880.[36] On the eve of the third Reform Act, the Tories comprised more than one-third of the members returned from the Metropolitan boroughs.

The third Reform Act was to transform London's political landscape. As part of the complex negotiations by which the Conservative majority allowed the Liberals' Franchise Bill through the House of Lords, a complete redrawing of the boundaries of constituencies took place throughout Britain on the principle that constituencies ought to be of roughly comparable size.[37] This had particularly important implications for London, where boroughs such as Chelsea had a higher population than either Manchester or Leeds. As Sir Charles Dilke, radical member for the Borough and chief negotiator of boundary changes on the Liberal side, told an audience in 1884, 'We here in the metropolis are more governed by parliament, in which we are less represented in proportion to our numbers or our wealth, than any other city.'[38] The 1884–85 legislation rectified this: 63 MPs were assigned to the Metropolitan area. The older constituency boundaries were kept, the population within them calculated and each constituency divided accordingly: Lambeth was split into four seats returning ten MPs; Marylebone, three with eight representatives; Finsbury, four with seven, Hackney, three with seven; Tower Hamlets, four with six; Southwark four with four; Chelsea, three with four; and Westminster three with three. The only constituency to lose out was the City. Its registered electorate had fallen to just 26,000, and so its traditional representation was halved, and henceforth it returned two members, not four. However, it was decided not to divide the constituency, with the consequence that the City remained one of the few two-member constituencies in parliament. Liverpool (with nine divisions), Birmingham (seven) and Manchester (six) all expanded, too; however, as the *Times* put it, these cities were 'dwarfed into insignificance by the aggregate of the metropolitan boroughs'.[39]

According to Dilke, both Joseph Chamberlain and Lord Salisbury believed that the substitution of two-member by one-member seats in

London would damage the Liberal party.[40] So it proved. The new system ushered in a period of strong Tory revival in London.[41] In the five elections between 1885 and 1900, the Conservatives never took fewer than 59 per cent of the metropolitan borough seats; in 1895 and 1900 the figure leaped to over 80 per cent.[42] Dilke himself lost his Chelsea seat in 1886. Until very recently, the historiography of London politics in this period has been dominated by accounts which focus on the complexities of liberal and labour politics, and ponder the strange deafness of the working classes to the appeals of socialism.[43] More recent scholarship, however, has started to investigate the positive factors that motivated the late-Victorian poor to embrace Conservatism. This book develops the trend.[44] Thus while the earlier chapters in this collection explore the dynamics of the Liberals' ascendancy in London, three of the last four contributions are devoted to a consideration of late Victorian Conservatism.

In Marc Baer's longitudinal study of politics in the Borough of Westminster between 1800 and 1890, the dramatic shift in metropolitan political allegiances is addressed directly. Baer begins his analysis at the dawn of the heroic age of 'Radical Westminster'. He examines the way in which Whig interference in the by-election of October 1806, caused by the death of Charles James Fox, provoked a backlash among the Borough's middle-class radicals, who accordingly revived the famous Westminster Committee and turned it into a vehicle for the return of the radical baronet, Sir Francis Burdett. For the next 50 years, the Committee, or its lineal descendants, was the borough's acknowledged kingmaker. By mid-century, however, demographic changes were beginning to work their influence, and the once safe Liberal seat became vulnerable to Tory takeover. The famous Strand bookseller, W. H. Smith, supported by a well-funded Westminster Conservative Association wrested one seat from the Liberals' grasp in 1868 and the Association secured both in 1874. The Third Reform Act cemented the Tories' domination. Reflecting on the change, Baer highlights the central role of associational politics in underwriting both the radicals' success in the first half of the century and that of the Tories after 1867.

Marc Brodie explores similar themes in his re-examination of 'slum conservatism' in the capital. The Conservatism of the East End poor has been ascribed by historians such as Henry Pelling, Gareth Stedman Jones and Duncan Tanner to their poverty which, it is said, made them easy prey for unscrupulous populist politicians promising to protect jobs and focusing popular anxiety concerning economic security on neighbouring Jewish minorities. Brodie, however, like historians working in other parts of the country, notably Patrick Joyce and Jon Lawrence, rehabilitates working-class Conservatism in the capital, and finds at its heart a series of more positive qualities linked to personal and community identity. It was, he says, a specific local interaction of identities of class, religion and race, which turned a potentially progressive area of the metropolis into a stronghold of Toryism.

Another prominent aspect of *fin de siècle* Conservatism is addressed by Alex Windscheffel: the impact of imperialism on the party's fortunes. Through an examination of the previously unconsidered political career of the explorer and geographer, Henry Morton Stanley, Liberal Unionist MP for Lambeth North between 1895 and 1900, Windscheffel highlights the ambiguities inherent in the Conservatives' promotion of the empire. His chapter foregrounds the imperial images and markers in Conservative understandings of the metropolitan cityscape and investigates the diverse ways in which the party sought to harness the 'imperial' to national and local contexts. Yet, as he points out, Stanley's candidature also highlights the limits and ambiguities of imperialist discourses at grass-roots level. For many Londoners, Stanley was not the triumphal imperial hero, but rather a symbol of the sensationalist, selfish and violent tendencies of the 'new imperialism'. Many would have agreed with the dire warning offered to the inhabitants of Lambeth by Henrietta Colenso, daughter of the former Bishop of Natal, during Stanley's 1892 campaign: 'Men who, believing in might rather than right, disregarded the rights of Africans would do the same, if they could, in the case of whites'.[45] Nevertheless, while Stanley lost in 1892, he won the seat in the Conservatives' London landslide of 1895.

As Baer, Brodie and Windscheffel demonstrate, therefore, Metropolitan London had become a bastion of Conservatism by 1900. But what had become of radicalism? In Chapter 10, Tim Cooper provides an answer: it had moved to the suburbs. As he points out, by the 1890s, the outer ring of London suburbs, East Ham, West Ham, Leyton, Tottenham and Willesden represented the fastest growing communities in the country.[46] As a consequence, it was in areas like this, rather than in the centre of the city, that late nineteenth-century politicians were obliged to come to terms with problems of rapid social and political change. In a forensic dissection of Walthamstow, he challenges traditional accounts of suburban politics which represent them as segmented and effectively de-politicised. On the contrary, he argues, it was in the new suburban towns like Walthamstow that radicalism was able to resurrect and adapt a politics of class that in urban centres was becoming difficult to maintain; as a consequence, the fierce battles that took place in Walthamstow over the developing image of the new suburb took a distinctly political form, radicals identifying with London and moderates clinging to an organic view of Walthamstow rooted in its rural past. If radicalism had been extirpated from London by the end of the century, its spirit survived in 'London over the border'.

Conclusion

To Francis Place, stalwart of Westminster politics and quintessential London radical, the political life of the nation's capital city was unique. As he explained to the foremost provincial radical of the century, Richard Cobden, in 1840:

> London differs very widely from Manchester, and, indeed, from every other place on the face of the earth. It has no local or particular interest as a town, not even as to politics. Its several boroughs in this respect are like so many very populous places at a distance one from another, and the inhabitants of any one of them know nothing, or next to nothing, of the proceedings in any other, and not much indeed of those of their own. London in my time, and that is half a century, has never moved [politically].'[47]

If London proved difficult terrain for Cobden's Anti Corn Law League, so too has it become for historians who build their narratives of nineteenth-century politics around the Manchester model of Liberalism. For although London remained a radical stronghold for much of the century, its radicalism differed from that which prevailed in the north, being much more concerned with traditional goals such as 'freedom' than with the essentially economic and religious goals of middle-class provincial radicalism. The great battles of the century in relation to free trade and the civil rights of dissenters found little resonance here.

Nevertheless London continued to occupy a central place in the mental map of nineteenth-century political activists. The chapters in this volume aim to highlight that sense of London's national importance, and, while reclaiming aspects of the capital's lost political history, act as a catalyst for a wider rethinking of London's place in the world of nineteenth-century British politics. Much, inevitably, remains to be done. The volume ends with some suggestions as to the directions future researchers might follow.

Notes

1. L. Nead, *Victorian Babylon: People, Streets and Images in Nineteenth Century London* (London, 2000), pp. 149–215 ; R. Allen, 'Observing London Street Life: G.A. Sala and A. J. Munby', in T. Hitchcock and H. Shore (eds) *The Streets of London from the Great Fire to the Great Stink* (London, 2003), pp. 198–214; B. Assael, 'Music in the Air: Noise, Performers and the Contest over the Streets in the Nineteenth Century', in ibid., pp. 183–97.
2. P. K. Gilbert, 'The Victorian Social Body and Urban Cartography' in Gilbert (ed.) *Imagined London* (New York, 2002); M. H. Port, 'Government and the Metropolitan Image: Ministers, Parliament and the Concept of a Capital City', in D. Arnold (ed.) *The Metropolis and Its Image: Constructing Identities for London c.1750–1950* (London, 1999), pp. 101–26, S. Koven, *Slumming: Sexual and Social Politics in Victorian London* (New Jersey, 2004), ch. 1; E. D. Rappaport, *Shopping for Pleasure: Women in the Making of London's West End* (London, 1999); J. R. Walkowitz, *City of Dreadful Delight: Narratives of Sexual Danger in Late-Victorian London* (London, 1992), ch. 1, and idem, 'The Indian Woman, the Flower Girl, and the Jew: Photojournalism in Edwardian London', *VS*, 12 (2001) 3–36.
3. J. Davis, *Reforming London: The Local Government Problem, 1855*–1900 (Oxford, 1988); S. D. Pennybacker, *A Vision for London 1889–1914: Labour, Everyday Life and the LCC Experiment* (London, 1995); S. Halliday, *The Great Stink of London: Sir Joseph Bazalgette and the Cleansing of the Victorian Metropolis* (Stroud, 1999); C. Wolmar, *The Subterranean Railway* (London, 2004).
4. R. Thorne (ed.) *The House of Commons, 1790–1820* (London, 1984), 4 vols; P. Thompson, *Socialists, Liberals and Labour: The Struggle for London, 1885–1914.* (London and Toronto, 1967); Marc Brodie, *The Politics of the Poor: The East End of London, 1885–1914* (Oxford, 2004); J. Vernon, *Politics and the People: A Study in English Political Culture c.1815–1867* (Cambridge, 1993), for Tower Hamlets. Much of the best work remains locked away in unpublished PhD theses: D. D. Cuthbert, 'The Redistribution Act of 1885' (Monash University 1968); M. Baer, 'The Politics of London, 1852–68: Parties, Voters and Representation' (Iowa University 1976); R. S. Draper, 'Democracy in St Pancras: Politics in a Metropolitan Parish, 1779–1849' (Harvard University 1979); A. Windscheffel, 'Villa Toryism? The Making of London Conservatism' (University of London 2000).
5. P. Joyce, *Work, Society and Politics: The Culture of the Factory in Later Victorian England* (Brighton, 1980); J. Lawrence, *Speaking for the People: Party, Language, and Popular Politics in England, 1867–1914* (Cambridge, 1998).
6. H. Kearney, *The British Isles: A History of Four Nations* (Cambridge, 1989), p. 149.
7. H. J. Dyos, 'Greater and Greater London: Metropolis and Provinces in the Nineteenth and Twentieth Centuries', in D. Cannadine and D. Reeder (eds) *Exploring the Urban Past: Essays in Urban History by H. J. Dyos* (Cambridge, 1982) pp. 37–55, D. Read, *The English Provinces c.1760–1960: A Study in Influence* (London, 1964), chs 1–2; D. Russell, *Looking North: Northern England and the National Imagination* (Manchester, 2004), ch. 2.

8. E. G. Burrows and M. Wallace, *Gotham: A History of New York City* (New York, 1999), pp. 786–1038 and S. Wilentz, *Chants Democratic: New York City and the Rise of the American Working Class, 1780–1850* (New York, 1984), pp. 3–60.
9. S. Inwood, *A History of London* (London, 1998), p. 217.
10. Quoted in R. Porter, *London: A Social History*; N. Rogers, *Whigs and Cities: Popular Politics in the Age of Walpole and Pitt* (Oxford, 1989).
11. G. Rudé, *Hanoverian London, 1714–1808* (London, 1971), chs 8–10.
12. Thorne, *House of Commons*, ii, pp. 263–6.
13. Thorne, *Commons*, i, p. 30.
14. *Times*, 4 August 1831.
15. Thorne, *Commons*, ii, p. 258.
16. N. Gash, *Politics in the Age of Peel: A Study in the Technique of Parliamentary Representation, 1830–50* (London, 1953); F. O'Gorman, *Voters, Patrons and Parties: The Unreformed Electoral System of Hanoverian England* (Oxford, 1989).
17. Porter, *London*, p. 191.
18. D. Kynaston, *The City of London, I: A World of Its Own, 1815–1890* (London, 1994), p. 22; Francis Sheppard, *London 1808–1870: The Infernal Wen* (London, 1971), p. 301.
19. Ibid., p. xviii.
20. PP1831–32, XXXIX, *Boundary Reports*, pp. 109–21 for this paragraph.
21. G. Crossick, *An Artisan Elite in Victorian Society: Kentish London, 1840–1880* (London, 1978).
22. Sheppard, *London*, pp. 312–18.
23. M. Taylor, *The Decline of British Radicalism, 1847–1860* (Oxford, 1995), pp. 71–6.
24. Figures based on F. W. S. Craig, *British General Election, 1832–1885* (London, 1977).
25. D. Southgate, *The Passing of the Whigs, 1832–1886* (London, 1962), p. 96.
26. A. Briggs, *Victorian Cities* (London, 1968), p. 120.
27. J. Vincent, *The Formation of the Liberal Party, 1857–1868* (London, 1966); M. Cragoe, *Culture, Politics and National Identity in Wales, 1832–86* (Oxford, 2004).
28. Sheppard, *London*, pp. 339–44.
29. *Times*, 11 March 1867; For its enduring impact in London: D. Tanner, 'The Parliamentary Election System, the "Fourth" Reform Act and the Rise of Labour in England and Wales', *Bulletin of the Institute of Historical Research*, 56, 134 (1983), 205–19.
30. *Times*, 2 July 1867, debate in parliament.
31. *Times*, 4 June 1867, editorial; 18 June 1867, debate in parliament.
32. J. Parry, *The Rise and Fall of Liberal Government in Victorian Britain* (Yale, 1993), p. 210.
33. *People's Paper*, 24 March 1855, p. 4.
34. *Times*, 9 October 1868.
35. T. O. Lloyd, *The General Election of 1880* (Oxford, 1968), p. 137; N. Blewett, *The Peers, The Parties and the People: The General Election of 1910* (London, 1972), p. 6.
36. Kynaston, *City of London*, pp. 369–70; R. Shannon, *The Age of Disraeli, 1868–81* (London, 1992), pp. 176–7.
37. M. E. J. Chadwick, 'The Role of Redistribution in the Making of the Third Reform Act', *HJ*, 19, 3 (1976), 665–83.

38. *Times*, 21 October 1884. R. Jenkins, *Sir Charles Dilke: A Victorian Tragedy* (London, 1968), pp. 185–95; S. Gwynn and G. Tuckwell, *The Life of the Rt Hon Sir Charles Dilke, Bart., MP*, 2 vols (London, 1918), II, pp. 63–79.
39. *Times*, 2 March 1885, p. 9.
40. Gwynn and Tuckwell, *Dilke*, II, p. 74.
41. D. Brooks, 'Gladstone and Midlothian: the Background to the First Campaign', *SHR*, 64 (1985), 42–67; J. Davis, 'Radical Clubs and London Politics, 1870–1900', in D. Feldman and G. Stedman Jones (eds), *Metropolis – London: Histories and Representations Since 1800* (London, 1989), p. 107.
42. Figures based on F. W. S. Craig, *British Election Results, 1885–1918* (London, 1974).
43. R. Price, *An Imperial War and the British Working Class* (London, 1972); G. Stedman Jones, *Outcast London: A Study in the Relationship between Classes in Victorian Society* (London 1976); Davis, 'Radical Clubs'; A. Taylor, ' "A Melancholy Odyssey among London Public Houses": Radical Club Life and the Unrespectable in Mid-Nineteenth Century London', *HR*, 78 (2005), 74–95.
44. Brodie, *Politics of the Poor*; P. Readman, 'The Conservative Party, Patriotism and British Politics: The Case of the General Election of 1900', *JBS*, 40 (2001); J. Schneer, *London 1900: The Imperial Metropolis* (New Haven, 1999), ch. 10; Windscheffel, 'Villa Toryism?'.
45. *South London Press*, 2 July 1892. For Colenso, Douglas Lorimer, *Colour, Class and the Victorians* (Leicester, 1978).
46. Briggs, *Victorian Cities*, p. 86.
47. Quoted in Sheppard, *London*, p. 319.

1
Metropolitan 'Radicalism' and Electoral Independence, 1760–1820

Matthew McCormack

Late Georgian radicalism used to be regarded as an uncomplicated business. The period from John Wilkes's noisy entry onto the political stage to Queen Caroline's subdued exit was glorified by Whig and Marxist historians alike as being one in which political theory and participation were inexorably democratised. In contrast with the Victorian period, much of this 'radical' activity was focused upon London, which has tended to lend even greater coherence to historical accounts of the phenomenon. As we will see, the capital had a proud tradition of political heterodoxy and most scholars have been content that this provided the logical set of conditions for the emergence of radical politics. Furthermore, Georgian radicals themselves were mostly London-centric. Many moved in the same circles and even provincial radicals gravitated towards the capital for election campaigns, meetings and ceremonial dinners, often appearing together on our sources' ubiquitous lists of attendees. Many subsequent commentators have bought into this co-ordinated picture, and the imposition of labels like 'Westminster radicals' has lent London radicalism – and Georgian radicalism itself – a unity that it may not in fact have possessed.

London had a long tradition of opposition to the court and the government. In part, this was an institutional phenomenon. The City of London was an ancient unit of government, which used its financial muscle and political influence to extract privileges and immunities from monarchs and ministers down the centuries. As a jurisdiction it only accounted for a relatively small proportion of the late Georgian conurbation, but it possessed an administrative role and political clout well beyond its formal boundaries. It also possessed a range of representative institutions, which were relatively democratic in their makeup: the Court of Common Council was elected by ratepayers and the Common Hall, which elected their four MPs, was open to all freemen. These could provide a forum for radical debates and resolutions, and had a considerable legal license to do so: during the 1790s, they were immune to the legislation suppressing radical meetings.[1] Although the City played an important role in the early development of radicalism in the second half of the eighteenth century,[2] by the nineteenth century their stance was more anti-government than 'radical' and they were primarily concerned with defending their privileges. The radical Francis Place complained of 'our corrupt, rotting, robbing, infamous Corporation of London' and by the 1820s it would itself become the subject of a campaign for reform.[3]

Most historians of radicalism therefore concentrate on more informal settings, and explain how London provided the conditions for radical thought in terms of its demography, cosmopolitanism and intellectual vibrancy. Radical London was a relatively small world, which consisted of overlapping (and often competing) networks of personal contacts. John Horne Tooke's home in Wimbledon, for example, provided a meeting place for his circle of moderate radicals, and his famous Sunday dinners were the occasion for many auspicious introductions and discussions.[4] Conviviality also played a central part in the 'radical underworld' vividly described by Iain McCalman, a world of debating clubs, coffeehouses and speakeasies that was inhabited by the capital's ultra-radicals.[5] Taverns had several functions: large venues like the Crown and Anchor hosted numerous ceremonial dinners and constituency meetings, whereas the location of other public houses near places of industry made them convenient for informal associations of radical working men.[6] Clubs and societies could also be more formalised, and the model of the Corresponding Society was employed to promote and co-ordinate the national (and even international) pursuit of liberty.

Radicals in the capital employed a range of methods to pursue their aims. As the hub of the nation's printing industry, London's presses, printshops and booksellers provided a focus for radical activity. Print was an inherently radical medium since it promoted openness, involved rational engagement on the part of the reader and could be widely disseminated. It was also a political issue in itself, since the freedom of the press was held to be a fundamental constitutional liberty, and radicals had to struggle against (or evade) government efforts to suppress it.[7] Radicals also made use of the capital's public spaces. As the reaction to the arrest of Sir Francis Burdett shows, the London crowd was still a force to be reckoned with in the 1810s, and Henry Hunt used the monster meeting to present the movement's 'mass platform' later in the decade.[8] Finally, London's status as the capital and the seat of Britain's governing institutions also made it the focus for radicals who wished to challenge the system. London was the obvious location for conventions – national gatherings of radical delegates – that sought to rival the authority of parliament, and insurrectionary plots that sought to overthrow it.

After 1820, the radical initiative passed from the capital to the provinces, and historians have offered a range of explanations for this phenomenon. For historians who equate radicalism with social class, this shift makes sense, since London's artisan economy contrasts with the apparently more 'mature' northern industrial working class.[9] Some identify the agitations on behalf of Queen Caroline as the last time that a single cause was able to draw the diverse metropolitan radical groups together.[10] Others suggest an intellectual change in this period, as the Westminster radicals embraced utilitarianism and moved politically towards the constitutional opposition.[11] Place himself pointed to the sheer size of the capital as the obstacle to effective radical mobilisation.[12] Radicalism in the capital, then, was far from being a unified or coherent phenomenon in the early nineteenth century. It was socially and intellectually diverse, employed a range of methods and milieux, and comprehended a wide variety of rival groups and individuals over an unwieldy geographical area. Given this heterogeneity, 'London radicalism' is a more problematic phenomenon than the label suggests.

London aside, it is only fairly recently that the notion of 'radicalism' itself has been subject to proper scrutiny. 'Radical' was a current term in this period, although in the earlier period it was more usually employed as an adjective – as in 'radical reformer' – rather than as a noun. In the 1790s, vaguer formulations such as 'a friend to moral and political improvement' were also in use, which suggest that senses of identity in this area were experimental and provisional.[13] We can see that 'radical' was an accepted term of identification by 1820 in this speech to the Westminster electors by Sir Francis Burdett. He responded to a heckler who called him a 'Radical':

> For my own part (said the hon. baronet), *I am one*. – (*Loud cheers*.) A radical is a person who would apply an effectual remedy to an inveterate disease. Every physician professes to be a radical, though few of them are found to be so. – (*A laugh*.) To *eradicate* means to root up. Now the tree of corruption has taken such deep root – its branches have extended themselves so far – that none but an idiot would think of merely lopping its exuberance, which would only strengthen the tree, and make it strike its roots still deeper.[14]

As Burdett argues, 'radical' literally means going back to the roots.[15] This could have both progressive and restorative implications, suggesting that change for the better happens either by moving forward or by returning to first principles: as we will see, this is appropriate since both commonly coexisted in Georgian reformist ideologies. Burdett's horticultural distinction between rooting up and 'lopping' also helps us to understand the difference between 'reformer' and 'radical'. The former sought to remove abuses in order to preserve the system, whereas the latter insisted on the necessity of a more fundamental change (although in practice the distinction was blurred, and historians as well as contemporaries use the two labels interchangeably).

'Radical', then, was a term of identification. 'Radicalism', on the other hand, was not and would have been a conceptual anachronism. It misleadingly suggests that 'the radicals' comprised a unified movement with a coherent ideology (an '-ism'). As such, many historians today tend to de-emphasise the distinctiveness of Georgian radical thought and activity. Rather than reducing a radical 'consciousness' to a socioeconomic base, they instead consider their languages and ideas on their own terms. This in turn leads to an acknowledgement of their debt to older oppositional traditions, which were then passed by the late Georgian radicals to their successors. Some scholars subscribe to the notion that there was a 'radical continuum' from the Civil War, through 'Country party' theory, to radicalism and then on to Chartism, Liberalism and even Labourism.[16] A related argument runs that the radicals, rather than proffering a wholly new ideology, inhabited essentially the same discursive terrain as their opponents, that of 'popular constitutionalism'. All sides had the sanctity of the ancient constitution and the interests of 'the People' in view: political activity consisted of laying claim to these powerful legitimising ideas in the interests of their cause.[17]

This chapter seeks to engage with this revisionist work in order to critique our understanding of late Georgian 'radicalism', and 'London radicalism' in particular. It will argue that historians need to pay more attention to the *electoral* dimension of radical London. London radicals were heavily involved in fighting elections in the prestigious metropolitan constituencies, but these contests are usually claimed for the history of metropolitan radicalism rather than examined in their own right. Rather than being a sideshow or a pragmatic use of existing political structures, I will argue that local electoral conflict was fundamental to the radical experience and, to a certain extent, constituted it. In particular, I want to examine the London radicals' debt to the Georgian tradition of electoral independence: the customary means by which a constituency sought to emancipate itself from local electoral oligarchy. Many key radicals such as John Wilkes, John Horne Tooke and Sir Francis Burdett adopted this 'independent' tactic and, by paying attention to the language and rituals of these election contests, we can learn much about radical notions of citizenship, manliness and the constitution. Indeed, their debt to the nationwide culture of electoral independence calls into question the 'metropolitan' character of Georgian radicalism as a whole.

Electoral independence and radical London

Modern historians acknowledge that many of the leading Georgian radicals were periodically involved in fighting election contests in the metropolitan constituencies of Westminster, Middlesex and – to a lesser extent – the City and Southwark. The significance of these battles, however, tends to be underplayed. For Francis Sheppard, the 'mood of democratic protest' surrounding Burdett's victory at Westminster in 1807 was a fleeting phenomenon, and 'was never strong enough to command the radical aspirations of all London.'[18] John Wilkes's earlier victories in Middlesex are better known, but tend to be treated as colourful Wilkite set pieces rather than as elections in their own right, and the historians who have taken them seriously have been primarily interested in the demography of his support.[19] Rather than prioritising the social and economic aspects of radicalism, however, it is useful to focus instead on radical languages and strategies.[20] When we 'return to the political' in this way, it is possible to make a case for the centrality of parliamentary elections to metropolitan radicalism.

Elections in the metropolitan constituencies were high-profile affairs. Westminster and Middlesex were the most prestigious seats in the country (rivalled only by Yorkshire because of its disproportionate size). Their location in the nation's capital and their proximity to the court and the Houses of Parliament undoubtedly gave the constituencies a unique importance, and contested elections in the metropolis were closely followed throughout the country. Their dense populations and wide franchises delivered large electorates, which made them vastly difficult and expensive to contest but gave their sitting members popular weight in the House. The Whig leader Charles James Fox certainly appreciated all of this, and his status as 'the man of the people' owed much to his 26 years as member for Westminster. The radicals, too, realised the symbolic importance of these seats: winning in the capital was both a democratic statement and placed additional pressure on the institutions that they sought to reform. In the absence of a reformed House of Commons, William Cobbett regarded Burdett at Westminster as the official delegate of the people of England.[21] Even Southwark could possess a national prestige. We should admittedly make allowances for electoral flattery, but one visiting speaker at a freeholders' dinner described it as 'the first Borough of the Empire, being a branch of that metropolis in which liberty and independence should make their sacred stand'.[22]

It is this preoccupation with 'independence' at the constituency level that I wish to explore further. In sources relating to London elections, as with those from constituencies throughout the country,[23] we see repeated reference to 'independence'. Voters are conventionally addressed as 'the independent freeholders', are urged to cast their votes 'independently' and to behave in an 'independent' manner; candidates proclaim their 'independence' in speeches and printed addresses; and everyone claims to have the 'independence' of the constituency in view. Quite what this means in this context is not immediately clear. 'Independence' entailed more than just voter freedom. A key meaning of 'independence' was freedom from party, at a time when 'faction' was regarded as a threat to the public good: radicals were indeed able to draw upon this connotation, but members of parliamentary parties were also able to claim 'independence' at the constituency level,[24] so we should perhaps focus more locally. Frank O'Gorman offered an effective interpretation of this phenomenon in his 1989 study of the Hanoverian electoral system, *Voters, Patrons and Parties*. O'Gorman argued that a system dominated by oligarchy was tempered by expectations of independence among voters, and he conceptualised independence primarily as a model of electoral conflict. In particular, when powerful interests sought control of both of a constituency's seats, or tried to prevent a contest by sharing them in a behind-the-scenes pact, voters could launch an 'independent' protest by seeking a third candidate to break the local monopoly. Independence was a legitimate customary resort when relations with local representatives broke down and, although the independents rarely succeeded, they forced many contests where otherwise there would have been none.[25]

When we apply O'Gorman's model of electoral independence to the metropolitan constituencies, the key radical contests of the period 1760–1820 appear in a new light, as populist efforts to emancipate the constituency from the forces of oligarchy. We should not read this as an immature form of radicalism, as some historians have suggested.[26] As we will see when we examine the contests in detail, 'independence' was central to the radical critique of the political system. Parliament could only be expected to govern for the general good if the electorate were freely able to select men of talent and disinterestedness. In order to understand why this was so we need to turn to the broader connotations of 'independence' within Georgian culture. As historians of political thought have demonstrated, the Georgian preoccupation with independence suggests that they conceived of political virtue and freedom in classical terms. Freedom from obligation was the precondition for political citizenship, whereas 'dependence' absolutely prevented an individual from acting freely and conscientiously, placing them in a position analogous to slavery.[27] A constituency that was denied a free choice, and which entirely depended upon a patron for its political representation, was therefore fundamentally unfree and required emancipating. 'Independence' also tells us a great deal about masculine values and how they operated in the political world. The term had a wide range of connotations in this period, suggesting patriotism, forthrightness and straightforward manliness, and was the personal virtue that was expected of voters and representatives alike in a constitutional system that relied upon checks and balances. Electoral independence is only comprehensible in this broader context, and we will see how Wilkes and Burdett in particular powerfully drew upon this culture of 'the independent man' in their electoral battles.

It is first worth outlining the history of electoral independence in the metropolitan constituencies. In early Georgian Britain, independents often made common cause with the Tories in opposing the Whig hegemony at the local level, and pioneered many of the later reformist methods and critiques in the process, promoting voters' rights and extracting pledges from candidates. As Nicholas Rogers has shown, electoral independence was a powerful factor in Westminster's politics in the 1740s. A society known as the Independent Electors of Westminster mobilised trading interests in the constituency against the dominance of the court faction and the government Whigs, leading to a series of acrimonious contests.[28] In the 1750s the independent party became defunct and the two seats were dominated by government candidates for two decades. Middlesex was also uncontested in this period until – as we will see – John Wilkes broke the Whig-Tory pact in 1768. Inspired by his example, Westminster elected Sir Robert Bernard at a by-election and Wilkites were returned in the City in the 1770s. From 1780, Charles James Fox became the focus for popular aspirations in Westminster: although a party man, he was able to play the part of the 'independent man' to perfection at Westminster elections. By 1790 however these huge contests against government-resourced candidates had become ruinously expensive, so Fox and the government candidate formed a pact to share the two seats.

Radicals in Westminster were appalled at this turn of events, and so John Horne Tooke revived the tradition of electoral independence in the name of radicalism: he stood as a classic 'third man' to force a contest and 'to raise the electors if possible to a sense of their own degradation'.[29] Tooke was soundly beaten, but to poll 1697 votes with few resources and no election committee was a huge achievement, and demonstrated both the potential of electoral independence and its usefulness as a platform for promoting parliamentary reform. Later in the decade the Foxites and the radicals in Westminster drew closer together in their opposition to the war and government repression so, when Tooke stood again in 1796, he therefore emphasised that his quarrel was with the government candidate, Sir Alan Gardner. The radicals formed a committee, largely from members of the London Corresponding Society, and polled 2819 in a high turnout.[30] In his study of this key contest, Timothy Jenks argues that Tooke firmly situated himself as an 'independent'.[31] As a contemporary account of the election observed, Tooke emphasised that he was 'unsupported by any power or connection: neither power or inclination to influence any single vote, nor any money to bribe with – he gave them [the electors] an opportunity, if they pleased, to be effectually represented'.[32] At the next election in 1802, radical energies focused on Burdett's independent challenge at Middlesex, but a third candidate again forced a contest at Westminster. John Graham, an auctioneer who presented himself as 'a man of business', stood on a platform of independence and constituency instructions. His presence irritated the other candidates, who nevertheless were unable to criticise his claim to serve 'the independence of the city', and he kept the poll open for nine days before conceding.[33]

The election of 1806 has been described as a 'watershed' in Westminster's electoral politics.[34] Radicals had become further disillusioned with the Whigs during their participation in the coalition government, and the death of Fox removed the popular hero from Westminster's electoral scene, bringing the two groups into direct opposition. The Whigs hoped that Sheridan would be able to take up Fox's mantle in the constituency, but a nabob named James Paull forced a contest by offering the electors his candidature, 'for the purpose of rescuing you from the disgrace of being transferred from one great man to another, like the debased inhabitants of a venal borough'.[35] Paull had the support of the capital's leading radicals, but was not himself a particularly impressive radical candidate. He had been involved in a long-running dispute with the Marquess of Wellesley regarding his conduct in India, so was able to present himself as a victim and scourge of government oppression.

As Burdett explained to the electors, however, his primary attraction was as an electoral independent:

> if he had no other merit, than that of being unconnected with, and independent of the other two [this] would give him a decided preference to both. He comes forward to afford the electors of Westminster an opportunity of maintaining the independence of their City; so that, upon that foundation alone, I think you cannot doubt which of the three candidates is best entitled to your support.

Paull presented his cause as being that of 'the truly independent and virtuous men in the middle class of society' against the government, the court, coalitions (national and local) and 'the dependent clergy', arguing that his votes were freely won rather than extracted through networks of clientage. He was narrowly beaten but, in the true style of an electoral independent, his effort was presented as a moral victory: whereas Sheridan and Hood's ceremonial car was drawn by horses, Paull's carriage was symbolically 'drawn home in triumph by the populace'.[36]

In 1807, Burdett was approached to fight Westminster on behalf of the radicals and the independent electors. The subsequent history of the two movements in the capital is best told through Burdett and his election campaigns, but independence efforts continued in the other metropolitan constituencies. In 1804, the Middlesex Freeholders' Club had been established by the veteran radical 'Major' John Cartwright, to support Burdett's candidature. They were also intended to be a permanent organisation 'to support the Independence of the County' on the model of the old Independent Elector societies, and they remained active into the 1810s.[37] In Southwark, too, radicalism and independence made common cause in this decade. The two seats had effectively been shared – 'a yoke of party and domestic tyranny' – until Sir Robert Wilson arrived in 1818 to challenge the monopoly. He presented himself to the electors as 'the humble instrument of their Independence, who broke the chain of slavery, so long existing in the Borough of Southwark'. His victory was celebrated at a huge anniversary dinner the following year, an event that underlines the fundamental links between radical reform, parliamentary elections and independence in the capital. Burdett was in attendance, and the impact of this victory upon his own electoral fortunes at Westminster was acknowledged. The City members were honoured in the toasts, as were the exertions of John Cam Hobhouse in the election. Other reformers and independents from around the country were honoured guests, and all present reaffirmed the necessity of parliamentary reform, hoping that the victory in 1818 would stimulate them to 'future exertions in the cause of Liberty'.[38]

After 1820, the momentum gained by radical reform and electoral independence in the capital was on the wane. We have already discussed the range of reasons usually given for the decline in radical activity in this period: the lack of unifying issue, intellectual divisions, or the difficulty of mobilising the capital and its working population. One further possible explanation is the lack of general elections in that decade – with only a notably quiet one in 1826 – which denied radicals a public and concrete opportunity to reaffirm their commitment to parliamentary representation with an 'independent' contest. Being an electoral independent, however, involved more than just standing as a third man: it was a complex public persona, which drew upon a wide range of political and cultural references. As such, it is worth examining two of London's most adept practitioners of electoral independence in more detail: namely John Wilkes and Sir Francis Burdett.

John Wilkes

John Wilkes is commonly credited with being the first English radical, and his famous elections for the county of Middlesex in the 1760s are usually claimed for the history of radicalism. On the other hand, his 'radicalism' is commonly derided as being accidental, opportunistic or the product of his more right-minded fellow travellers. Given the difficulty of pinning down Wilkes's politics, it is temping to suggest an alternative interpretation: that in 1768–69 Wilkes was primarily an electoral independent, and that electoral independence partly constituted his radical critique of the political system.

Wilkes had not always been an independent. His first (failed) attempt to get into parliament was with the support of a powerful patron, and when he did eventually get returned for Aylesbury in 1757 he had to employ the other traditional method of paying voters handsomely for the privilege: as he noted to his friend John Dell, 'I will give two guineas per man, with the promise of whatever more offers. If you think two guineas not enough I will offer three or five.'[39] By the early 1760s, when he had established a national reputation as a libertarian and the scourge of the government, he was addressing his Aylesbury constituents in rather different terms. Speaking the language of an independent, he assured them that 'I have always found a true pleasure in submitting to you my Parliamentary conduct', promising to uphold their 'liberty, safety, property' and electoral privileges.[40]

Wilkes's real engagement with the tactics and idiom of electoral independence came after his return from French exile in 1768. It is easy to be cynical about his motives: with the authorities and his creditors bearing down upon him, he needed both to stay in the public eye and to obtain the legal immunity that a seat in parliament conferred. As he famously put it, 'I must raise a dust or starve in gaol.'[41] By running as an independent in a high-profile constituency he also could enhance his popular reputation, cock a snoot at the establishment and (crucially) avoid spending much money. First he attempted to get elected for the City of London, and hastily joined a Guild in order to qualify as a candidate. From the start, he played the part of an independent to the letter. He stood forward as 'a private man, unconnected with the Great, and unsupported by any Party' and portrayed the status quo as a corrupt oligarchy:

> Will you then look tamely on, and not show yourselves free and independent, when you hear, from undoubted authority, that orders are issued from above, directing the Livery to vote for the four old members; a circumstance which puts this capital city upon a level with the lowest and most corrupt boroughs.[42]

The Livery were not persuaded by this diagnosis. Reluctant to entrust their ancient liberties to a newcomer of Wilkes's reputation, they placed him at the bottom of the poll.

Undaunted, Wilkes then immediately stood for the county of Middlesex. Middlesex was more amenable to Wilkes's independent challenge. Since the 1750s the two seats had been routinely carved up by Whig and Tory candidates, a tacit agreement that ensured that the county did not go to the polls. Wilkes was therefore able to present himself as the classic 'third man' by forcing a contest and persuading the freeholders that their privileges had been devalued by an unconstitutional and unmanly deal. Historians have tended to emphasise the national and constitutional issues raised by Wilkes at Middlesex, but Wilkes was very adept at concentrating on local political grievances. In a typical handbill he urged the freeholders to consider 'in what manner your independence in this great county hath been overlooked these twice seven years past. Hath any one of your late members vouchsafed even to bespeak your support at any other moment than at the eve of a new election?' He asked the 'independent freeholders of the county of Middlesex' to 'shew their resentment', and they responded by giving him more votes than either of the two sitting members.[43]

Notoriously, the Commons voted to expel him, and so Wilkes was repeatedly re-elected and thrown out until they declared him 'incapable of being elected a member of the present Parliament'. This made a mockery of the whole principle of popular election, and raised the issue of whether the Commons' membership was chosen by the electorate or by the government. As Wilkes argued,

> by a second choice of me for this county, you, Gentlemen, the independent freeholders, will assert the clear right you derive from the constitution of naming your representatives. If ministers can once usurp the power of declaring who *shall not* be your representative, the next step is very easy, and will follow speedily. It is that of telling you, whom you *shall* send to parliament, and then the boasted constitution of England will be entirely torn up by the roots.

This was the ethos of electoral independence, to which radicalism and reform were later to be indebted: parliament could only be said to represent the people if the electorate in the constituencies were given the opportunity to elect community representatives freely. As an independent, Wilkes always linked the wider constitutional issues to local electoral conditions, stressing that the new election was an 'injury' to the freemen, pledging to protect their ancient 'privileges and franchises' and offering to submit his parliamentary conduct to his constituents.[44]

Throughout these contests, Wilkes not only played by the rules of electoral independence, but also acted the part. If 'independence' was the quality that was expected of Georgian public men, then the election contest was the most tangible opportunity to put it into practice. Although he could play up his modest origins if the occasion demanded it, he often proclaimed the political independence of a man of rank. Unlike the squires on the backbenches who railed against the capital as the seat of luxury and corruption, however, Wilkes was emphatically a city rather than a country gentleman, and London voters identified with his urbanity and disdain for rural pursuits. During elections, Wilkes maintained the independent propriety of insisting that he was acting for the constituency rather than himself, claiming (not entirely truthfully) that he disdained party and patronage.[45] He also played the stock character of the heroic independent candidate to perfection, and was lauded as 'the most manly and intrepid defender of the general rights and privileges of Englishmen in our times'. In the electoral melodrama, he also succeeded in portraying the 'enemies of freedom and independency' – his electoral and ministerial opponents – in the mould of stage villains.

He accused them of 'clandestine and dark' deeds, 'meanness and artifice', 'low cunning' and 'weak malice'.[46] The battle between independence and oligarchy was invariably portrayed as a struggle of good against evil, which would eventually restore a lost era of freedom and consensus to the community.[47]

A protest of independency required independence on the part of the voters as well as the candidate and, famously, the Middlesex freeholders did not disappoint. As George Rudé has demonstrated, many middling voters valued their franchises and appreciated the opportunity to exercise them, coming out strongly in favour of Wilkes in the urban wards in particular.[48] There was more to independent voting than just defying the political wishes of one's local betters, however. In an open voting system this was a hugely significant act and had to be approached in a particular way. Wilkes and his supporters drew upon the long tradition that presented 'independence' as the behavioural ideal for voters at election time, connoting the manly bravery, conscientiousness and patriotism of the freeborn Englishman. Voters were urged demonstratively to 'shew yourselves free and independent', leaving themselves and their neighbours in little doubt that their small act of heroism was both legitimate and essential to the preservation of a higher ideal.[49]

Many aspects of Wilkes's radicalism therefore owed much to electoral independence. It has often been remarked that Wilkite thought took a very different direction from the late 1760s, shifting from a rather elitist defence of civil liberties to a focus upon political reform and the rights of the small man. Historians have variously attributed this change to the American question or his more radical colleagues, but arguably it was his engagement with the electoral culture of the large metropolitan constituencies that was crucial. From this point on, Wilkes began to emphasise the 'independence' of the humble citizen-voter, a central tenet of later Whig, radical and Liberal reformism. Less than a decade later, he would table the first motion for parliamentary reform in the House of Commons, declaring that 'every free agent in this kingdom ... should be represented in Parliament'[50]: he arguably never would have done so if he had not stood as a third man at Middlesex.

Sir Francis Burdett

As we have seen, Sir Francis Burdett's career encapsulates the travails of London radical politics in this period. He remains, however, an enigmatic figure who highlights both the flexibility of the late-Georgian political spectrum and the difficulty of talking about 'radicalism'.

He started out as a radical in the romantic, restorative mould. Although he later associated with Bentham, in his emphases upon the role of the aristocracy and the perfectibility of the organic ancient constitution he arguably had more in common intellectually with Burke. Like the Lake Poets and many other radical young men of the 1790s, he had turned to Toryism by the 1830s without substantially changing his ideology.

Burdett dominated the London radical scene in the early nineteenth century – where 'Burdettite' was practically synonymous with 'radical reformer'[51] – and had pretensions to be its national figurehead. Paradoxically, it was his very rank that conferred this role. John Belchem and James Epstein have examined the notion of the 'gentleman leader' in this period: radicals emphasised the gentlemanly independence of their leaders in order to license their unprecedented populist and public activities, and to underline the separateness of their platform from interest and conventional party politics.[52] As his nominator at the 1802 Middlesex election noted:

> Sir Francis Burdett was already well known to the county and the kingdom, through his public conduct, which had at all times been actuated by the public weal. His general character was esteemed for the many virtues which governed his conduct. If fortune was an object in the minds of the Electors, his was large enough to secure independence. He inherited from nature an independent spirit, and this advantage had been cultivated by education.[53]

Only a disinterested aristocrat could unite high and low against the false aristocrats, the *parvenus* and the clients, the personnel of Old Corruption. Burdett himself saw gentlemanly independence as central to his radical politics. In his view, he was an old-style patriot in the Bolingbroke mould, one of 'the Tory gentry under Anne',[54] the ancient landed nobility who had a natural duty to lead and defend the people.

Burdett was therefore well placed to present himself as an electoral independent. Like Wilkes, his first seat came at a cost: he came in for Boroughbridge in 1796 on the Newcastle interest. Being married to a Coutts heiress, however, it was not beyond his means, and he was soon able to take an independent line in parliament, criticising Pitt and supporting the more radical Whig initiatives.[55] He became involved with Tooke and his Wimbledon circle, and took an especial interest in the treatment of political prisoners at the nearby Coldbath Fields Prison. One of the sitting members for Middlesex was William Mainwaring, who was both a Pittite and chairman of the county magistrates' bench, which had written a report commending the conduct of the prison governor, Aris. When an election approached in 1802, a group of radicals therefore approached Burdett to contest the county.

For historians of radicalism, the prison issue dominated the 1802 election: Burdett's fight was against the government and their policy of legal suppression.[56] Burdett's challenge, however, was essentially that of an independent. Middlesex had been uncontested since Wilkes's quiet withdrawal in 1790, returning Mainwaring and George Byng (a Whig) unopposed. Burdett therefore broke the monopoly by running as a third man, capitalising on the freeholders' desire to be polled and their disillusionment with the existing members. When a freeholder named Britten seconded his nomination at the hustings, he made no apologies for proposing a third candidate: 'it was one of the few privileges which Englishmen had left, and God knows there are few enough, of calling to account their Representatives, and investigating their past conduct'. Burdett himself reiterated that he 'would stand forward in support of their rights and liberties to the last' and assured them that a vote for him 'was the most sure way to secure their own liberty and independence'.[57]

The prison issue was certainly important at the election, but it was not the sole reason for Burdett's success as his opponents claimed.[58] Rather, it drew attention to the liberty of the subject, a theme that dominated electoral culture. Burdett was interested in legal liberty throughout his career but he always viewed it in political terms. At his nomination speech he asked the freeholders to consider 'whether they would, by making their choice, give effect to a system much complained of; or on the contrary, by supporting him, furnish an opportunity for a fair enquiry into that abominable scene of horror, the Bastille!'.[59] In a broader sense, the 'system' was 'Old Corruption' itself, of which Coldbath Fields was but a symptom. Change in the legal, social and economic spheres would only come about if the governing system reflected the independent will of the people: therefore the subject would only be free from oppression if parliament was reformed. As he later explained to his constituents, 'Laws to be entitled to respect and willing obedience, must be pure – must come from a pure source – that is, from common consent, and through an uncorrupt channel – that is, an House of Commons freely elected by the People.'[60] Burdett was the product of a political tradition that had tremendous faith in the efficacy of representative politics, and therefore viewed radical action in fundamentally electoral terms.

Burdett succeeded in unseating Mainwaring, but the result was contested and declared void after a lengthy enquiry. In 1804 the two candidates therefore had to contest a by-election at which, as R. G. Thorne records, 'Burdett's basic theme was now "independence" '[61]: harking back to Wilkes four decades before, this contest was primarily concerned with whether the rights of the Middlesex electors had been usurped by a corrupt parliament. Burdett's nominator informed the freeholders that the question at issue was 'whether their political character and independence should be destroyed, and the County of Middlesex become a corrupt rotten borough'. Burdett lost narrowly, but the election was considered to be a moral victory for the cause of independence: the people drew Sir Francis into London in a specially decorated chariot, illuminating their windows as he passed, so he arrived in Pall Mall 'in a blaze of light'.[62]

In 1807, radicals in Westminster approached Burdett to stand there, inaugurating his leading position in radical Westminster and the nationwide reform movement. He ran on a platform of free election and topped the poll, unseating the Whig Sheridan and being returned with a fellow reformer Thomas Cochrane. He was to hold the seat for 30 years but, in spite of this dominant position, independence remained his theme. To the frustration of Francis Place and his radical sponsors, this independence often extended to his supporters since he refused to be dictated to by London's plebeian activists. His aloofness, timidity regarding reform and proprietorial attitude towards the constituency would even lead some radicals to stand against him – there were no fewer than five reformers in the field in 1818 – but his national status made him almost immune to local 'politicking'. Nevertheless, Burdett's supporters in Westminster were keen to emphasise the wider significance of his metropolitan electoral campaigns. In 1820 they published a 'brief Narrative of the Progress of PARLIAMENTARY REFORM' that placed the cause of free election in the capital at the heart of the history of British reformism. 1807 was commemorated as the year 'when Westminster first emancipated itself', and its mutual influence upon electoral campaigns in Southwark and Middlesex was underlined. Electoral independence was central to radical reform in the metropolis and Sir Francis Burdett – 'Westminster's pride and England's hope' – was its nineteenth-century champion.[63]

Conclusion

It is therefore clear that much of what we conventionally regard as 'radicalism' owed much to the traditional culture of electoral independence. Both causes argued that so long as the Commons was filled with members who were incapable or dependent upon powerful patrons, it could not be expected to provide a counterweight to the executive or to legislate for the general good. When constituents are denied the opportunity to select their representatives, they are entirely dependent upon the arbitrary will of their governors, with no means of redress. Instead, the return of MPs should rely upon the choice of suitably free and virtuous ('independent') persons. Electoral independence should therefore not be regarded as an immature form of nineteenth-century radicalism: rather, it was absolutely central to it. Indeed, given the definitional difficulties inherent in talking about 'radicalism' and 'London radicalism', it is arguably more productive and less anachronistic to consider Wilkes and Burdett primarily as electoral independents.

With regard to the capital itself, it is clear that the metropolitan constituencies had a unique status nationally, which lent greater significance to the election battles that were fought there. As the chapters in this collection will testify, London remained a privileged stage for political activity into the 1820s and beyond. London played an important role in constructing radical politics in Georgian Britain, and radical politics also had a role in constructing 'London' (which was not yet a static or well-defined administrative and political unit): as we have seen, radical involvement in election contests helped to draw Middlesex in particular into a 'metropolitan' political sphere. On the other hand, the importance of electoral independence in the capital's radical scene leaves us with an alternative reflection. How far is it useful to talk in terms of 'London radicalism' when reformist political activity in the capital was fundamentally indebted to a long-established electoral tradition that was present throughout the country?

Acknowledgements

I would like to thank Matthew Cragoe, Tony Taylor and Drew Gray for commenting on this chapter, and the Economic and Social Research Council and University College Northampton for funding the research upon which it has been based.

Notes

1. J. A. Hone, *For the Cause of Truth: Radicalism in London, 1796–1821* (Oxford, 1982), p. 130.
2. L. Sutherland, 'The City of London and opposition to government, 1768–1774', in A. Newman (ed.) *Politics and Finance in the Eighteenth Century* (London, 1984), pp. 115–47.

3. F. Sheppard, *London 1808–1870: The Infernal Wen* (London, 1971), p. 45.
4. James Paull recalls his visits in *A Refutation of the Calumnies of John Horne Tooke* (London, 1807), p. 22.
5. I. McCalman, *Radical Underworld: Prophets, Revolutionaries and Pornographers in London, 1795–1840* (Oxford, 1988).
6. Hone, *For the Cause*, p. 7.
7. K. Gilmartin, *Print Politics: The Press and Radical Opposition in Early Nineteenth-Century England* (Cambridge, 1996).
8. J. Belchem, *'Orator' Hunt: Henry Hunt and English Working-Class Radicalism* (Oxford, 1985).
9. Sheppard, *London*, p. 300.
10. J. Stevenson, 'The Queen Caroline Affair', in J. Stevenson (ed.) *London in the Age of Reform* (Oxford, 1977), pp. 117–48.
11. W. Thomas, 'Whigs and Radicals in Westminster: The Election of 1819', *Guildhall Miscellany*, III (1970), 213–14.
12. Francis Place to Richard Cobden (4 March 1840): Add. Ms. 35151, ff. 230 and 233.
13. T. Holcroft [and W. Hazlitt,] *The Life of Thomas Holcroft*, ed. E. Colby, ii (London, 1925), p. 12.
14. F. Burdett, *Reform of Parliament. To the Electors of Westminster* (London, 1820), p. 7.
15. J. Belchem, *Popular Radicalism in Nineteenth-Century Britain* (Basingstoke, 1996), p. 1.
16. J. G. A. Pocock, *The Machiavellian Moment: Florentine Political Thought and the Atlantic Republican Tradition* (Princeton, 1975); G. Stedman Jones, *Languages of Class* (Cambridge, 1983); E. Biagini, *Liberty, Retrenchment and Reform: Popular Liberalism in the Age of Gladstone, 1860–1880* (Cambridge, 1992).
17. J. Vernon (ed.), *Re-Reading the Constitution: New Narratives in the Political History of England's Long Nineteenth Century* (Cambridge, 1996).
18. Sheppard, *London*, p. 299.
19. G. Rudé, *Wilkes and Liberty: A Social Study of 1763 to 1774* (Oxford, 1962).
20. T. Jenks, 'Language and Politics at the Westminster Election of 1796', *HJ*, XLIV (2001), 419–39.
21. Thomas, 'Whigs and Radicals', p. 186.
22. *Triumph at Southwark. A Full Report of the Speeches delivered at the Anniversary Dinner given by the Free Electors of Southwark ...* (London, 1819), p. 8.
23. M. McCormack, *The Independent Man: Citizenship and Gender Politics in Georgian England* (Manchester, 2005), ch. 2.
24. The Pittite William Mainwaring, Burdett's opponent at Middlesex in the early 1800s, claimed to be defending the 'independence' of the constituency against the 'faction' of the radicals. *History of the Westminster and Middlesex Elections in the Month of November, 1806* (London, 1807), p. 294.
25. F. O'Gorman, *Voters, Patrons, and Parties: The Unreformed Electorate of Hanoverian England* (Oxford, 1989), pp. 259–85 and *passim*. R. Sweet, 'Freemen and Independence in English borough politics, c.1770–1830', *P & P*, 161 (1998), 84–115.
26. O'Gorman, *Voters*, pp. 281–4; G. Rudé, *Hanoverian London 1714–1808* (London, 1971).
27. Q. Skinner, *Liberty Before Liberalism* (Cambridge, 1998).

28. N. Rogers, 'Aristocratic Clientage, Trade and Independency: Popular Politics in Pre-radical Westminster', *P & P*, 61 (1973), 70–106. See also L. Colley, 'Eighteenth-century English radicalism before Wilkes', *TRHS*, 5th series: 31 (1981), 1–19.
29. Francis Place, quoted in R. G. Thorne, *The House of Commons, 1790–1820*, 4 vols (London, 1986), ii, p. 267.
30. Thorne, *House of Commons*, ii, p. 268.
31. Jenks, 'Language and Politics', p. 429.
32. *Westminster Election. Speeches (Out of Parliament) Addressed to the Electors of the City of Westminster* (London, c.1796), p. i.
33. Anon., *The Picture of Parliament; Or, A History of the General Election of 1802* (London, 1802), pp. 82, 84.
34. Thorne, *House of Commons*, ii, p. 296.
35. *History of the Westminster and Middlesex Elections*, p. 3.
36. Ibid., pp. 9, 10, 265, 304.
37. Thorne, *House of Commons*, ii, pp. 261–3; *History of the Westminster and Middlesex Elections*, p. 307.
38. *Triumph at Southwark*, p. 3.
39. Quoted in Rudé, *Wilkes and Liberty*, p. 18.
40. 'To the Electors of Aylesbury' (1764), reprinted in *English Liberty: Being a Collection of Interesting Tracts, From the Year 1762 to 1769, Containing the Private Correspondence, Public Letters, Speeches and Addresses of John Wilkes, Esq.* (London, c.1769), pp. 125–35.
41. Quoted in L. Namier and J. Brooke (eds), *The House of Commons 1754–90*, 3 vols. (London, 1964), iii, p. 640.
42. John Wilkes, *The Battle of the Quills: Or, Wilkes Attacked and Defended* (London, 1768), pp. 40, 55.
43. Ibid., pp. 68, 69.
44. *English Liberty*, pp. 243–4, 291.
45. 'To the Gentlemen, Clergy, and Freeholders of the County of Middlesex', in *English Liberty*, pp. 192–4 (p. 94).
46. *Battle of the Quills*, p. 69; *English Liberty*, p. 307.
47. M. McCormack, ' "The Independent Man" in English Political Culture', unpublished PhD thesis (University of Manchester, 2002), ch. 3.
48. Rudé, *Wilkes and Liberty*, p. 181.
49. *Battle of the Quills*, p. 55.
50. 21 March 1776: *The Parliamentary Register*, III (London, 1802), p. 185.
51. J. Dinwiddy, 'Sir Francis Burdett and Burdettite Radicalism', *History*, 65 (1980), 17–31 (p. 22).
52. J. Belchem and J. Epstein, 'The Nineteenth-century Gentleman Leader Revisited', *SH*, 22, 2 (1997), 174–93.
53. *Picture of Parliament*, p. 54.
54. Quoted in Thomas, *Philosophic Radicals*, p. 58.
55. Thorne, *House of Commons*, iii, pp. 302–3.
56. Hone, *For the Cause*, ch. 3.
57. *Picture of Parliament*, pp. 54, 63–4.
58. *The Middlesex Election Candidly Considered in its Causes and Consequences* (London, c.1803), p. iii.

59. *Picture of Parliament*, p. 57.
60. *Letter from Sir Francis Burdett to his Constituents* (London, 1810). *A Full Report of the Proceedings of the Electors of Westminster* (London, 1809), p. 15.
61. Thorne, *House of Commons*, ii, p. 261.
62. *A Full Account of the Proceedings at the Middlesex Election* (London, 1804), pp. 6, 17; *A Full Report of the Speeches of Sir Francis Burdett at the Late Election* (London, 1804), pp. 88–9.
63. *Westminster Election, 1820* (London, 1820), p. 7; *Reform of Parliament*, p. 4.

2
'Policing the Peelers': Parliament, the Public, and the Metropolitan Police, 1829–33

David A. Campion

> Because the English Bourgeois finds himself reproduced in his law, as he does in his God, the policeman's truncheon ... has for him a wonderfully soothing power. But for the workingman quite otherwise.
>
> [Friedrich Engels, 1844[1]]

> 'Liberty' does not consist of having your house robbed by organised gangs of thieves, and in leaving the principal streets of London in the nightly possession of drunken women and vagabonds.
>
> [Sir Robert Peel, 1829[2]]

The year 1833 was a difficult one for the Metropolitan Police. In August, the House of Commons convened two separate committees of inquiry to investigate alleged misconduct and abuses of authority among the rank and file of the organization. Prompted by concerns raised in these investigations, parliament then convened a third committee to review the overall state of the police. The 1833 investigations constituted the first significant governmental scrutiny of law enforcement after the Police Act of 1829 that had replaced London's localized networks of night watchmen and parish constables with Sir Robert Peel's centrally controlled and organized Metropolitan Police. The subsequent investigations brought to the forefront of British public attention the acute political controversies that had surrounded the 'New' Police since its inception four years earlier. They helped determine, as much as the establishment of the Metropolitan Police itself, the model that urban policing would follow in Britain for the rest of the nineteenth century and into the twentieth century.

The creation of the Metropolitan Police was a signal event in the political history of London, though perhaps with consequences that its founder, Secretary Peel, had not anticipated but of which the patrolling constables would soon become acutely aware. This chapter focuses on the 1833 parliamentary investigations as a window into the larger issue of the politicization of law enforcement in London that followed the decision to place the most basic functions of public safety within the domain of the Home Office. Indeed, few developments in the history of London managed to narrow the distance between the politics of the street and the politics of Westminster to the same degree as the creation of the Metropolitan Police. Moreover, at various stages this body of men served as both conduit and insulator between these two political spheres. They were the point of contact – in the physical sense as much as any other – between the political elite and the general public whom that elite sought to protect and be protected from at various times. This was a reality that both Engels and Peel understood keenly, though they perceived it from vastly opposing political viewpoints.

The specific complaints brought before the two select committees in 1833 addressed both systemic and incidental problems of police misconduct. The first complaint accused the police of routinely deploying plainclothes constables as political spies for the state. The second charged the police with excessive use of force in dispersing crowds during an unlawful political assembly earlier that year. In each case, senior police officials answered the charges by claiming they had employed the least intrusive and coercive methods necessary for the proper enforcement of laws and the maintenance of the public peace. The reports of the two investigations, though they dealt with specific grievances against the police, illustrated the larger, underlying political problems that accompanied the introduction of the New Police. These included the gaining of respect and acceptance by the people being policed as well as reconciling the desire for greater uniformity and efficiency in urban policing with the need for local accountability and the preservation of traditional English liberties. They also included enforcing laws evenhandedly and maintaining the peace while minimizing the intrusiveness of the state in the social and political affairs of private citizens. The 1833 House of Commons inquiries into the conduct of the Metropolitan Police addressed in exacting detail many of the ambiguities regarding the New Police and its social role that had persisted in the early years since its founding. Following both investigations, the select committees exonerated the

Police but cautioned its members to be especially vigilant against abuses within their ranks. They cemented the legitimacy of an active, centralized police department while also reinforcing the limits of its power and warning that the perceived tyrannies of continental police forces would not be tolerated among the free people of England. Lastly these investigations helped define the identity and sense of mission of the New Police. They legitimized the rightful use of police power while warning constables and their supervisors that oppressive or abusive enforcement of the law would not go unchecked.

Ultimately, the investigations set a tone for policing in London that spread across Britain during the mid-nineteenth century as other industrial urban centers such as Manchester, Birmingham, and Liverpool modeled their police departments on the 'Peelers' of London. The reform of provincial police departments throughout Britain followed much the same pattern. In the latter half of the nineteenth century, the example of the Metropolitan Police expanded beyond the British Isles to its colonies and to other industrializing nations. The example of London's Metropolitan Police came to influence the development of large urban police departments in such diverse cities as Toronto, Cape Town, Bombay, Sydney, New York, Chicago, and Tokyo. Thus, the investigations and reforms of the Metropolitan Police during the 1830s were instrumental in setting modern law enforcement in London and cities throughout the Western democracies along the path that it has followed to the present day.

Sir Robert Peel and the creation of the 'New' Police

To fully appreciate the significance of the 1833 investigations of police misconduct one must first assess the dramatic changes in policing in London that had occurred as a result of the Police Act of 1829, as well as considering the state of the police before and after the passage of that act. The very existence of the 'New' Police and the controversies surrounding it factored directly into the climate of public opinion in 1833 when the police misconduct investigations occurred. Before 1829, London and its environs had been policed by multiple networks of night watchmen and constables organized locally by parish. Many of those arrangements had not changed appreciably for over a century.[3] Parish constabularies were funded directly by the local residents and answered only to local magistrates and other parish leaders. In law enforcement, the parishes were entities unto themselves, each setting its own guidelines for how the locality would be policed. Parishes often relied upon volunteer constables, whose part-time service meant that many neighborhoods were patrolled only at night. It remains a truism among traditional historians of the police that this patchwork quilt of law enforcement bodies that blanketed the greater metropolitan area had become irrevocably worn by the beginning of the nineteenth century. The steady influx from the countryside into London of thousands of people during the early period of industrialization, the rise of the 'labouring' classes, the growth of overcrowded slums and increasing levels of poverty all contributed to an alarming rise of crime – especially theft – and a perceived lack of public morality against which the parish constables proved incapable of effectively combating.[4] The solution lay in a radical restructuring of both the organization and philosophy of policing.

The primary innovation of the New Police, upon which most historians agree, was the radical change in organization. In 1829, the 'Bill for Further Improving the Police of the Metropolis' abolished the parish system and replaced it with one department, the Metropolitan Police. The jurisdiction of the Metropolitan Police extended in a 12-mile radius from Charing Cross and was composed of 19 'divisions', each designated by a letter of the alphabet. These corresponded not to traditional parish boundaries but rather to geographic areas measured in square miles.[5] The Police Act also completely overhauled the system by which policing had been previously financed. Where the parishes had once controlled their own budgets and determined rates among local residents for the operational costs of their constabularies, the government introduced a new universal rate paying system throughout London in which funds were allocated to the various divisions at the discretion of the central police administration. Additionally, it mandated uniform standards of recruitment, training and attire among its men. Most importantly, the Police Act placed administrative control of the 'New' Police under the Secretary of State for the Home Office.

The introduction of the Metropolitan Police in 1829 was received with mixed feeling among the various segments of London society. In November of that year, the Duke of Wellington wrote effusively to his colleague Peel, 'I congratulate you upon the entire success of the Police in London.' He added, 'it is impossible to see anything more respectable than they are'.[6] Yet, others were more sparing in their praise while some unleashed a torrent of opposition. Some Whig leaders in parliament saw in the New Police the dangerous tendencies of Peel's brand of Toryism, since the new legislation championed the centralized power of the state and undermined the traditionally English virtues of local self-government.

Affluent Londoners also reacted negatively to the universal ratepaying scheme whose equalizing tendencies forced the wealthier parishes to pay for policing in the poorer sections.[7] Most importantly, local municipal leaders protested that the city's law enforcement officers were now no longer answerable, either politically or financially, to the people whose neighborhoods they patrolled, but instead walked their beats as cogs in the impersonal and unfamiliar machinery of a centralized state. For these critics, as well as many other Englishmen, the very word 'police' had unpleasant connotations of continental absolutism and carried the sinister odour, however slight, of Bourbon and Bonapartist spying.[8] From such a perspective, Peel's creation of a quasi-military, centralized *gendarmerie* to replace the traditional system of locally appointed constables marked a first step down a dangerous and slippery path.[9] Moreover, the fires of British patriotism during the previous generation had been so consistently stoked by the experience of total war with France and her continental allies that some historians have argued that Britons actually shaped much of their identity as a people in opposition of the worst perceived depredations of revolutionary France.[10] Concerning the 'police', one English critic, J. P. Smith, in 1812 wrote that they could not help but evolve into 'a system of tyranny; an organized army of spies and informers, for the destruction of all public liberty, and the disturbance of all private happiness'. He added, 'every system of police is the curse of despotism'.[11] This persistent feeling is especially significant when considering the nature of the complaints brought against the Metropolitan Police in 1833.

Just how much of an improvement the Metropolitan Police was over what had preceded it remains the subject of historical debate. Traditional historians of the police emphasize the efficiency of the new force, the higher standards of professional conduct and training, and the marked decrease in crime and public indecency.[12] Revisionists, on the other hand, insist that the New Police introduced few innovations and that many of the chronic problems in policing persisted after 1829 or, in some cases, worsened.[13] The latter claim that many of the supposed corrective actions, such as a paid constabulary and daytime patrols, had already existed in the parishes. The widely accepted accounts of the inadequacy of the old methods of policing, they argue, say more about the propensity among police historians to validate the creation of the New Police than about the realities of London's political and social order prior to 1829.[14] Revisionists also point to the fact that under the new system, rates for policing increased significantly while the police actually had fewer constables on patrol at any given time than before 1829.[15]

They further argue that many of the Metropolitan Police constables were as poorly paid as their parish predecessors and that the turnover rate in the first years of the new organization remained alarmingly high as the problem of recruiting and retaining good men persisted.[16] The poor quality and unprofessional comportment of some of the new constables certainly tarnished the image of the Metropolitan Police in the eyes of many Londoners in the years leading up to the 1833 investigations.[17]

Such an image, recently offered in histories of the police, contradicts the longstanding historical portrayal of Peel's police as efficient, impartial and highly professional public servants. The revised portrait of the Metropolitan policeman as a man hastily trained and often careless in executing his new duties helps explain the low levels of public confidence in the New Police in its earliest years.[18] Mindful of this, one can see the 1833 misconduct investigations not simply as occasions for adjudicating isolated incidents within the organization. Instead, they offered signs of a systemic crisis of identity and public acceptance of the New Police as an institution, and as a crossroads for determining the future of modern, urban law enforcement in Britain. It was these investigations and subsequent reforms that shaped the nature of policing in London, and, by extension, in cities throughout the Western liberal democracies that followed London's example. It remains now to address the substance and implications of the specific accusations made against the police.

Sergeant Popay: plainclothesman or political spy?

On 6 August 1833, the first of two House of Commons select committees that had been convened to investigate allegations of police misconduct presented their report.[19] The committee, which included Sir Robert Peel, former Home Secretary and architect of the 1829 Police Act, had met to answer a petition alleging that the police had employed plainclothes constables as political spies for the government. The complaint had been lodged by Frederick Young and other members of the National Union of the Working Classes, a radical political organization (also referred to in the investigation report as the 'Political Union'). They testified that a certain William Popay, who they later learned was a sergeant in the police, had infiltrated their organization under a false identity and acted as an *agent provocateur*, inciting them to acts of rebellion intended to justify police retaliation.[20] Young and the other petitioners further testified that Popay had occasionally been accompanied by other plainclothesmen. They complained that such practices, rather than stemming from a legitimate need to preserve public order, amounted to a government-sanctioned, ratepayer-supported spy network that deprived law-abiding citizens of their most basic liberties.[21]

Sergeant Popay, in his own defense, testified before the committee that he had been directed by his supervisor, Superintendent Andrew McLean of 'P' Division, to attend Political Union meetings in plainclothes and report on what transpired.[22] His testimony was followed by that of McLean, who attested to Popay's competence and good character and stated that it was common practice in the police to employ plainclothes constables in certain circumstances.[23] In accordance with the New Police's emphasis on crime prevention, divisional superintendents used these specially selected constables to 'look after characters suspected of intent to commit a felony'.[24] The plainclothesmen made regular written reports to their divisional superintendents, who then passed on the information to the commissioners. McLean stated that plainclothesmen were used for observation only and were never to interact with or deceive in any way those being monitored. When asked to account for his behavior, Popay told the committee that he had had no choice but to engage in conversation, accept invitations to join the Union and socialize with its members, and create a false identity when pressed for personal information. He stated that aloof behavior at the meetings would, over time, have raised suspicions and made it impossible for him to carry out his surveillance effectively.[25] Following the investigation, the select committee concluded that Sergeant Popay's conduct had been 'highly reprehensible' since he took an active part in that which he had only been instructed to observe.[26] It also blamed his superiors, though less strongly, for not supervising his work closely enough and detecting such obvious breaches of plainclothes protocol. Most importantly, the committee reinforced the acceptability of limited undercover policing but warned that abuses of the practice would not be tolerated.[27]

The investigation underscored the contentiousness of using undercover policemen as a means of preventing crime. Proponents of the practice within the New Police argued that while uniformed patrolmen constituted a valuable deterrent to crime, they simply could not function as effectively as plainclothesmen in certain situations.[28] These officials maintained that the infiltration of clandestine groups that threatened the public peace was a legitimate activity of an organization dedicated to the continued maintenance of law and order not merely the restoration of the same after acts of criminal mischief. Such undercover work, argued Sir Charles Rowan, one of the joint commissioners of the police, violated no one's liberties since the constables did not interfere with the lawful rights of citizens to assemble or speak, but rather ensured the security of the overall population of London against the secret planning of criminal activity. According to Rowan and other officials, the police understood the sensitive nature of undercover work and were extremely temperate in its use, always mindful of the rights of citizens and handpicking only their most competent and mature men for such duty. Nevertheless, they insisted that undercover surveillance represented an indispensable component in the philosophy of modern policing that sought to prevent criminal activity rather than merely reacting to it after the fact.

The opposition to plainclothes surveillance that Young and the other petitioners voiced to the investigation committee gave a completely different account of the matter regarding Sergeant Popay and his associates. Several members of the Political Union testified that their organization stood for nothing more than greater political representation for the working classes and that they had been marked for state surveillance solely for their political views. They maintained that Popay had not merely observed the proceedings of their law-abiding organization but had overstepped the supposed restrictions that the police had placed on its plainclothes constables. He had created a false identity, misled them at every turn, and incited them with inflammatory language and provocations towards revolutionary violence designed to give their organization an image as a perceived threat to public safety – one that would conveniently justify a police crackdown.[29]

Apart from Popay's questionable conduct, there was a larger concern among the petitioners about the nature of the Metropolitan Police itself. The fact that the undercover constables in question were no longer commissioned locally to enforce the law but were instead under orders from a centrally controlled, state bureaucracy meant essentially that the New Police was little more than a state spy network underwritten by London taxpayers. Thus, under the pretense of keeping the peace, the state could at its own discretion intervene in and secretly undermine any organization that threatened to alter the existing political and social power structures. In voicing these concerns, the Political Union petitioners were not alone. Some magistrates had earlier expressed concern to the Home Secretary and police commissioners that the use of plainclothesmen set a dangerous precedent for state intervention in the private lives of citizens.[30] Evidently the line between effective undercover crime prevention and the more sinister activities of a secret police was a fine one (see Figures 3 and 4).

The police at Cold Bath Fields: preservers of order or blue brutes?

Later that month, on August 23, another House of Commons select committee presented its final report on its inquiry into the separate allegations of excessive use of force by the police in dispersing an outdoor political assembly at the Cold Bath Fields in the Clerkenwell section of London on May 13 of that same year. The Cold Bath Fields Report was the second major investigation of the Metropolitan Police that year, coming only 17 days after the select committee inquiring into the spying charge had presented its findings. The Cold Bath Fields report, like the spying report before it, addressed a sensitive dimension of modern urban policing, namely, what exactly constituted an 'acceptable' use of force by the police in preventing public disorder and in keeping the peace. How far could constables go in using violence and other coercive measures to ensure compliance with the law and restoration of order in the midst of civil unrest? As with the spying charge, the justifiable use of force by the police became a particularly controversial issue owing to the assertive, centralized, and state-directed nature of the New Police.

The incident in question was not unrelated to the earlier investigation of spying, since the assembly at the Cold Bath Fields had been organized by the same Political Union that had been infiltrated by Sergeant Popay earlier that year. The outdoor assembly, a political rally that had given itself the politically loaded name 'National Convention', had been scheduled by the Political Union to occur at the Cold Bath Fields on May 13.[31] In the days prior to the meeting, the Home Secretary had declared it an unlawful assembly and posted flyers warning the King's subjects not to participate.[32] On the morning of the assembly, 70–80 constables of 'A' Division under Superintendent Mays were stationed in a nearby livery as several hundred people gathered in the Cold Bath Fields to hear the assembled speakers. The constables of 'A' Division were joined by reinforcements from other divisions and units of the Horse Guards until there were approximately 440 constables present. Shortly thereafter, Superintendent Mays gave the signal for his men to move in. A confrontation occurred in which scores of policemen and civilians were injured and one constable, Robert Culley, was killed.[33]

What actually happened at the Cold Bath Fields is still unclear. Eyewitness accounts printed in *The Times* the next day and testimony given before the committee from civilians and constables tell two conflicting stories.[34] According to Superintendent Mays, constables armed only with batons began to march down Calthorpe Street from the livery towards the speaker's platform in the Cold Bath Fields. This had been done by a prearranged signal with plainclothes constables in the crowd. The plan, which had been approved the day before by the Home Secretary and the joint commissioners of the police, was for the plainclothesmen to arrest the speakers and for the uniformed constables to disperse the crowd and provide any necessary assistance to the arresting officers.[35] Mays stated that the advance of his men had been intentionally slow to allow those in the crowd ample opportunity to leave the area. Having done that, the constables were left to subdue with their batons only the most openly combative members of the crowd. During the advance, stones were thrown at the police.[36] Mays maintained that, at all times, the degree of force used by the constables had been the very minimum necessary to restore order and that his men had demonstrated remarkable restraint given the deadly force which they had faced. He stated that many in the crowd had waited for the police with concealed weapons, among them knives and loaded pistols, and in the confrontation several constables had sustained stab wounds, including Culley, who had died almost immediately after being stabbed through the heart.[37]

Civilian eyewitnesses testifying before the committee provided an entirely different account of the events.[38] Many of them stated that the police had charged the crowd from all directions and had relentlessly and indiscriminately attacked men, women, and children – many of whom were not involved in the political rally but had merely been passersby in the wrong place at the wrong time. Some witnesses to the event testified that the constables had taunted their victims as they clubbed them.[39] At no point did police supervisors rein in their men and any acts of violence among members of the crowd had not been premeditated, but rather desperate attempts at self-defense in what today might be called a police riot. Numerous witnesses agreed that the wilful and reckless actions of the police had created an atmosphere of chaos and violence rather than preventing one, and that excessive and gratuitous use of force by the police resulted in scores of injuries and the unfortunate death of Constable Culley that would otherwise have not occurred.[40]

There is no conclusive way to know who was to blame for what occurred at Cold Bath Fields, but the incident is revealing beyond the question of culpability. Traditional historiography tends to take Superintendent Mays at his word when he said that he cautioned his men to advance slowly, not to lose their tempers, and to arrest only the leaders of the rally.[41] Historical accounts of the incident also rely heavily on the report of the select committee, which exonerated the police of any blame for the incident. The report concluded that the police did not employ greater force than that which they encountered, that occasional lapses into excessive use of force by individual constables could be attributed to the confusion and heat of the moment, and that the police had given members of the crowd ample opportunity to walk away from any confrontation had they so chosen.[42]

The investigation of the Cold Bath Fields incident and the controversy surrounding it again points to the question of accountability of a centralized police organization to the people being policed. Civil unrest was nothing new in nineteenth-century London, but prior to 1829 it had generally been dealt with by the army, often more harshly and with substantially more loss of life than by the police later on. Objections to the police handling of the problem stemmed largely from the fact that as riot control, they served primarily as a *de facto* standing army, but one dedicated exclusively to internal security.[43] As policemen, they combined this function with the day-to-day patrolling of the neighborhoods as the parish constables had once done. The most troubling difference with the Metropolitan Police was that the constables and their supervisors, answering to the state, had no direct accountability to the people residing within their divisions and it was difficult for local residents to lodge complaints against individual policemen or the system as a whole. Most constables patrolled beats outside their own neighborhoods and many had been recruited from outside London and often as far away as Ireland. Thus, they could act with wanton cruelty and general irresponsibility knowing that their victims did not have the same recourse that had earlier existed in the days of local law enforcement. From the perspective of the members of the Political Union, it must have been extremely disconcerting to see their group being both spied upon and physically assaulted by members of the same state apparatus – all under the nebulous pretext of keeping the peace.

The emergence of the 'New' Police as a historical problem

To understand the full import of the police misconduct investigations of 1833, one must situate them among the various strands of historical scholarship on the police in Britain. The investigations by themselves have never been the subject of historical study, but they have been repeatedly accounted for and assimilated into two competing historiographical schools of thought.[44] The first of these is the longstanding, traditional scholarship that situates the creation of Metropolitan Police along the linear path of progress and rationality in the evolution of modern Britain.[45] The second is a more recent, revisionist trend that identifies the New Police as the arm of the industrial elites in maintaining and enforcing conformity among the working classes to the social and economic realities of industrial capitalism.

Traditional histories of the police in Britain tend to represent the foundation of the Metropolitan Police as a landmark in the advancement of reason and order in modern British society.[46] This Whiggish view of social progress generally hails the foresight of Peel and his realization of a modern, professional police organization capable of maintaining law and order in a rapidly changing society. Traditional scholarship of the New Police also rests upon the presumption that the preexisting law enforcement bodies, many of which had changed little since the eighteenth century, were anachronistic and obsolete in an urban setting characterized by the dynamic transformations of industrialization and a rapid population increase – and with them the attendant problems of crime and social unrest. From this view, the 'New' Police represented an appropriate and wholly positive response by the government to the alarming threats of crime and social chaos and to the inadequacies of the existing preindustrial constabularies in dealing with these problems effectively. As a rational, Weberian bureaucracy, Peel's 'New' Police elevated law enforcement from overly personal, arbitrary, and inefficient parochial bodies and infused it with a degree of organization, professionalism, and impartiality that would ultimately make it the pride of Londoners and the envy of other cities in Britain and throughout the Western world.

Traditional historians of the police include the 1833 investigations in their writings to valorize the New Police. They argue that the Police, when scrutinized in the most exacting detail, demonstrated the foresight of its founder, the wisdom of it leaders, and the temperance of its constables. They further maintain that the open and honest accounting of itself before parliament validated its existence and proved that it played an essential role in the modernization of urban Britain. This school of historical scholarship emphasizes the fact that both investigations exonerated the police and that the 1833 House of Commons Select Committee to review the general state of the Metropolitan Police offered unqualified praise for that organization.[47] It also stresses that the investigations are evidence that the New Police always remained accountable to the citizens of London, even the most politically marginal, and that their reorganization into one department under the Home Office did in no way diminish the responsibility of the police for the actions of its men, nor did it lend itself to inhumane behavior or a disregard for England's traditional civil liberties.

Revisionist historians of the Police in Britain, however, have often focused on the development of the Metropolitan Police and its offspring in other industrial cities of Britain as an outgrowth of the industrial elites' concerns about the protection of private property and the prevention of violent uprisings by the lower classes – occurrences that were becoming more frequent as the social and economic effects of industrialization were being more deeply felt.[48] Marxist historians, in particular, are apt to describe the New Police as symptomatic of the fear of industrial capitalists over the anxiety and rising class consciousness of their workers.[49] Echoing Friedrich Engels, these scholars view the modern, urban policeman as a reflection of modern industry itself: impersonal, alienated from the people, serving a capitalist master and upholding laws that reinforced that master's power over the means of production and the institutions of political control. Moreover, the distinctly lower class composition of the constabulary merely underscores the working man's muscle and sweat driving the machinery of his own oppression. For Marxists, historically, the New Police are little more than the clichéd thin blue line between an uneasy English bourgeoisie and the inevitable proletarian revolution.

Non-Marxist revisionists take a somewhat different view. Most agree that the vision of New Police did owe much to the industrial middle class. The Metropolitan Police was the brainchild of Robert Peel, a man whose Tory politics embodied the aspirations of a rising and assertive middle class. As former Chief Secretary in Ireland, Peel had returned to England with notions of state control through police power and of coercive methods of keeping order in society that proved not entirely suited to the traditions and political sensibilities of the residents of London.[50] This resulted in some considerable growing pains for the New Police in its early years. Apart from the political shift to centralized control over its administration, Peel and his supporters sought to achieve the same streamlined and efficient results in law enforcement that industrial production had done in the economy. Revisionists such as R. D. Storch argue that the New Police served as enforcers not only of the law but also of acceptable social behavior (sobriety, sexual restraint, deference to organized religion) and a respect for private property that reflected the values of the politically ascendant middle class.[51] From this view, the police functioned as a *political* and *moral* force as much as one dedicated to the prevention of crime and the preservation of the peace. Its greatest opponents were not common criminals, but the radical political groups and lower class London ratepayers who bore the burden of financing a state-controlled body of men whose sole function was to preserve the social and political status quo.[52]

From the perspective of many revisionists, the exoneration and praise of the Metropolitan Police by the investigating committees are hardly surprising given the social and political background of the members of parliament and the other men represented in the committees.[53] Former Home Secretary Peel was a member of both select committees as was Commissioner Byng, the head of the very organization being investigated. More significant, perhaps, is the fact that these investigations came on the heels of the Reform Act of 1832 that extended the franchise to members of the commercial and professional elites. Historians have traditionally interpreted this event as a victory for the middle classes – a segment of society from within whose folds Peel himself had emerged – and a notable milestone along the path of their political and social ascendancy. This was a victory gained at the expense of the landed gentry and aristocracy and with virtually no regard paid to the political aspirations of the working classes, the overwhelming majority upon whose simmering discontent the lid of law enforcement would be kept firmly pressed. Consequently, when it came to meaningful reform and restraint of the police, the new elite of industrial Britain could not have been expected to bind the hands or demoralize in any significant way the sentinels guarding their lives and property.

Conclusion: police reform in the aftermath of the 1833 investigations

Six years after the police misconduct investigations, Parliament introduced a bill calling for reforms within the Metropolitan Police. The 1839 'Bill for Further Improving the Police of the Metropolis' called for greater penalties for constables who were derelict in their duties, including fines of up to ten pounds and one month in jail.[54] It abolished all remaining ward constables and solidified the jurisdiction of the Metropolitan Police over the greater London area. The bill gave constables greater latitude to search suspects and make arrests for 'disturbing the peace' and also increased penalties for anyone who assaulted a constable. Overall, the 1839 Police Reform Act reinforced the idea of the public accountability of the police, both as an institution and as individuals, while simultaneously reinforcing their authority and extending the limits of their power. It was this model, later infused with Victorian notions of progress and probity, which other British urban police organizations would soon follow.

The 1833 investigations of police misconduct and the 1839 reforms lead to two conclusions. The first is that the Metropolitan Police in 1829 did not start out as the benign, efficient, and responsible civic organization that traditional police historians have long described. At the outset, Peel's 'New' Police had the flavor of the Anglo-Irish authoritarian and coercive tendencies of its founder. The direction in which the New Police first headed, with its substandard recruits and lack of local accountability, may account for much of the popular backlash among Londoners to the new constables. The second conclusion is that the investigations themselves reveal that the police were ultimately made to be accountable to the people as a whole by a democratic government, more so than many revisionists acknowledge. The House of Commons investigations showed that those being policed, even political outcasts like the members of the Political Union, could have their grievances formally addressed and taken seriously by the political leadership of the country. Although the police were exonerated in 1833, they were shown to be not completely beyond blame, and the final reports of the spying charge and the Cold Bath Fields incident warned the New Police that the limits of their power, even as these were being expanded, would be strictly enforced thereafter.

The 1833 investigations corrected many of the abuses and inconsistencies within the Metropolitan Police. They validated the presence of a centralized police department while ensuring that constables and their supervisors, as civil servants and fellow citizens, would remain accountable to the people amongst whom they patrolled for their behavior and the manner in which they enforced the people's laws. It was this model upon which other cities in England built up their own police departments and, it may be argued, later allowed Britain to weather the Chartist uprisings with less of a threat to public order and political stability than occurred in most other European countries during the revolutions of 1848.[55] And while radical opposition to the police remained consistently high throughout the nineteenth century and into the twentieth century – predictably so since their criticisms of government had not waned either – the Metropolitan Police did eventually manage to overcome the initial hostility and ambivalence of most Londoners and win their respect, grudging at first but given more freely over time.[56] A telling example of this pattern of public perception would later arise in the establishment by the police in 1883 of a 'Special Branch' to combat the Fenian bombing campaigns that had terrorized the metropolis. This development reignited old radical fears of a secret paramilitary subset of police armed with exceptional powers of surveillance and coercion. However, the overwhelming majority of frightened Londoners cheered on the initiative of their police in tackling the ubiquitous and sadly persistent problem of urban terrorism.[57] Radical criticism of the police did serve to remind MET officials that they and their men were themselves under scrutiny and perhaps this prevented excesses that a more cowed or complacent public would have tolerated among its police. Yet the criticisms of radicals should be seen as atypical rather than symptomatic of a more generalized hostility among the people of London towards their police that in all likelihood was not there. At the very least, the evolution of the 'Peeler', the nature of modern policing, and the intersection of law enforcement, public order and the dynamics of London politics emerge as a more complex and nuanced historical problem than is often acknowledged either in the laudatory histories of traditionalists or in the scathing critiques of revisionists and the political left.

In the popular imagination, the English policeman in the nineteenth and twentieth centuries often emerges paradoxically as both a symbol of English exceptionalism and an example of Britain's considerable influence in the development of modern urban communities throughout the Western liberal democracies. The blue-coated servant of the people, approachable and helpful, is often held up by the English, rightfully, as the fruit of a democratic society, and thus the English policeman as an object of national pride has predominated in most popular and scholarly history up to the present day. Whether or not this is an accurate portrayal of the police will continue to remain the subject of debate among historians. Certainly Engels' caution about the power of the policeman's truncheon has lost none of its potency even in our own age. However, it has been the more modest objective of this chapter to show that the image today of the English 'bobby' – the quintessential public servant, benign but vigilant, conscientious but impersonal, readily identifiable in his distinct but notably unmilitary uniform, and armed with the people's respect and deference rather than a firearm – owes as much, if not more, to the political controversies, public pressure, parliamentary investigations and reforms of the 1830s than to Peel's Police Act of 1829 that created him and sent him out onto the street.

Acknowledgements

I am grateful to my colleagues at Lewis & Clark College whose suggestions helped me formulate many of the ideas and much of my approach to the topic of this chapter. I also wish to acknowledge the financial support I received from the college to conduct the necessary research in London. Finally, I am indebted to

Matthew Cragoe and Tony Taylor who commented on an earlier draft of this chapter.

Notes

1. F. Engels (W.O. Henderson and W.H. Chaloner, trans.), *The Condition of the Working Class in England* (Stanford, 1958 [1844]), p. 258.
2. Letter to the Duke of Wellington, 5 November 1829. R. Peel (C.S. Parker, ed.), *Sir Robert Peel, from his Private Papers, Vol. II* (London, 1891), p. 115.
3. R. Paley, ' "An Imperfect, Inadequate, and Wretched System?" Policing London before Peel', *Criminal Justice History*, 10 (1989), 95–130.
4. T. A. Critchley, *A History of the Police in England and Wales 900–1966* (London, 1967), p. 42.
5. 'Bill for Improving the Police in and Near the Metropolis', House of Commons, 15 May 1829, pp. i, 1–2, 169, 425.
6. Paley, 'Policing London', 117.
7. Ibid.
8. C. Emsley, *The English Police: A Political and Social History* (London, 1991), p. 3.
9. For the large secret police network in Metternich's Austria, A. Sked, *The Decline and Fall of the Habsburg Empire, 1815–1918* (London, 1989), pp. 41–88.
10. L. Colley, *Britons: Forging a Nation, 1707–1837* (New Haven, 1992).
11. J. P. Smith, *An Account of a Successful Experiment* (1812) quoted in E. P. Thompson, *The Making of the English Working Class* (New York: Vintage, 1963), p. 82.
12. For traditional accounts of British police history, C. Reith, *British Police and the Democratic Ideal* (London, 1943) and *A Short History of the British Police* (Oxford, 1948); Critchley, *A History of the Police*; D. Ascoli, *The Queen's Peace. Origins and Development of the Metropolitan Police, 1829–1979* (London, 1979). Public indecency included drunkenness, loitering, prostitution, cockfighting, bearbaiting and gambling. For the policeman as enforcer of social morality, R. D. Storch, 'The Policeman as Domestic Missionary: Urban Discipline and Popular Culture in Northern England, 1850–1880', *JSH*, 9 (1976), 481–509.
13. R. D. Storch, 'The Plague of the Blue Locusts: Police Reform and Popular Resistance in Northern England, 1840–57', *International Review of Social History*, 20 (1975), 61–90 and 'The Policeman as Domestic Missionary'.
14. Paley, 'Policing London', 114–16.
15. Ibid., 115.
16. For teething troubles, ibid., 116.
17. National Archives [N.A.], London, Home Office, HO 65/12, S. M. Phillipps to Select Committee on the State of the Police, 27 July 1833; Metropolitan Police Daily Reports, 1833–38.
18. N.A., Metropolitan Police: Office of the Commissioner: Correspondence and Papers, MEPO 2/38, letter of Sir Robert Peel, 10 December 1829, for attempts to institute screening mechanisms.
19. PP, 627, xiii, 407, *Report from the Select Committee on the Petition of Frederick Young and Others*, 3–5 (hereafter *Frederick Young Report*).

20. *Frederick Young Report*, pp. 7–10, evidence of J. B. Brown. Popay apparently masqueraded as a landscape drawer and encouraged the Political Union members to obtain weapons, even offering them training in swordsmanship.
21. Ibid., pp. 3–5, petition.
22. Ibid., pp. 58–80, evidence of Sergeant W. Popay.
23. Ibid., p. 47, evidence of Supt. A. McLean.
24. Ibid., p. 47, McLean.
25. Ibid., p. 60, Popay.
26. Ibid., p. 3, 'Resolution 1'.
27. Ibid., p. 3, 'Resolution 3'.
28. Ibid., p. 81. Plainclothesmen were particularly useful in apprehending pickpockets at large public gatherings.
29. Ibid., pp. 4–5, petition.
30. Ibid., p. 80, evidence of Rowan.
31. PP, 718, xiii, 589, *Report from the Select Committee on Cold Bath Fields Meeting* [hereafter *Cold Bath Fields Report*].
32. *Cold Bath Fields Report*, p. 16.
33. N.A., MEPO 4/2, 'Return of Deaths in the Metropolitan Police'. PC Robert Culley (No. 1044) is listed as the second member of Metropolitan Police to be killed in the line of duty.
34. *Times*, 14 May 1833, 'Meeting of the National Union'.
35. *Cold Bath Fields Report*, p. 7.
36. Ibid., p. 29.
37. N.A., HO 65/11, letter of S. M. Phillipps to Col. Rowan, 30 May 1833, for delays in payment of a £200 death gratuity to Culley's widow.
38. N.A., HO 61/9, 'Metropolitan Police Correspondence'. An anonymous undated letter threatened the Home Secretary after the 'murders in Calthorpe Street': 'You infernal villain ... Thou shalt be tried yet'.
39. *Cold Bath Fields Report*, p. 29.
40. The verdict of 'justifiable homicide' on those tried for the death of Constable Culley shocked both the Police Department and London society: it was overturned on appeal. Critchley, *A History of the Police in England and Wales*, p. 55.
41. *Cold Bath Fields Report*, pp. 29–30, evidence of May.
42. Ibid., pp. 3–4.
43. For the tensions this could provoke, D. Philips and R. D. Storch, 'Whigs and Coppers: the Grey Ministry's National Police Scheme, 1832', *Historical Review*, 67 (1994), 75–90. The London Metropolitan Police adopted blue uniforms to differentiate its constables from red-uniformed soldiers, Critchley, *History of the* Police, p. 51.
44. The orthodox ('cop-sided') view, and the revisionist ('lop-sided') view, are compared in R. Reiner, *The Politics of the Police*, (Brighton, 1985), pp. 9–47.
45. C. D. Robinson, 'Ideology as History: A Look at the Way Some English Police Historians Look at the Police', *Police Studies*, 2 (1979), 35–49.
46. Critchley, *A History of the Police*; Ascoli, *The Queen's Peace*.
47. PP, 675, xiii, 401, *Report from the Select Committee on Metropolitan Police*, p. 5.
48. Storch, 'The Plague of the Blue Locusts', Reiner, *The Politics of the Police*, and Paley, 'Policing London'.

49. Thompson, *Making of the Working Class in England*; E. J. Hobsbawn, *The Age of Revolution* (London, 1962) and *The Age of Capital* (London, 1975).
50. Paley, 'Policing London', 124–5. Among the first Joint Commissioners of the Metropolitan Police was Col. Rowan, a former Irish magistrate and ex-army officer.
51. Storch describes the New Police as the 'all purpose leveler of urban discipline' as constables waged campaigns against public drunkenness, prostitution, gambling, selling liquor outside allowed hours, and creating disturbances outside churches during services. See 'The Policeman as Domestic Missionary'.
52. Storch, 'The Plague of the Blue Locusts', 66–7.
53. The authors of these reports hardly represented a cross-section of society, and would have been unlikely to entertain inflammatory accusations against the police. Archived police reports also tend to give filtered and sanitized versions of events. D. J. V. Jones, 'The New Police, Crime, and People in England and Wales, 1829–1888', *TRHS*, 5th series, 33 (1983), 151.
54. PP, 58, iv, 409, *Bill for Further Improving the Police*, 15 February 1839.
55. F. C. Mather, *Public Order in the Age of the Chartists* (Manchester, 1959).
56. S. Inwood, 'Policing London's Morals: the Metropolitan Police and Popular Culture, 1829–1850', *London Journal* 15 (1990), 131–5.
57. B. Porter, *The Origins of the Vigilant State. The London Metropolitan Police Special Branch Before the First World War* (London, 1987).

3
Metropolitan Whiggery, 1832–55
Ben Weinstein

Historians of early and mid-Victorian politics have tended to characterize London as city dominated by an independent, artisanal, anti-statist, and anti-aristocratic radical political culture.[1] Whiggery's role in the construction of London's Victorian political culture, meanwhile, has been almost entirely ignored.[2] Yet, while it is true that elements of 'old radicalism' were central to London's early Victorian political culture, it is equally true that Whiggery wielded significant influence over metropolitan politics during this same period. In fact, it can be argued that the anti-statist and anti-aristocratic agenda promoted so successfully by what Patrick Joyce describes as '*Reynolds's*-style' radicalism in the 1850s remained resonant in London precisely because the Whig aristocracy, and the Russellite vision of an enlarged state, remained such prominent influences on metropolitan political culture in the 1840s and 1850s.[3] Although metropolitan radicalism was by no means merely reactive to Whig policy, Whiggery did exert a powerful 'negative influence' over the construction of the early Victorian metropolitan radical identity. The decline of Toryism in the metropolitan boroughs after 1832, and Whiggery's simultaneous elevation into a creed of government, enhanced and ensured this influence. Each of these developments remobilized metropolitan radicals into more direct confrontation with Whiggery in the metropolitan constituencies and this newly antagonistic relationship altered electoral strategies for Whig and radical alike. In this context, metropolitan radicals promptly began to portray the Whigs as the party of administrative centralization while loudly promoting themselves as the defenders of English 'local self-government'. Despite these attacks, Whiggery remained a potent force in the metropolitan boroughs. During the two decades following the Great Reform Act of 1832, some 30 per cent (12 out of 40) of all metropolitan MPs harboured strong ties to either the Melbourne or Russell administrations.

In the absence of early Victorian metropolitan psephological evidence, how do we explain the metropolitan electoral success enjoyed by high-profile Russellites such as Lord Robert Grosvenor, William Clay, Hugh Fortescue, Benjamin Hawes, Charles Lushington, and C. R. Fox in the 1840s and 1850s?[4] This chapter suggests that these successes owed a great deal to the popularity of the Russellite social reform programme among metropolitan professionals. While Whiggery remained an important element of metropolitan political culture during the 1830s, its most distinctive contribution to London's politics was not felt until the mid-1840s, when Russell's answer to the 'condition of England question' found a receptive and politically powerful metropolitan audience among London's professional classes. In addition to winning the support of key figures from philanthropic-minded metropolitan literary bohemians (Douglas Jerrold, Henry Mayhew, Charles Dickens and Leigh Hunt were all enthusiastic supporters), the Russellite social reform programme was also embraced by lower order medical professionals who hoped that its proposed reforms might advance scientific specialization and enhance the status of the expert.

Yet, if Russell's social reform programme recruited the support of many metropolitan professionals it also alienated important groups of commercialist metropolitan liberals. The popular perception that Russellite Whiggery was single-mindedly intent on enlarging the central government, *polarized* the liberal community in London between Whigs and *Reynolds's*-style radicals.[5] From the late 1840s, this process was exacerbated by Russellite solutions to the ongoing 'London Government Problem', which further enhanced Whiggery's reputation for centralization and state paternalism.[6] State centralization was seen by many radical critics as the logical outcome of Whiggery's inherently paternalistic and aristocratic perspective.[7] Of course, Whiggery was understood by many of its retrenchment-minded critics as a fundamentally aristocratic political creed, and many of the Whigs who were most active in metropolitan politics during the early Victorian period happened to be members of the so-called 'sacred circle of the great grandmotherhood' – the ultimate articulation of Whig aristocratic exclusiveness. It was precisely these elitist associations that prompted the Middlesex radical MP Ralph Bernal Osbourne to condemn Russellite Whiggery as 'a snug family party'.[8] Such views were further reinforced by Whig identification with metropolitan high society, especially as embodied in Brooks's Club and Holland House. But London was much more to Whiggery than a playground – just as Holland House and Brooks's were much more than sites of fun and fashion. In a very real sense, London was central to the whole Whig self-understanding and identity.

With this in mind, the following section examines London's importance to the construction of Whig identity and self-understanding, while simultaneously making the case for Whiggery's metropolitan political influence. It will be suggested that the support of an important constituency of metropolitan professionals enhanced Whiggery's influence over metropolitan political culture and ensured its continued electoral success in the metropolitan constituencies.

Whiggery in early Victorian London

In July 1843, the *Edinburgh Review* published T. B. Macaulay's review of Lucy Aikin's *Life of Addison*. In keeping with the format favoured by the *Edinburgh Review*, Macaulay's essay said very little about Aikin's work and a great deal about Addison's.[9] Not surprisingly, given Addison's place in the Whig cosmology, Macaulay's assessment was unreservedly admiring. In Macaulay's view Addison deserved to be 'considered not only as the greatest of the English essayists, but also as forerunner of the great English novelists.'[10] The essay supported this claim by illustrating the precocious novelistic qualities of the *Spectator* series, and by praising Addison's two greatest characters: Mr. Spectator (considered by Macaulay to be Addison's greatest 'serious' character) and the *Freeholder*'s 'Foxhunter' (considered by Macaulay to be Addison's greatest 'satirical' character). But while Macaulay's *Review* essay purported to judge Addison's work on purely literary grounds, much of its real interest lay in politics. In particular, Macaulay's decision to contrast Mr. Spectator against the Foxhunter seemed to reveal much more about Macaulay's hopes for contemporary Whiggery than it did about Addison's literary talents. The essay recognized in Mr. Spectator a 'faultless' articulation of the ideal Whig. It held up the Foxhunter, meanwhile, as Mr. Spectator's 'perfect' Tory foil. Importantly, Macaulay's description of Mr. Spectator emphasized the character's metropolitan sophistication and urbanity vis-à-vis the provincial narrow-mindedness of the Foxhunter. Macaulay wrote,

> The Spectator is a gentleman who, after passing a studious youth at the university, has traveled on classic ground, and has bestowed much attention on curious points of antiquity. He has, on his return, fixed his residence in London, and has observed all the forms of life which are to be found in that great city, has daily listened to the wits of Will's, has smoked with the philosophers of the Grecian, and has mingled with the parsons at Child's, and with the politicians at St. James's. In the morning he often listens to the hum of the Exchange; in the evening, his face is constantly to be seen in the pit of Drury Lane theatre.[11]

The Tory Foxhunter, on the other hand, was 'ignorant, stupid, and violent ... the original of Squire Western.'[12]

Addison's various attempts to define Whiggery by its metropolitan sophistication and urbanity, and against the self-interested and narrow-minded parochialism of the Tory squirearchy, delighted Victorian 'advanced Whigs' like Macaulay, who, according to Leslie Mitchell, themselves had a tendency to 'characterize Whig and Tory in terms of London against an unsophisticated countryside'.[13] Unsurprisingly, Macaulay often described Addison as a member of 'our caste', but while Addison's metropolitan prejudices fitted nicely with Foxite Whiggery's 'unabashed urbanity', and although Lord Holland was always mindful of honouring Addison's Holland House connections,[14] one must acknowledge that the brand of Whiggery promoted by Addison was nonetheless far removed from that practiced by Russell, Macaulay or even Fox, a century later. Yet throughout the 1830s and 1840s, Whigs like Russell, Morpeth and Grosvenor stayed true to the conviction that London was the *essential* context for Whiggery's self-realization. These cultural attachments kept London at the very heart of both the Russellite political mission and of Whig identity and self-understanding.

The Addisonian devotion to London had, of course, been strengthened by Charles James Fox during the late eighteenth-century when Fox had been known as the 'Westminster Watchman' and when he had, in turn, described Westminster as his 'refuge and protection' and his 'citadel'.[15] It is no coincidence that these views were shared throughout the 1840s and 1850s by Russell and many of his closest associates, each of whom had long worshipped at the alter of Fox.[16] In the wake of Romilly's suicide in 1819, Russell himself contemplated standing for Westminster as heir to the Foxite legacy. Ultimately, Russell's attempts at nomination failed, prompting Fox's old enemy Francis Place to observe happily that 'it is now no use to talk of old Foxey, who was always insincere, always a friend of the people, when out of office, always willing to sacrifice them to get into place.'[17] But Place's judgment was ill made, for the 'radical' candidate (John Cam Hobhouse) was himself one of Fox's greatest admirers – a trait which, if kept relatively secret in 1818, would be dramatically exposed in years to come. Indeed, when Hobhouse first offered himself to the Westminster electors, he revealed to Place that 'he should endeavor to tread in the steps of that illustrious man the late Charles James Fox.'[18]

Almost 30 years later, the Foxite legacy still played in important part in metropolitan political culture. When the third Baron Holland's eldest son, C. R. Fox, finally entered politics in 1841, as a candidate for Tower

Hamlets, he professed to be standing on exactly the same principles that had motivated his father and uncle before him,[19] and when he was returned to parliament Lady Holland attributed this success to his unique genealogy and the unique political training he had received within the walls of Holland House. 'His name, his father's son,' she claimed, 'gave the impetus to their [the electors] zeal. They remembered how warmly their cause had been advocated by him, who lived but to promote peace and amity among mankind.'[20] The *Times* was incredulous that the largest and most plebeian of all the metropolitan constituencies should fall under the Foxite spell, and immediately began referring to the borough as 'the Whig rotten borough of Tower Hamlets.'[21] It did not help the borough's reputation that, at around the same time, the supposedly radical MP for Tower Hamlets William Clay had also begun working closely with Russell's administration on sanitary reform.[22]

During the first half of the nineteenth century, the intense Whig attachment to London was also sustained by ties of immediate self-interest. Four of early Victorian London's largest and most rapidly developing estates were owned by aggressively Whig families – namely the Russells in Bloomsbury, the Grosvenors in Westminster, the Portmans in Marylebone and the Foxs in Holland Park. In the early nineteenth century, as these estates were developed, their owners began to take an ever greater interest in what kind of place London would eventually become.[23] In addition to the financial incentives for development, therefore, Whig Grandees often felt sharp social obligations to improve the quality of metropolitan life. According to Henry Trelawny Boodle, agent for the Grosvenor and Northampton estates, the Earl Westminster carried out his developments not for personal or financial gain, but 'chiefly … on public grounds … because he desires better houses, and he is a great lover of architecture and likes a handsome town, and he would sacrifice enormously to carry that out on his estate. By far the most important element, in his mind, is the present improvement of London quite irrespective of what his children or grandchildren may succeed to.'[24] The Seventh Duke of Bedford, meanwhile, did his utmost to have Bloomsbury developed into a socially balanced yet uniformly respectable district, and he disapproved strongly of the negligence of his neighbours Lord Somers and the Earl of Southampton, who had let their lands be used for third- and fourth-rate housing.[25]

The attitudes displayed by the Grosvenors and Russells hint at their paternal interest in wider metropolitan culture. Unsurprisingly, this paternal interest was often extended into metropolitan politics. There is compelling evidence, for instance, that during the early nineteenth century the great Whig metropolitan landowners went to some lengths to secure Whig victories in a number of metropolitan elections. Various incidents attest to this. In early June, 1818, to take one example, Francis Place suggested that Parry, then the editor of the Whiggish *Morning Chronicle*, had been making 'a list of persons, and he was hunting them out to make a requisition to Romilly. He and Barber Beaumont, who had been consulting with the steward of the Duke of Bedford and had listed out the names of some leasees whose term was nearly ended and who were consequently in a state of dependence for a renewal of their leases, and to them they both went, and obtained their signatures – this trick was also played on the estates of other Noble Whig Grandees [sic]'.[26] In a later diary entry relating to the same incident, Place implicated both the Duke of Bedford and Earl Grosvenor, claiming that 'Richards and Allen, both of Tavistock street, signed it [the requisition] on being urged in the way above named – both were negotiating for new leases.'[27]

In the wake of the Reform Act, Edward Berkeley Portman took a somewhat more straightforward approach to influencing the political culture of Marylebone, a constituency in which he was a large landowner. Portman had represented Dorset, where he was also a large landowner, and had proved a very popular figure within that constituency. On the creation of the new metropolitan boroughs in 1832, however, Portman immediately quit Dorset to stand for election in his much more valuable metropolitan land holding. Radical disquiet over Portman's borough influence eventually prompted Portman to promise publicly that he 'should not himself use any influence whatever over the votes of any man'.[28] After the election, however, the radical candidates made numerous objections to the 'bribery' and intimidation used by Portman and his Whig cronies to secure Whig returns. The ultra-radical St. Pancras vestryman Thomas Murphy, who polled a mere 900 votes to Portman's 4000 plus, went so far as to claim that he would have been returned 'if they [the electors] could have given their votes free from corrupt influence ... in this election, corruption had been used to defeat me, and to ensure the triumph of the ministerial candidates'.[29] In his lengthy condemnation of the election proceedings, Murphy linked Portman's extensive borough proprietorship with Whig bribery and intimidation, and in doing so exposed both the degree to which landownership and politics overlapped and the lengths to which Whigs would go to win important metropolitan constituencies.

Given Whiggery's high metropolitan profile, many Whigs had understandably high hopes for success in the new metropolitan boroughs created by the Reform Act. In fact, many of the candidates returned to parliament by these new metropolitan constituencies at the first reformed election had attachments to Grey's (admittedly mixed) Whig government, and the results of this election hint at the extent to which Whiggery's metropolitan electoral strength has been underestimated. William Horne, for instance, who was elected for the new borough of Marylebone in 1832, had been solicitor general since 1830, and was raised to the post of attorney-general shortly after the election. Not surprisingly, Horne pushed a strict party line in parliament and was often criticized by Marylebone radicals for a perceived over-reliance on the influence of his aristocratic Whig friends.[30] Largely on account of these connections, Marylebone radicals categorized Horne as a 'Whig of the old school'.[31] As we have seen, Marylebone's other representative, Edward Berkeley Portman, exceeded even Horne's considerable Whig connections. Portman's membership in the so-called 'sacred circle of the great-grandmotherhood' gave him unquestionable Whig credentials. According to his radical critics, Portman was 'of so aristocratic a temper, that he would not condescend to mix freely and confidentially with the electors'.[32] Despite this aloofness, however, Portman polled more votes in 1832 than any other candidate in the metropolitan constituencies, including Joseph Hume in Middlesex.

Marylebone's relatively wealthy electorate could have been expected to return a pair of Whigs in 1832. But that 'opulent and extensive quarter' (as the Earl Grey called Marylebone) was by no means alone in its appreciation of Whiggism. In Tower Hamlets, which was certainly the poorest and most solidly plebeian metropolitan borough in 1832, Stephen Lushington was returned at the head of the poll.[33] Lushington, like Horne, was a Whig legal placeman who had formed strong links to Brougham during their shared defence of Queen Caroline in 1820.[34] Throughout the 1820s Lushington had worked within the Whig opposition to abolish West Indian slavery and to repeal the civil disabilities of the Jews. These causes brought Lushington into close working relationships with a number of leading Whigs, including Lord John Russell, who Lushington claimed to be particularly closely allied to.[35] In Finsbury, Robert Grant struck a very similar figure. Like Lushington, Grant had worked closely with Russell on Jewish emancipation and was a legal placeman.[36] During the 1832 election, Grant flaunted his desire to work even more closely with the government. When asked to justify his candidacy, he made no mention of serving Finsbury's interests. Instead, he simply advertised the fact that he 'was identified with the present administration, and it was upon this ground that I solicit the support of the electors'.[37] Grant's defection to Whiggery, a move which disappointed many metropolitan radicals, was all but ensured by the promise of further patronage.[38] Shortly after the election, Grant was appointed judge advocate-general. Together with the Southwark representative William Brougham, brother of the ambitious Lord Chancellor, Grant, Horne and Lushington were quickly labeled by the radical press as 'the place holding and place coveting members for the metropolis'.[39]

Somewhat surprisingly, Benjamin Hawes, MP for Lambeth in 1832, was not included by the radical press in this group of place holders and place seekers. Yet Hawes was every bit as friendly to Whiggery as Horne, Grant or Lushington, and in 1832 he sought out his own place energetically.[40] 'I cannot better describe my political principles', he claimed in 1832, 'than by stating that they are in strict accordance with the policy pursued by his majesty's present government'.[41] Westminster and Middlesex, meanwhile, returned Whigs of their own, for by 1832, John Cam Hobhouse had officially fallen back into league with the Whigs[42] and the old Foxite, George Byng, had once again been returned for the metropolitan county. This meant that in 1832, *every* metropolitan constituency returned at least one Whig.[43] In the wake of these metropolitan victories, Lord Tavistock could not help but gloat, "I cannot say how much pleasure these triumphs have given me ... what an answer to conservative foreboding has been furnished by the metropolitan districts."[44]

Importantly, Whig electoral strength and mass appeal in the metropolitan boroughs remained robust throughout the 1830s and into the 1840s, paving the way for the metropolitan success of Russell's social reform programme. The 1842 publication of Edwin Chadwick's *Report on the Sanitary Condition of the Labouring Population of Great Britain* led almost immediately to a welter of philanthropic activity, and then, from 1844, to an avowedly *political* movement for sanitary reform and implementation of the Chadwickian agenda for overhaul of Britain's urban administration. The Health of Towns Association (HOTA) was the first institutional manifestation of this politicized movement.[45] Among Chadwick's biographers, much has been made of the HOTA's bi-partisan membership.[46] However, this emphasis on political bipartisanship tends to mask the important fact that the HOTA's essential agenda was for state centralization. Consequently, the organization's prominent Whig members tended to be Russellites (Morpeth, Grosvenor, Ebrington and Normanby for instance), while its Tories were either high evangelicals like Ashley or Young Englanders like Disraeli and Lord John Manners. Peelites and liberals were noticeably absent, and by the time of its 1847 mutation into the Metropolitan Sanitary Association (MSA), the HOTA had become unmistakably Russellite. With the arch-Russellite, Robert

Grosvenor (who, from 1847, sat for Middlesex), at its head, the MSA used its *First Report* to announce a commitment to Chadwick's original vision of a centralized and rationalized sanitary administration for all of London.[47] Unsurprisingly, the MSA took a correspondingly dim view of London's parochially administered system, and never failed to use its platform to make ideological attacks on vestry government.[48] From the very beginning, the MSA publicized its paternalist sympathies for London's most destitute residents by identifying itself as an enemy of narrow middle-class municipal penny-pinching and retrenchment.[49] Attitudes such as these reinforced Whiggery's paternalist reputation while simultaneously enhancing Whiggery's popularity among London's poorest as well as among London's philanthropically minded professional community.

Although politicized organizations such as HOTA and the MSA were patronized by paternally minded social elites, many of their most active and important members were drawn from the professions. The Chadwickean/Russellite programme promoted by HOTA and the MSA appealed to professionals in two ways. First, it exploited elements of philanthropic culture, which boomed in the years following the publication of Chadwick's *Report* and which, in the 1840s and 1850s, was particularly pronounced among social elites such as physicians, barristers, clerics and members of metropolitan literary scene.[50] Second, the Chadwickean/Russellite programme promoted codification, rationalization and the rise of the expert – all of which appealed to lower order professionals such as the surgeons, who by the mid-nineteenth century were caught in a battle for professional recognition.[51] The *Lancet*, for instance, initially endorsed the Russellite sanitary reform programme explicitly on the basis that it would aid the rise of the medical expert.[52] Although the *Lancet* was ultimately disappointed with the way in which Morpeth's Public Health Bill used professional expertise, medical and engineering 'experts' such as Thomas Southwood Smith and Henry Austin were eventually promoted to important positions within the Chadwickian administrative apparatus. In light of these promotions, it is little wonder that prominent metropolitan critics of Russellite sanitary reform often described the MSA and other Russellite social reform organizations as being dominated by a 'coterie of patentless doctors, briefless barristers, and better employed engineers'.[53]

Crossover appeal to both elite (established) and low (emerging) professional cultures won a widespread and balanced foundation of support for the Russellite social programme amongst the metropolitan professional community. This was an extremely important coup for Russell.

While London certainly was a city of artisans and traders, it was also *the* centre of the professional world, and contained more doctors, lawyers and journalists than the rest of the country put together.[54] In 1851, nearly 30 per cent of all professionals employed in England and Wales (or 84,738 in gross numbers) were employed in London.[55] Of course, as home to the Inns of Court, the Royal Colleges and central government, London had traditionally been the focus of professional development. Peter Earle has estimated that as much as one-third of the early Georgian metropolitan middle class were professionals. A century later, professionals no longer accounted for such a high proportion of the expanding metropolitan middle class, but still wielded an enormous amount of influence in metropolitan society and politics.[56] Gareth Stedman Jones, for one, has described London's mid-Victorian professional community as 'the new London Gentry' because of the great influence that they exerted on metropolitan culture.[57] Moreover, because of its wealth, this new London gentry accounted for a relatively large proportion of the metropolitan electorate. From the 1820s, the London University medical school in particular began producing what Adrian Desmond has called 'the future medical electorate who would carry through Benthamite social objectives in health, welfare, and management reform'.[58] In London, this newly influential 'medical electorate' played an important role in the unfolding of Russell's plans.

Societies such as the MSA introduced Russellite social policy to members of the London medical elite like Sir James Clark, Hector Gavin and Joseph Toynbee while appealing simultaneously to lower order Benthamite surgeons like Thomas Southwood Smith and R. A. Grainger. It is worth noting, for instance, that roughly one-third of the MSA's lay, non-titled membership were medical men.[59] Moreover, if these doctors joined the MSA as politically neutral philanthropists, many quickly became loyal Russellites. Joseph Toynbee's example is instructive. Toynbee, a fairly prominent metropolitan aural surgeon and fellow of both the Royal Society and the Royal College of Surgeons, had been an enthusiastic, but politically neutral, supporter of organizations like the National Philanthropic Association and the Metropolitan Association for Ventilation for the Poor since the early 1840s. During this early phase of his philanthropic involvement, Toynbee confessed that he worked merely to 'confer a good deal of happiness ... on the labouring classes'.[60] In 1845, Toynbee joined the executive committee of the Russellite Society for Improving the Conditions of the Labouring Classes and in the same year he became a general committee member of both the HOTA and the MSA. In the following year, he became treasurer of the Metropolitan Association for the Improvement of the Dwellings of the Industrious Classes, in which capacity he began to work closely with Lord Morpeth.

From this point on his philanthropy became strongly politicized, and when Morpeth introduced his Public Health Bill in March, 1847, Toynbee threw all his weight behind it. He believed Morpeth's Bill to be a 'very comprehensive one', and revealed further the extent to which his involvement in social reform had been politicized by warning that while the Bill would 'do great good ... if it passes; it will no doubt create great opposition in interested parties, but we must break it down'.[61] At around this time Toynbee began to loath the radical cry for local self-government, which he believed had been used to mislead and manipulate working-class opinion. Toward the end of his life, he recalled with regret how a fundamentally *middle-class* anti-centralization agenda had blinded working men to their true interests. Speaking of the radical rebellion against the Russellite social reform programme, Toynbee claimed that, 'after blandly smiling at all our commissions, committees, lectures, evidence, speeches, books, and statistics, which showed the evils arising from defective sanitary legislation John Bull suddenly became alarmed ... so he jumped up, cudgel in hand, beating about him right and left, and of course threw blame on the wrong parties'.[62] Toynbee hoped that his commitment to the Russellite plan, and his loyalty in the face of the radical onslaught, would be repaid with an appointment to whatever authority would arise from the proposed reforms.[63] After all, his expertise had been integral to the functioning of the Russellite social reform organizations, and he, among others, expected the Russellite programme eventually to produce a centralized, bureaucratic government of experts and specialists.

This prospect was especially attractive to Benthamite lower order professionals, who looked forward to a professional world based on merit and specialized knowledge rather than social connections, and whose commitment to the Russellite programme is powerfully illustrated by the workings of the Health of London Association (HLA). The HLA advertised its professional character repeatedly, and claimed to speak particularly on behalf of London's surgeons, solicitors, architects and surveyors. Although the HLA claimed to admire the work that had been carried out by organizations like the HOTA, it still 'considered that the idea of endeavoring to obtain the sentiments and opinions of that portion of the public who were, from their professions or avocations, best fitted to afford information, had not been sufficiently carried out',[64] which suggests that the organization's motivations might have had less to do with philanthropy than with the rise of the expert.

In 1847, the HLA issued a report that claimed to represent the opinions of over 3000 professionals from across the metropolis on how London ought to be governed. The report's conclusions were a ringing endorsement of Lord Morpeth's Sanitary Bill and of the need for a central Council of Health to preside over London.

> It is universally declared [by respondents to the Association's survey] to be essentially necessary for the benefit of the community at large, that such a central board be constituted ... many express their surprise that government has never yet instituted such a council, or that the philanthropic portion of the public has not insisted on it ... sanitary measures, in order to be effectual, must be carried out on a large scale; and unless the Legislature gives encouragement to public bodies to carry out efficient measures for sanitary improvements, they will never be effectually promoted, for it is impossible for private contractors to undertake very extensive works. The powers invested in the various existing commissions are wholly inadequate for the purpose of promoting the public health. The legislature should encourage sanitary improvements in every possible way, either by giving more power to the existing boards, controlled by a central board, or by creating new powers.[65]

Many of the HLA's most prominent members (including, for example, Thomas Southwood Smith, R. A. Grainger and Henry Austin) were Benthamites. Throughout the 1840s and 1850s metropolitan medical men were especially drawn to Benthamism. This was partly a consequence of private medical training in London, which was given at places such as the Webb street school in Lambeth, the Aldersgate school in the City and Dermott's school in Soho. According to Adrian Desmond,

> by the 1830s many of these schools were staffed by Benthamites and Wakleyans. The teachers supported the gamut of Benthamite reforms, moving beyond calls of state control of medicine or a minister of health (as mooted by Bentham). The Webb street school was the most obviously Benthamite, and its anatomists publicly examined the master's constitution in more ways than one.[66]

This group was understandably drawn to a movement that promoted the Benthamite virtues of codification, rationalization, and the rise of the expert, and as prominent members of the HOTA and HLA, Thomas Southwood Smith and R.A. Grainger were living bridges between London's Benthamite surgical culture and Russellite health reform. In the 1820s and 1830s, Smith and Grainger both taught at the Webb street school, where they and their fellow radical medics were at that time in the thick of a debate about the first principles of life. Both rejected the Anglican (or Cuverian) conception of vital powers and creative influence, and posited instead that life depends only on certain physical conditions (the Lamarkian attitude). At the same time, Smith and Grainger were unremittingly hostile to the laissez-faire attitude contained within the Cuverian view.[67]

Like Chadwick, Smith understood social and sanitary reform as necessary prerequisites for creating a level playing field upon which anything close to a deregulated society or 'free' competition could be fought out on. In Smith's view, the Chadwickian/Russellite health reformers had

> taken the lead in proclaiming that nothing can be done for the improvement of the people as long as these sanitary miseries are allowed to exist; that no efforts on the part of the people for their own improvement can be successful until they are raised above these degrading influences; that no increase in the demand for labour, no rise in wages, no success in the management of those wages can give health and comfort to their families until their dwellings cease to be dark, damp, and filthy dens; that the admission of pure air to their houses, and the bright sun, and an abundant supply of wholesome water, must precede and preface the work of the schoolmaster and the minister of religion.[68]

Tellingly, the debates that informed these views (views which predisposed radical medics like Smith toward Benthamism) were almost unique to the medical profession, and hence largely absent from other professions such as engineering.

Importantly, many of the Whigs who won electoral success in metropolitan constituencies during the 1840s and 1850s were closely associated with the Russellite social reform movement. The political career of one of Southwood Smith's fellow members on the governing council of the Metropolitan Commission of Sewers illustrate this point and provides a final testament to the strength of Whiggery in the early Victorian metropolitan constituencies. Like Lord Robert Grosvenor in Middlesex, who had long been a high profile member of the MSA, and who consistently advocated Chadwick's 'centralized' solution to the London government and sanitation problems, Hugh Fortescue was one of the first Commissioners appointed to the new metropolitan administrative body.[69] In the wake of Chadwick's fall, Fortescue managed to win a seat for Marylebone (1854), even as the constituency's vestry radicals strongly criticized his past life as a Chadwickian 'centralizer'.[70] During the late 1840s and early 1850s, Marylebone had been at the very heart of the radical vestry opposition to Russellite 'centralization'. Now it was to be represented by an arch-Russellite and arch-Chadwickian. Importantly, Fortescue won the Marylebone election without making a single pledge – an extremely unusual feat in a reformed metropolitan borough, and an even more unusual feat in Marylebone, which had long since turned its liberal MPs into delegates for vestry interests.[71] In fact, Fortescue criticized the idea of pledges at every opportunity, thereby further revealing his fundamentally paternalist outlook.[72] Upon retiring from Marylebone five years later, Fortescue reiterated his belief that 'bidding for the honest votes of ignorant voters by dishonest professions and servile pledges, demoralizes candidates even more than their constituencies and sacrifices the Members to the electors' independence, making him their delegate rather than their representative.'[73]

Very little separated Fortescue's views from those put forward in Westminster by Francis Burdett 30 years earlier. Paternalism lay at the core of both approaches, and it underpinned the wider metropolitan strength of Whiggery. Just as the promise of 'scientific paternalism' won a constituency of support for Russellite Whiggery among London's large and influential professional community, so social paternalism ensured the success of men like Fortescue and Grosvenor. As one vestry radical derisively put it, Marylebone had 'always hankered after the honour of being represented by a scion of the aristocracy'.[74] We have seen that this 'hankering' was shared by many of the metropolitan constituencies. Russellite Whigs such as Ebrington, Grosvenor, Fox and even Lord John Russell himself in the City, recognized the opportunities presented for aristocratic paternalist leadership by the metropolitan constituencies in the 1840s and 1850s. During these decades, London politics (and particularly the fight over sanitation reform and the London government problem) gave Whiggery a chance to preserve and even revitalize its metropolitan credentials and identity by casting itself as a paternal defender of those without voices in London's vestry government. At the same time, Whiggery's revitalization gave London a chance to reject the narrow localism and political economy of vestry and *Reynolds's*-style radicalism.

Notes

1. M. Taylor *The Decline of British Radicalism* (Oxford, 1995), p. 71; I. Prothero, *Artisans and Politics in Early Nineteenth-Century London: John Gast and his Times* (Hassocks, 1979); E. P. Thompson, *The Making of the English Working-Class* (London, 1968).
2. D. Southgate, *The Passing of the Whigs, 1832–1886* (London, 1962), p. 97. P. Mandler, *Aristocratic Government in the Age of Reform, Whigs and Liberals 1830–1852* (Oxford, 1990) emphasizes connections between Whiggery and popular support. L. Mitchell, *Holland House* (London, 1980); Richard Brent, *Liberal Anglican Politics: Whiggery, Religion, and Reform 1830–1841* (Oxford, 1987); T. A. Jenkins, *Gladstone, Whiggery, and the Liberal Party, 1874–1886* (Oxford, 1988); I. D. C. Newbould, 'The Whigs, the Church, and Education, 1839', *JBS*, 26 (1987), 332–46; idem, 'Whiggery and the Dilemma of Reform: Liberals, Radicals, and the Melbourne administration, 1835–39', *BIHR*, 53 (1980), 229–41; J. P. Parry, *The Rise and Fall of Liberal Government in Victorian Britain* (New Haven, 1993); idem, 'Past and Future in the Later Career of Lord John Russell', in T. C. W. Blanning and D. Cannadine (eds) *History and Biography* (Cambridge, 1996).
3. P. Joyce, *Visions of the People: Industrial England and the Question of Class, 1840–1914* (Cambridge, 1991), pp. 67–70.
4. No pollbook exists for any London borough after 1841.
5. The idea of Whig centralization is articulated in: B. Disraeli, *Whigs and Whiggism*, ed. William Hutcheon (London, 1913); Mandler, *Aristocratic Government*; W. Lubenow, *The Politics of Government Growth* (Newton Abbot, 1971); D. Roberts *The Victorian Origins of the British Welfare State* (New Haven, 1961). Cf. Parry, *Rise and Fall of Liberal Government*; J. Prest, *Liberty and Locality: Parliament, Permissive Legislation, and Ratepayer Democracies in the Nineteenth-Century* (Oxford, 1990).
6. J. Davis *Reforming London* (Oxford, 1988); D. Owen, *The Government of Victorian London* (London, 1982).
7. For the radical critique of Whig patronage, P. Harling, *The Waning of 'Old Corruption': the Politics of Economic Reform in Britain, 1779–1846* (Oxford, 1996), pp. 208–12; David Roberts, *The Social Conscience of the Early-Victorians* (Stanford, 2002). Cf. W. D. Rubinstein, 'The End of "Old Corruption" in Britain, 1780–1860', *P & P*, 101 (1983) 55–86. For Russellite paternalism, Mandler, *Aristocratic Government*, pp. 71–85, 236–75. D. Roberts, *Paternalism in Early-Victorian England* (London, 1979), pp. 229–36.
8. R. B. Osbourne, *Speech ... on Mr. Hume's Motion for Reform of Parliament* (London, 1848), p. 15. Mandler, *Aristocratic Government*, esp. 'Part One'; Southgate *The Passing of the Whigs*, appendix III.
9. J. Shattock, *Politics and Reviewers: The Edinburgh and the Quarterly in the Early Victorian Age* (London, 1989), pp. 109–10.
10. T. B. Macaulay, 'Life and Writings of Addison', in E. A. Bloom and L. D. Bloom (eds) *Addison and Steele: The Critical Heritage* (New York, 1995), p. 420.
11. Ibid., p. 419.
12. Ibid., pp. 426–7.
13. Mitchell, *Holland House*, p. 174.

14. Addison's portrait hung even above Fox's at Holland House: J. Hamburger, *Macaulay and the Whig Tradition* (Chicago, 1976), p. 251 fn. 76; L. Sanders, *The Holland House Circle* (London, 1908), p. 91.
15. P. Corfield, E. Green and C. Harvey, 'Westminster Man: Charles James Fox and His Electorate' *PH*, 20, 2 (2001), pp. 162, 167, 182–4; P. Kelly 'Radicalism and Public Opinion in the General Election of 1784', *BIHR*, 45, 111 (1972), 75; J. Dinwiddy, 'Charles James Fox and the People', *History* 55, 185 (1970), 342.
16. F. Sitwell 'The Fox Club', in P. Ziegler and D. Seward (eds) *Brooks's: A Social History* (London, 1991), pp. 150–1.
17. British Library, London, Add. Ms. 27842 (Place Papers), fo. 42 and Add. Ms. 56540 (Broughton Papers), diary entry, 17 November 1818.
18. Place Papers, Add. Ms. 27843, fo. 391 (Place's memorandum of 1818 election, written 1 June 1826).
19. *Times*, 10 June 1841.
20. E. Vassall, Baroness Holland (ed.), *Elizabeth, Lady Holland to Her Son, 1821–1845 Earl of Ilchester* (London, 1946), p. 193: Lady Holland to Henry Holland (4th baron Holland), 2 July, 1841.
21. *Times* 5 July 1841, p. 4.
22. S. E. Finer, *The Life and Times of Sir Edwin Chadwick* (London, 1952), p. 330. W. Thomas, *The Philosophic Radicals: Nine Studies in Theory and Practice, 1817–1841* (Oxford, 1979), pp. 206–07.
23. For the wider ideals pursued by the Russells and Groveners in developing their estates, D. Olson, *The Growth of Victorian London* (Harmondsworth, 1979), chs 2–3; J. Summerson, *Georgian London* (London, 1970), ch. 14.
24. Quoted in D. Olson, *Town Planning in London: the Eighteenth and Nineteenth-Centuries* (New Haven, 1982), p. 23.
25. H. Hobhouse, *Thomas Cubitt: Master Builder* (London, 1988), ch. 4.
26. Place Papers, Add. Ms. 27841, fo. 17.
27. Place Papers, Add. Ms. 27841, fo. 124.
28. *Morning Chronicle* (MC) 10 December 1832, p. 3.
29. *MC* 12 December 1832, p. 3; *Morning Herald* 13 December, 1832, p. 3.
30. *Morning Herald*, 12, 13 December 1832, p. 3.
31. T. Murphy, *A Letter to the Radicals of the United Kingdom* (London, 1838), p. 7.
32. *Times*, 4 October 1832, p. 3.
33. The ancient Foxite, Lincoln Stanhope, secured nearly 3000 votes in 1832, but finished third.
34. E. Helevy, *History of the English People* (London, 1926), ii, p. 104.
35. S. M. Waddams, *Law, Politics, and the Church of England: The Career of Stephen Lushington, 1782–1873* (Cambridge, 1992), p. 78.
36. Grant was appointed to the board of control (1830) and the privy council (1831).
37. *Times*, 7 December 1832, p. 3.
38. Burdett cursed Grant's decision, writing in September 1830 that 'the Grants and Palmerstons will join the devil – after all our rage are the best men going'. Broughton Papers, Add. Ms. 47222, fos 260–1.
39. *Spectator*, 4 May 1833, p. 401.
40. Thomas, *Philosophic Radicals*, p. 332.
41. G. Hill, *The Electoral History of the borough of Lambeth Since its Enfranchisement in 1832 with Portraits and Memoirs of its Representatives During 46 Years* (London, 1879), p. 17.

42. Disraeli, *Whigs and Whiggism*, pp. 294, 296, thought that Hobhouse's rapprochement with Whiggery exposed him as the worst kind of Whig placeman. Cf. Brent, *Liberal Anglican Politics*.
43. Even Greenwich, which in many ways stood outside of early Victorian London, returned the loyal Whig, J. W. D. Dundas.
44. Broughton Papers, Add. Ms. 47223, fo. 62., Lord Tavistock to Hobhouse, 12 December 1832.
45. Health of Towns Association, *Abstract of Proceedings of a Public Meeting, Held at Exeter Hall, 11 December 1844* (London, 1844), p. 1.
46. S. E. Finer, *The Life and Times of Edwin Chadwick* (London, 1952), pp. 238–9; C. Hamlin, *Public Health and Social Justice in the Age of Chadwick* (Cambridge, 1998).
47. Metropolitan Sanitary Association, *First Report of the Commissioners* (London, 1847), p. 24.
48. University College London, Chadwick Papers, box 54, Metropolitan Sanitary Association, 'Considerations as to House and Town Drainage', p. 9.
49. Chadwick Papers, MS 608 fos 16–16b, Chadwick to Delane, 24 March 1848; and fos 58–60, Chadwick to Delane, 27 November 1850.
50. Harold Perkin, *Origins of Modern English Society* (London, 1969), pp. 256–7 describes the Victorian professional elite as a class of 'ready made social crank[s] who could be relied on to come to the aid of any class but their own'.
51. M. J. Peterson, *The Medical Profession in Mid-Victorian London* (London, 1978), pp. 284–7.
52. *Lancet* (1848), vol. 1, pp. 169, 216.
53. Sir R. Broun, *Extramural Interment and the Metropolitan Sanitary Association* (1852), p. 10.
54. P. Corfield, *Power and the Professions on Britain, 1700–1850* (London, 1995).
55. L. Schwarz, *London in the Age of Industrialisation* (Cambridge, 1992), pp. 4, 263.
56. P. Earle *The Making of the English Middle-Class* (London, 1989), p. 60. In 1851, professionals made up around 6 per cent of the entire metropolitan labour force: Schwarz, *London in the Age of Industrialisation*, p. 23.
57. G. Stedman Jones, *Outcast London: A Study in the Relationship between Classes in Victorian Society* (London 1976), p. 269.
58. A. Desmond, *The Politics of Evolution* (Chicago, 1989), p. 27.
59. Metropolitan Sanitary Association, *Public Health a Public Question: First Report of the Metropolitan Sanitary Association on the Sanitary Condition of the Metropolis* (London, 1850), for a membership list.
60. Bodleian Library Oxford, Toynbee Family Papers, MS Eng. lett. c. 535, fo. 1, Joseph to Charles Toynbee, 1 March 1844.
61. Toynbee Papers, MS Eng. lett. c.535, fo. 6b, Joseph to Arnold Toynbee, 30 March 1847.
62. J. Toynbee, *The Breath of Life and the Breath of Death and a People Without a Country* (London, 1866), p. 4.
63. G. Toynbee (ed.), *Reminiscences and Letters of Joseph and Arnold Toynbee* (London, n/d), p. 18.
64. *Report of the Health of London Association, on the Sanitary Condition of the Metropolis* (London, 1847), p. ix.
65. *Ibid.*, pp. 22, 63.

66. Desmond, *Politics of Evolution*, pp. 163–4. The last line refers to the public autopsy performed on Bentham's corpse by Southwood Smith in 1832.
67. B. Hilton, 'The Politics of Anatomy and the Anatomy of Politics, 1825–1850', in S. Collini, R. Whatmore and B. Young (eds), *History, Religion, and Culture: British Intellectual History, 1750–1950*, p. 189.
68. British Library(BL), Add. MS. 44919, fo. 133.
69. Fortescue (Viscount Ebrington), *Unhealthiness of Towns: Its Causes and Remedies* (London, 1851). For Fortescue's commitment to Russellite Whiggery, J. Vincent (ed.), *Disraeli, Derby and the Conservative Party: Journals and Memoirs of Edward Henry, Lord Stanley* (Hassocks, 1978), p. 55.
70. Fortescue's opponent referred to him as 'the centralizing noble Lord' throughout the contest: *Times* 19 December 1854, p. 10.
71. *The Vestryman and Metropolitan Parochial Gazette*, 28 June 1834; J. W. Brooke, *The Democrats of Marylebone* (London, 1839).
72. *Times*, 19 December 1854, p. 10; 21 December 1854, p. 7.
73. H. Fortescue, *Parliamentary Reforms: Lord Ebrington's Address to the Electors of Marylebone* (London, 1859), pp. 6–7.
74. *Times*, 10 December 1854.

4
Post-Chartism: Metropolitan Perspectives on the Chartist Movement in Decline 1848–80

Antony Taylor

In recent years, the 'cultural turn' has stimulated a move away from the micro-level studies of Chartist activity produced in the 1960s and 1970s.[1] In such work the notion of a broader 'radical culture' has flourished with an emphasis on the congruences, rather than the differences, between Chartism, radicalism and political Liberalism. In this space, political identities have blurred. Moreover, despite their ambitions to weave a national narrative of reform politics, much of this work remains rooted in the local case study with a strong bias towards the small mill towns of the North-West and the West Riding. It could be argued that what characterizes this new historical literature is its subscription to an ideal-type of Liberalism. Following the tradition established by nineteenth-century Liberal standard-bearers like Henry Jephson, Patrick Joyce and James Vernon in particular re-create an idealized picture of provincial Liberalism as represented by and for the consumption of contemporaries.[2] Following the view of nineteenth-century Liberals themselves, it shows Liberal culture as an untroubled unity, drawing on a shared political culture with radicalism, and celebrating an untroubled Gladstonian 'Age of Equipoise'.

This view is rather different from the periodic alarms of government and the moral panics of some Victorian commentators in the city that really mattered to contemporaries: the national and imperial capital of London. Recently a new metropolitan analysis has problematized London as a site of conflict over places of public meeting, gender, town planning, local government and anxiety about the relief of poverty.[3] From an early stage London was seen as outside the norms of political, social and moral behaviour. A tension is thus apparent between those historians who see the ascendancy of Liberal reformism at mid-century as uncontested, and those who detect a fault-line in the relationship between Liberalism and the radical constituency over reform, accentuated by the stresses of policing, and weak local government in the metropolis. Embracing a London-centred emphasis, this chapter examines the continuing vitality of late Chartism and popular reformism in the capital as a corrective to a historiography that draws too derivatively on a regional perspective. It argues that current debates about continuity in radicalism may be modified by an analysis that considers the persistence of a vibrant radical identity existing outside Liberalism and expressed through club life, concern for the preservation of open spaces, and a culture of riotous assembly. In this it is informed by recent cultural readings of London.[4] Here the city acts as a lens, highlighting the divisions between the regions and the capital, and seeking to explain the apparent vitality of radicalism in the metropolis in terms of its proximity to central government, and through the absence of those religious and cultural factors that favoured the formation of a popular Liberal consensus in the provinces.

It is the purpose of this chapter to remedy a deficiency in the historiography of popular politics. It begins by presupposing the longevity of popular radical traditions in London, explores their roots in older radical forms and puts the case for their long-term survival after Chartism. Chartism still emerges from much of the literature on the movement as a northern-orientated and profoundly regional phenomenon, irresistible to those historians preoccupied with heavy industry, the locality and/or Marxist notions of economic exploitation. Chartism, however, began in London. Moreover, it persisted there long after it had fallen into abeyance in the regions. In the great northern centres Chartism drew on subsiduary agitations like the Ten Hours movement and the Anti-Poor Law movement that had very little traction in the capital.[5] London is in part overlooked because of the weakness of these movements there. In contrast to the limited economic goals that preoccupied northern Chartists, metropolitan Chartists were conscious of their proximity to parliament, and of their role as standard bearers on the national stage. In addition, a number of structural and environmental factors gave their platform a vitality and resonance missing in the regions. Whereas the Chartist movement splintered in the north and further movements like co-operation and temperance that worked towards limited objectives drained the energy of the agitation, Chartism in London remained buoyant, sustained by local environmental factors and with a platform that remained undiminished by the successor movements that sapped their northern counterparts. The first part of this chapter explores what might be seen as the political factors which allowed Chartism to survive longer in the capital than elsewhere in Britain; and in the following section, attention turns to the environmental factors which guaranteed its continuing relevance into the 1860s. Against the background of the amorphous political culture of London, this chapter reviews the role of existing political groups and parties in either militating against, or, on occasion, encouraging, continuing traditions of mass participatory political engagement.

The Survival of London Chartism through the 1860s

The traditional view of metropolitan politics is that the capital was difficult to mobilize, proved highly resistant to organizational innovation, and seldom provided the base for a national leadership, the absence of which amongst so many bickering factions severely hindered the Chartist movement in its closing stages. Francis Place's much quoted remarks about the difficulties of stimulating a response in London show the capital as a vacuum, impeding, rather than encouraging, the cause of reform.[6] Yet, Place's comments grew out of his work as an agent for the Anti-Corn Law League (ACLL) and may reveal only the unpopularity of the League platform in London. As D. J. Rowe and others have noted, the growth of the Chartist movement was undoubtedly retarded by the sheer size of London and the attendant difficulties of organizing an agitation in such a huge area and amongst such a vast diversity of artisan trades and economic 'out' groups.[7] Nevertheless, historians have overlooked the degree to which Chartism did surmount these difficulties, both in 1842, and building on that success, in 1848.[8] Indeed, outside the West Riding of Yorkshire the one area of significant Chartist revival in 1848 was London. More recent interpretations of the nationwide movement have argued for the debilitating impact of central government's policing methods on Chartist fortunes in 1848–49.[9] Whilst this may be true of the regions, in London Chartist organization survived the backlash intact and successfully established an infrastructure of radical organization for its successor agitations to build on.

In the 1840s Chartists confounded Place's gloomy prognosis and provided a strong organizational base for the movement in the capital. The triumph of Chartism in London during these years was largely an organizational one. After 1844, the National Charter Association (NCA) was increasingly dominated by metropolitan delegates who monopolized all the key positions. Whilst boding ill for the national administration of the movement and contributing to the breakdown of national perspectives within Chartism, this development nevertheless preserved intact the agitational core of metropolitan radicalism.[10] Moreover, the movement's strong links with the metropolitan trades allowed it to create enduring branches rooted in individual trade associations that set up bridging groups between Chartist organization and radical trades like the bootmakers, and woodworkers. With their roots deep in the artisanal politics of the capital, organizations like the National Association of United Trades and the National Organisation of United Trades established a joint framework for collective action that consolidated the personnel in both camps.[11] An overemphasis on the clandestine revolutionary element grafted onto Chartism by its connection with Irish Confederate Clubs has also led historians to underestimate the organizational benefits conferred by mutual Irish and Chartist strategic planning during these years.[12] In London such benefits were considerable. Irish Confederate clubs augmented the activities of the NCA by providing a second more convivial tier of organization, through groups like the Ernest Jones Brigade and the Robert Emmet club. Even after the debacle of 1848 in some districts of the capital the movement was strong enough to flout government restrictions and meet in defiance of police guards and spies following the arrest of leading conspirators in the summer.[13] In the late 1840s in particular the metropolitan focus of the NCA meant that metropolitan Chartism retained a localized leadership structure and was able to sustain itself in the capital as it failed to do elsewhere. During this period it proved self-renewing: George Odger, William Newton, Peter Henriette, Charles Bradlaugh and George Howell (who were all to play a major part in the radical politics of the 1860s and 1870s) were amongst those radicalized in the early 1850s at a time when Chartism in the regions was fading. In marked contrast, the movement in Manchester collapsed after the arrest of 29 local leaders left local organization in disarray.[14]

In addition, the Chartist platform in the capital was able to sustain itself through its continuing relevance for voting culture in London. Throughout the nineteenth century, the metropolitan electorate had a reputation for volatility and apathy. Plebeian voters in particular were seen as detached from the political process. The persistent low turnout of those entitled to vote was depicted as a metropolitan disease, confirming the malaise at the heart of London's political process. Complaints about the indifference of the working-class electorate were commonplace amongst unsuccessful radicals who exhibited a marked tendency to blame the voters. The *Bee-Hive* complained of the candidature of the land reformer, Captain Frederick Maxse, for Tower Hamlets in 1874:

> At that election, out of 32,000 voters, scarcely 17,000 went to the poll, such was the amount of public interest evinced by a constituency, said to be radical, in the great interests of the day, and in the earnest thoughtful politician who appealed for support. It is true that the hours of polling are such as to disenfranchise thousands of working-class voters, and various vexatious restrictions hamper their registration; but nevertheless, some efforts at self-sacrifice should be forthcoming on the part of those who have so much to gain by the representation of progressive ideas.[15]

Such complaints of a fickle and febrile crowd politics obscure the position of the metropolitan franchise. Existing franchise provision played an especially important role in laying down the foundations for a durable movement of radical protest. Indeed, the very problems arising from the limited nature of the franchise, and the difficulties attendant on utilizing the vote outlined by the *Bee-Hive*, made London fertile ground for radical activism in the 1850s and 1860s when the Chartist movement was in abeyance elsewhere. London already had a small pool of working-class voters before 1832. In Southwark and Westminster occupational franchises had created a group of traditionally radical electors supportive of opponents of 'Old Corruption' like Wilkes and Burdett. In theory the high price of property in the capital meant that any franchise measure tethered exclusively to the value of property favoured the extension of the vote. Most metropolitan houses were rated at £10 and above in the 1840s.[16] However, it was London's heterogeneous shopkeeping and small tradesman element that profited the most from the 1832 Reform Act. Elsewhere the working-class vote was shrinking. In the larger boroughs like Lambeth and Tower Hamlets working-class voters did exist, but anomalies in the metropolitan franchise kept their numbers small.[17] Under the terms of the 1832 Reform Act, lodgers, defined as those who rented rooms from a non-resident landlord, were not entitled to the vote. As contemporaries made clear lodging was the norm for working-class households in the poorer parts of London.[18] Most working-class families lived not in London's £10 houses, but in individual rented rooms. Compounding provided a further barrier to the extension of the metropolitan franchise. Compounding occurred where vestries claimed rates on property from the landlord, not the tenant. Compound householders were eligible for the franchise, but could register for the vote only when they applied to pay their own rate, a process that had to be repeated as many as six times a year when the rates were due. This acted as a deterrent to compounders who applied for voter status. In 1849 Sir William Clay estimated that as many as 16,000 householders were disenfranchised by compounding in Tower Hamlets alone.[19] Finally, the 12 months residence clause in the 1832 Reform Act disadvantaged a shifting, itinerant labour force dependant on casualized or seasonal work patterns. Here movement and mobility, part of the traditional rhythm of London employment, artificially depressed the numbers of working-class voters.[20] Where movement occurred within a borough, electors faced the problem of re-registering their vote, but lost it altogether for the full 12-month period if they moved outside its boundaries. Metropolitan radicals condemned the injustices of a voting system in which 'the exercise of the right to vote in the making of the laws we are bound to obey should depend on the state of a rent book' and noted the detrimental effect of itinerancy on enfranchisement in the capital where 'there were whole parishes in which not a single lodger had taken the trouble to have his name placed on the register'.[21]

These factors not only kept the metropolitan electorate small in areas in which it was already tiny, but also ensured that the franchise remained a contentious issue in the London boroughs. Under-representation in London was chronic. In contrast to Manchester or Leeds, where enfranchisement rates were rising steadily in the 1850s as property increased in value, in London they were in decline.[22] Moreover the fact that all property in London was already rated at £10 or above, meant that simply lowering the property threshold at which householders became eligible for the vote would not address London's enfranchisement problems. In 1860 a £6 franchise proposal in John Bright's reform bill of that year was opposed by metropolitan reformers on these grounds and was acknowledged by Gladstone in the mid-1860s to have been entirely inadequate to meet London's needs: 'The bill of 1860 was, it might almost be said, of no use at all in London. Such was the scale of rents in the metropolis that a descent from £10 to £6 was of no importance whatever.'[23] London was thus the one area of the country where the number of voters per head of population was in decline. The limitations of the working-class franchise in London encouraged metropolitan reformers to favour radical solutions to the reform question. The only answer to the peculiarities and vagaries of the metropolitan franchise was an extended manhood suffrage. For this reason the Chartist platform remained a logical and acceptable one in London, with a continuing urgency it lacked elsewhere. In the regions as the number of plebeian voters increased, so too the franchise was ceasing to be an issue.[24]

The other important element in the metropolitan equation was religion (or the absence of it). Despite the fact that the headquarters of all the major overseas missionary societies were located in the capital, contemporary stereotypes of 'Godless London' were confirmed by the 1851 religious census. Church attendance was limited and intermittent. In larger boroughs like Lambeth and Tower Hamlets attendance rates were barely 30 per cent.[25] The major religious denominations were weak in London. Nonconformity in particular was almost non-existent in the inner London boroughs; in 1851 aggregate attendances for the Dissenting sects were smaller than anywhere else in the country.[26] Anglicanism did retain a presence but, as Henry Pelling has pointed out, by the 1850s the Church of England had all but abandoned its pastoral mission in the East End. Pew rents and absentee pastors had alienated much of its following heralding a retreat to the suburbs and the wealthier quarters of Westminster and the City.[27] Not until the 1880s did the experience of missionary work amongst the poor and dispossessed provide a model for a regenerated salvationism under Moody and Sankey and later William Booth who saw the East End as a place of opportunity, rather than of defeat.[28] Plebeian Catholicism was also marginal. It put down deep roots only amongst the settled Irish and Italian communities of Clerkenwell and Holborn in Central London.[29]

The weakness of organized religion in the capital meant that political factions tended not to be defined in religious terms. Increasingly in the regions the strength of religious adherence and the popularity of Anglican-inspired evangelism and Nonconformity meant that religious affiliation dictated the nature of political allegiance. Militant Nonconformity, however, whilst strong in the North, Midlands, Wales and West Country, was far less pronounced in London than elsewhere. Nor is there much evidence of the kind of politics traditionally associated with it. In contrast to Lancashire and Yorkshire there was little common identity of interest between London's radical MPs and the Nonconformist sects. Of the capital's 16 MPs in the 1850s only 3 actively identified with the Dissenting interest. Without the anti-tithe and burial agitation of Manchester and Leeds linked to the Whig anti-ritualism of the 1850s, metropolitan Liberalism lacked the religious dimension that nurtured a generation of Liberal activists in the provinces.[30] Nor is there much evidence of a reactive popular Conservatism buoyed up by the Orange interest and fuelled by anti-Irish feeling. In the absence of any cross-London local authority there was no outlet for sectarian tensions. School boards were not established until 1870, and the London County Council was resolutely non-sectarian, abolishing all religious discussion from its meetings. Religiously-based party conflict was thus quite alien to London in the 1850s. Ultimately, limited religious adherence in the capital meant that political allegiances were not defined in exclusively religious terms, either for Liberalism, or for Toryism, a factor that hampered the growth of formal party structures during this period.

The key electoral and religious elements that contributed to party formation in the regions were lacking in London. The capital provided an example of a near 'partyless' political culture. In part this was due to the collapse of metropolitan Toryism at mid-century. The Tories in London never recovered from the national malaise that afflicted the party after the rupture over the Corn Laws. Their only strongholds between 1847 and 1865 were in Westminster, in the City, which cemented their association with the unpopular Corporation, and as 'outsider' county representatives for rural Middlesex. Beyond these areas they brought forward no metropolitan candidates at all in 1857, and in 1859 only one solitary metropolitan Conservative who stood for Marylebone.[31] Witnesses testifying before the 1860 Parliamentary Select Committee on Reform concluded that Conservative voters were effectively disenfranchised in the London boroughs contributing to the notorious low-turn figures in the capital.[32] Not until the Jingo agitation of 1877–78 were metropolitan Conservatives able to break out of their strongholds and regain the political ground they had lost in the previous two decades.[33]

A fragmented Liberal/radicalism dominated London in the absence of a strong Tory opposition. These divisions between different Liberal factions ran deeper in London than elsewhere in the country. In the larger boroughs a multiplicity of Liberals could contest elections without the danger of a seat falling to the Tories. In Tower Hamlets in 1852 all five candidates for the borough's two seats were Liberals. In 1857 Finsbury was contested by four Liberals without any Tory opposition. Throughout this period London was distinguished by a remarkably low level of electoral contests in comparison to the regions. This was particularly marked during the general elections of 1859 and 1865 when, against the background of a Palmerstonian accord at national level, contests were few. Neither Westminster nor Marylebone were contested in 1857, and in 1859 there were no elections at all in four of London's seven central boroughs: Westminster, the City, Tower Hamlets and Lambeth.[34] Frequently 'gentlemen's agreements' were the order of the day, resolving unnecessary conflict within the Liberal elite.

Without religious cleavages, the dynamics of London elections tended to be driven by friction between Liberal splinter groups. More often than not these were the result of personal differences. In the absence of party strife, the apparatus of electioneering failed to evolve as it did in the provinces. Outside the City, where there was a Tory opposition, party apparatus was unknown. The highly sophisticated methods of canvassing, registration and candidate selection pioneered by the ACLL in Manchester were seldom employed in London until the 1880s. In these circumstances the sheer size of predominantly working-class boroughs like Lambeth and Tower Hamlets prohibited the development of effective electoral machinery. Most metropolitan Liberals dispensed with electoral management strategies altogether. In 1857 Thomas Slingsby Duncombe contested Finsbury with only a single paid secretary and a messenger in a campaign that cost him a mere £412.[35]

Politics in London remained recognizably eighteenth century in nature well into the nineteenth century. Without the discipline brought by party, London's Liberal MPs retained a strongly individualistic character. Most were wedded to an older radical tradition and continued to operate in a style reminiscent of popular demagogues like John Wilkes or Francis Burdett. The radical MPs for Finsbury, Thomas Wakley and Thomas Slingsby Duncombe, were survivors of the early nineteenth-century generation of radicals. Indeed Wakley had been a personal friend of Henry Hunt.[36] A non-aligned Whiggery also persisted into the 1860s, sometimes sustained against the patriotic backdrop of the capital, by a Palmerstonian concern for an imperilled national interest abroad.[37] As in the previous century, radicalism amongst London's MPs tended to be measured in terms of their distance from the court, the throne and the coffers of government patronage. This was the basis of the old 'Independent' position as outlined in Matthew McCormack's contribution to this volume. Even the outward trappings of 'Independency' persisted. In 1857 when the reformer W. A. Wilkinson contested Lambeth, he did so under the 'blue and buff' colours of the old Wilkite banner.[38] Into the 1870s and 1880s metropolitan Liberal MPs were noted for their idiosyncratic approach to party loyalties. W. A. Torrens, MP for Finsbury between 1865 and 1885, became the role model for the mid-Victorian 'private member', promoting numerous private members' bills, refusing cabinet office and flouting the wishes of his constituency party.[39]

In these circumstances electoral arrangements in London were haphazard. Most political activity was rooted in the public house, as it had been in the eighteenth century. During elections pubs were pressed into service as centres for canvassing, placarding and public meetings. Within each borough rival networks of pubs also served to delineate the territory of contending parliamentary candidates. The central role of the public house in London's political life retarded the bond that developed between Liberalism and the temperance movement in the regions. In the north of England, Liberalism cohered around the organizational framework of Liberalism, Nonconformity and temperance. In London, by contrast, it was almost unknown for Liberals to stand on a temperance platform. Whereas in the provinces the drink interest had become identified with popular Toryism by the 1860s, in London the main body of brewers were politically non-aligned, distributing their favours equally between contending factions, whether Tory versus Liberal, or Liberal versus Liberal, or Liberal versus radical. When the temperance campaigner Harper Twelvetrees contested Marylebone in 1852 he faced the combined power of the brewing interest and came bottom of the poll with a single vote.[40] As the metropolitan political agent W. A. James explained with regard to this campaign in 1860: 'in consequence of his determining upon high principles not to engage public houses, but to hold committee rooms at private houses ... no public houses were taken by him, and the consequence was that the whole of the publicans voted in a body against him'.[41]

When metropolitan MPs campaigned, they did so in the style of eighteenth-century electioneering. The public meeting in London retained a central importance as the space at which they were beholden to the electorate. It was a place, first and foremost, of unmediated contact, but also of popular theatre and accountability. Its attendant processions, hustings, effigy-burnings and even violence continued to matter in London as an integral part of the political process despite the changes introduced by the 1832 and 1867 reform acts. Without organized party to support them, London's MPs were excessively vulnerable to currents of opinion within the electorate. The absence of cushioning electoral machinery exposed them to the vagaries of non-electors, to the whims of militant radicals and, most important of all, to the caprices of the crowd. For crowd politicians the public meeting was a place where the sacred compact between the elected, the voter and non-electors was cemented. Here the collectivity of the people's will was on display (see Figures 8 and 9). Without political machinery the majority of working-class electors were never integrated into the political system and thus constituted an uncontrolled, ungovernable element within metropolitan politics. In this situation, parliamentary candidates vied with one another to acquire the mantle of the radical representative by appeasing militant supporters at the forum of the public meeting.

Metropolitan radicals were expert at working these crowd situations. The Chartists, in particular, were instrumental in establishing a hustings presence that exerted considerable pressure on MPs. The fact that the Chartists were one of the few well-organized political groupings in the metropolis placed them in a good position to cause large-scale disruption at public meetings. Equally, access to the popular platform gave them a much higher public profile than their provincial counterparts. In contrast to Manchester, where ticketing and indoor meetings enabled the ACLL supporters to keep disruption at public meetings to a minimum, the momentum of London politics still turned on issues of popular accountability debated openly before the people.[42] Moreover, metropolitan radicals were adept at orchestrating opposition to the popular and programmatic Liberal movements of London. Agitations like the Parliamentary and Financial Reform Association and the National and Constitutional Association founded in emulation of the ACLL in Manchester, rapidly succumbed to Chartist pressure. In 1852 Chartists invaded the national conference of the Parliamentary and Financial Reform Association in St. Martin's Hall and delayed proceedings for up to seven hours; at the inaugural meeting of the National and Constitutional Association at the London Tavern in 1855 resolutions supporting the programme of the body were overturned by amendments in favour of the Charter.[43] As late as 1859, metropolitan Liberals fought elections under near-siege conditions. In St. Luke's, Finsbury, in a traditional radical stronghold, a meeting held on behalf of the sitting MP, Sir Samuel Morton Peto, descended into chaos after a Chartist invasion. Light fittings were torn from the walls, and Peto was driven from the platform. As the *Cabinet Newspaper* reported:

> Bills were held up, circulars were thrown about and such a scene as has not been witnessed since the good old days of the Westminster election occurred. Men in fustian roared for the Charter, hats were knocked off, and the apprehension was that an indiscriminate fight would take place.[44]

Without a policy of 'packing' and 'ticket-only' assemblies, of the type less frequently deployed in the capital than in the regions, London's Liberals exposed themselves to harassment and attack by a well-organized Chartist rump. The pressure exerted by this style of crowd politics pushed most metropolitan MPs in a radical direction. William Newton of Tower Hamlets, Thomas Slingsby Duncombe and Thomas Wakley of Finsbury, were all heavily dependant on Chartist popular support; in 1859 all 16 London MPs were elected on a reform programme of varying shades of militancy. Even Gladstone noted the 'somewhat advanced Liberalism' of London's MPs in a speech in 1866.[45]

The survival of London Chartism

In those areas where Chartism lost the political argument it declined rapidly after 1848. In the provinces the collapse of Chartism enabled middle-class radicals to draw on many of the issues that had sustained the radical movement during the 1840s. In the process they created a broad radical coalition that provided the basis for Liberal successes into the 1860s and 1870s. In a marked contrast to the situation in the regions after 1848, the middle-class reform movement in London faltered and allowed the political initiative to remain with the Chartists. The model of an emergent grass-roots Liberalism that flourished in the provinces found only the shallowest purchase in the stony soil of the metropolis. There a broad popular Liberalism was slow to emerge, allowing older radical forms to retard the development of party. Liberalism was as a result weak in the metropolis, and London remained the home of a truculent radicalism grounded in surviving Chartist associations and memories, whose zeal was not tempered by popular Liberalism as in the regions.

This survival was in part the consequence of pressures on London's social and geographical space. The expense involved in hiring large opulent halls for political meetings was beyond the means of poverty-stricken radical organizations. Instead reformers were forced back on the bar rooms of public houses and London's areas of open ground. The classic London meeting was usually held on a brown-field site, on a redundant area of wasteland or common, or in a public park. In parks like Regent's Park and Victoria Park, there was a 'Sunday Right' allowing itinerant lecturers and monomaniacal enthusiasts to agitate and dispute[46] (see Figure 6). Through such institutions, the open ground of the capital became sacred space where the people met to assert their accumulated strength. Places like Primrose Hill, Bishop Bonner's Fields, Clerkenwell Green, Copenhagen Fields and Peckham Rye were sites steeped in the collective traditions of metropolitan radicalism. These were the spaces where atheists, blasphemers and 'radical spouters' tested the tolerance of the state and achieved notoriety in high profile cases.[47] Beatrice Webb recalled attending meetings at Victoria Park in the East End in the 1880s where 'the thickest crowd surrounded the banner of the social democrat'.[48] A description in the anarchist journal *Freedom* captures the flavour of one such meeting held in Hyde Park in 1888 to protest against the

Conservative Irish Coercion Bill:

> '*Justice! Justice!* One penny shows you how to get rid of all landlords and capitalists!' was the appropriate cry that fell upon one's ears when joining the huge crowd assembling around the platform erected beneath the 'Reformers' Tree' for the reception of T.D. Sullivan and Edward Harrington, two of 'Balfour's criminals'. The chance words heard whilst waiting for the heroes of the hour were instructive and portentous. To the right stood a sturdy workman propounding the doctrine of socialism as it seemed to him. Some high church dignitary was his text, and he strove to make clear to his auditors the iniquity of a man who pocketed £10,000 a year minus a paltry £90 which went to pay a 'miserable curate for doing the work the bishop ought to do, but didn't'. 'Ay, Ay, chimed in a comrade, they're a bad lot. You may be sure that you're in the right when the clergy's against you'. Then another took up the parable in a lighter vein, entertaining his hearers with his views concerning the royal squabble over the payment or non-payment of certain Jubilee travelling expenses, and the meanness of German personages who had to come to England to get a square meal, etc. etc.[49]

Even invasions of the West End were justified by a radical reading of London's geography and history. When rioters surged down the Strand in 1886 they saw themselves as the spiritual heirs to Wat Tyler's 1381 peasant rebels, responsible for the plunder of Savoy Palace, the London residence of the 'tax-exacter', John of Gaunt. Tyler was an iconic figure for metropolitan radicals. The democratic appropriation of the squares and boulevards of London by Tyler and the later peasant leader Jack Cade in 1450 held lessons for the more militant of the Chartists. At the alleged sites of his camps on Clerkenwell Green and at Smithfield, memories of Tyler inflamed the rhetoric used at these public spaces. Here, metropolitan radicals extracted their own version of history from the national narrative. Chartist branches were named after Tyler in 1848, and images of him killing the poll tax collector featured prominently on reform banners into the 1860s[50] (see Figure 5). For many reformers, the events of the Wat Tyler revolt became part of an alternative tourist trail in the capital in which the claim to a radical geography of London was established. Mark Starr wrote in *Lansbury's Labour Weekly*: 'It would be worthwhile, for example, on visiting the East End of London to trace Wat Tyler's march on the city, the subsequent attacks on the lawyers of the Temple, and the final incidents in Smithfield. We have no wall of the Communards as in *Père Lachaise*, but here is a fourteenth century memory of a deceived peasantry.'[51] As the metropolitan open spaces were enclosed or built over, so radicals mounted campaigns to preserve the people's land from occupation by 'commons' eaters'. In the 1870s this campaign preserved Wimbledon Common and Hampstead Heath for the people of London, although the methods used to defend them resulted in direct action protests that provoked brushes with the law and the police.[52] Those who were imprisoned for their part in these disturbances were celebrated as 'people's martyrs'. The spatial geography and social space of London in the 1850s favoured Chartist survival in a way that was unique to the metropolis.[53] Clashes over the open ground where radicalism had put down deep roots tended to the combustible.[54] The absence of metropolitan local government interposed between Londoners and Whitehall accentuated the distance between government and the governed in London. In addition control of policing by the Home Office transformed every conflict over open space into a dispute with central government itself. At a time when the regional centres were largely quiescent, London gained a reputation for ungovernability over public space. When the 'mobocracy' democratically appropriated London's ceremonial centres like Trafalgar Square, the Mall and the Strand, it threatened to overwhelm the imperial symbolism of the capital itself, substituting its own emblems and images of the people militant. Harry Quelch boasted of his part in the Trafalgar Square riots of 1887, bragging of 'the flag of the branch he had the honour of saving from the attack of the guardians of order, although it was the first to be unfurled on the plinth of the Nelson column'.[55] Moreover the heightened tensions surrounding such meetings created periodic flashpoints in which radicals adopted an aggressive and confrontational stance inimical to the pluralistic outlook of reform Liberals in the regions.

Chartism also managed to perpetuate itself through the network of clubs and debating societies that formed a staple component of the radical culture of the capital from the Regency period onwards. In London the club was integral to the survival of post-Chartist reform movements. As Ian McCalman demonstrates, after 1815 political radicalism was bound up with, and was in turn transmitted through, an artisanal culture of conviviality in London.[56] This pattern repeated itself in the 1850s. Pubs were important in this process, and Chartist branches continued to meet there. Radicals, however, found their strongest voice in London's long established debating club circuit. In the regions such clubs were all but dormant, in London they continued to thrive. The debating clubs, whose roots were in the Restoration period, provided an easy blend of conviviality and informal political debate. Cogers Club near St. Bride's Church, could trace its origins back to 1755; the Green Dragon in Fleet Street was founded in the 1650s.[57] Most had strong links with the city's radical tradition. Cogers was the most well known of these establishments. According to metropolitan lore, it occupied the premises of one of the famous Whig 'Mug Houses' of the reign of George I, at which drinking vessels were adorned with the likenesses of the Earl of Shaftesbury and other idols of metropolitan Whiggery, and irreverent toasts were drunk in opposition to the Stuarts following the Jacobite Rising of 1715. The debating clubs preserved intact the metropolitan tradition of underground debate and kept together a body of ideas and a clientele who provided a point of contact with earlier movements. Cogers counted John Wilkes and Henry Hunt amongst its former members. H. Barton Baker wrote: 'Many well-known orators have made their first essays in their art at Cogers Hall, which has echoed with the voices of Johnson, Goldsmith, Wilkes, Dan O'Connell, and in our own days with those of Stewart Parnell, T. P. O'Connor, Sir Edward Clarke, Bradlaugh and many another notoriety.'[58] The role of the clubs as centres of debate created an accessible lecture circuit where former Chartists like Thomas Cooper and Bronterre O'Brien found employment as lecturers. George Howell recalled of his exposure to such venerable radical presences in the clubs that 'for years I heard all they had to say and was conversant with their writings'.[59] A network of coffeehouses provided a further outlet for political debate. They not only stocked newspapers and even books, but were also free from the pressures exerted by landlords, brewers and Justices of the Peace. Beyond the coffeehouses and debating clubs was a penumbra of radical and ultra-liberal societies and associations rooted in the thriving club culture of London. Here unorthodox political and social views abounded. Charles Booth found in them a readership for radical weeklies like *Reynolds's Newspaper* and 'a good deal of vague unorganized socialism'. Some had associations with republicanism and other underground and heretical views. The Eleusis Club in Paddington, which became the headquarters of Sir Charles Dilke's local election committee for Chelsea, displayed a loyal address to the Queen captured in a *melée* from a loyalist platform during the anti-Dilke republican riots of 1871. This memento of the club's republican past was still proudly on display in 1905.[60] Visiting the 'Hole-in-the-Wall' Republican club in 1874, the metropolitan journalist James Greenwood challenged the popular demonology that surrounded the radical clubs, noting 'men who had seen service beneath the Reformers' Tree in Hyde Park, men who have spouted sedition to such an insane extent that compassioning their infirmity, government has refrained from shutting their mouths', but at the same time detecting a more measured and temperate demeanour amongst a majority of the respectable members present.[61]

The persistence of an infrastructure of radical activity in London prevented the dispersal and diffusion of energies that characterized Chartism in the regions. Outside London the 1850s was a critical period in the evolution of movements dedicated to limited economic aims, rather than to the overall transformation of society. Strategies like co-operation and temperance, which prospered particularly in Lancashire and the West Riding of Yorkshire, promoted the benefits of an accord with Liberalism for minimal social rewards. As J. K. Walton has noted, co-operatives, building societies and temperance groups in Lancashire held out the prospect of profitable sinecures for radicals in their declining years.[62] In London, where Chartism retained a significant agitational presence, this development was much less marked. Recent historiography has noted the absence of a strong co-operative tradition in the capital, and the failure of the Christian Socialist initiatives in retail co-operation that were so successful in the regions.[63] By the end of the 1850s there was still no cross-London clearing-house system for commodities on the model of the Cooperative Wholesale Society in Manchester. Metropolitan co-operatives faced immense problems in overcoming the barriers to retail provision posed by the sheer size of London and the immense diversity of its trading base. For this reason the lifespan of individual co-operative associations in London was short. In 1861 there were criticisms of the commitment of London's co-operators from within the movement, while Percy Redfern, the historian of the movement, was dismissive of metropolitan co-operation, writing of it as 'a galaxy of distinguished men (who) provided a force rich in colonels and generals, but (were) desperately short of common soldiers'.[64] Similarly Brian Harrison has described London as the 'bugbear' of the temperance movement.[65] The temperance campaign in London never succeeded in overcoming the central role of the public house in London's commercial, recreational and political life. Despite mid-century attempts to contest the grip of public house culture on plebeian life in London, it remained central.[66] Election committees campaigned from pubs, workmen were paid there, and trades unionists used them as ports of call, and as centres for discussion, organization and strike action. The sheer size of London meant that protest could only be orchestrated effectively through committees meeting in local pubs. Chartism used this method of mobilization in the 1830s and, despite

Ernest Jones' attempt to wean Chartist branches away from the public house, it persisted into the 1850s and 1860s.[67]

Dependency on the public house remained ingrained in Chartist culture in the capital to a degree that set the Chartism of London apart from its regional counterparts. In the 1840s regional Chartism had stabilized around a network of permanent club and meeting-house facilities; in London, however, high property prices precluded the construction of purpose-built premises for public meetings. As with trade societies, local Chartist branches continued to identify themselves with a particular pub long after the practice had died out elsewhere. Some of London's most prominent Chartists were publicans, amongst them the Engineers' leader William Newton, and the veteran reformer William Morgan. William Morgan's pub the 'Bull's Head', Crown Street, Soho provided a venue for unrepentant Chartists until the 1870s.[68]

Chartism's ability to act as a vehicle for popular discontents gave it a coherence and vitality in the capital that made it resistant to erosion by the movements that had arisen out of the disintegration of Chartism in the provinces. As late as the 1870s, members of 'Feargus O' Connor's Old Guard' were conspicuous at radical public meetings amongst the Positivists, secularists and foreign *émigrés*.[69] Loyalty to its memory and a continuing perception of the movement as an effective agent of change inhibited the development of a popular Liberal consensus in London throughout the period when a fused Cobdenite/Liberalism was in the ascendant in the provincial urban centres. Chartism survived in London through its continuing command of the political agenda. Dorothy Thompson has suggested that by the 1840s Chartism had lost the argument over free trade. Chartists predicted the baleful effects of Corn Law repeal, and of the unrestrained competition provided by free trade policies. Absence of protection, they asserted, would lead to the production of cheaper goods for sale in international markets, high food prices and a depression of domestic wage levels.[70] In the north after 1850 Chartist economic arguments were fallacious. The self evident prosperity of manufacturing industry in Lancashire and Yorkshire made the issue a difficult one to exploit for electoral gain. In such areas Cobdenite radicals were extremely successful in mobilizing popular support against Lord Derby's attempts to re-introduce a sliding scale on corn. Their manipulation of this issue re-opened the wider debate on protectionism, and resulted in the resurrection of the ACLL platform in 1852 to defend the benefits of freedom of trade.[71] In London, however, Chartists were more effective in highlighting the disadvantages of free trade policies for the casualized labourers and out-workers based in the declining industries of the Pool of London and the East End. Most of the industries which suffered disproportionately from the absence of protectionist policies were concentrated in London. Chartist radicalism retained the initiative amongst groups of outworkers including the slop-workers and the sweated trades who were the human casualties of free trade.[72] From the 1830s the emblem of these out-groups became the debased Spitalfields silk-weaver who the Chartists elevated into an icon of dispossession and internal exile at the hands of cheap imports and a cowardly government afraid to preserve domestic industries from undercutting by a revived Bonapartist France.[73] A Silk Weavers' Protection Society established in 1852 became a major propagandist vehicle in London against free trade doctrines. Henry Mayhew's articles in the *Morning Star* also exposed the suffering apparent amongst sections of the clothing, the boot and shoe, silk-weaving and dockside trades. At appearances on Chartist platforms he pointed to the undercutting of prices by foreign manufacturers, the resultant widespread casualization in London and employers' wage reductions to bring pay in line with falling bread prices. At meetings with tailors, coal heavers and carpenters he was highly critical of the free trade platform of Cobden and Bright.[74] The result was to seriously undermine the position of the restored ACLL in London in the short term, and to discredit free trade nostrums in London in the long term.

In London a febrile crowd politics, unmediated through Liberalism, became the hallmark of radical continuities. In 1855 Chartists were still conspicuous in the Sunday Trading Bill riots and in co-ordinating opposition to high grain prices during the Crimean War.[75] Nowhere else in Britain was the public sphere, and uncontested access to it, of such sensitivity as in London. Above all, metropolitan politics was slow to change. As late as the 1880s metropolitan Liberals were still dragged in a radical direction by the dynamics of ungovernable crowd politics and a strong grass-roots radicalism. Some historians have seen an element of populism in metropolitan crowd action that could drift in either a radical or a Tory direction, helping to account for the strength of Toryism in London from the 1890s.[76] Figures like the Social Democratic Leader, Henry Hyndman, embodied some of these contradictions of the metropolitan political platform, promoting socialism and radicalism on the one hand, and empire, patriotism and anti-Semitism on the other.[77] The Liberal Party certainly felt that London could not be mastered, even by the New Liberalism. Charles Masterman, amongst others, rooted his notion of a neurotic urban mass prone to fickle urges and periodic spasms of unrest in the 'New Town Type' created by rootless metropolitan living. Mediating his ideas through the work of the French theorist of crowd hysteria, Gustave Le Bon, Masterman feared for a future in which 'a new race ... the "street-bred" people of the twentieth century' proliferating in the great churn of London's population, drained the energy and vitality of the urban masses.[78]

Conclusion

This chapter has problematized the issue of London in recent literature concerning radical continuity in mid-nineteenth-century Britain. It provides fresh evidence on the strength and vitality of metropolitan Chartism in the period of the movement's decline. Through scrutiny of the local context of London Chartism it reappraises the value of a metropolitan approach, and prioritizes a reading that emphasizes the importance of a structural understanding of London. It is informed by a comparative methodology, highlighting differences and similarities with overlapping movements of political protest in the regions. By moving beyond Liberalism's own conception of itself, it argues for a closer analysis of the links between party forms, the political platform and the role of the franchise in curtailing or encouraging militancy over the vote. In so doing it seeks to modify the historiography of late Chartism, and to question recent assumptions about the continuities between popular radicalism and Liberalism in the period 1848–80.

Notes

1. E. Biagini, *Liberty, Retrenchment and Reform: Popular Liberalism in the Age of Gladstone, 1860–1880* (Cambridge, 1992); P. Joyce, *Visions of the People: Industrial England and the Question of Class* (Cambridge, 1991); idem, *Democratic Subjects: The Self and the Social in Nineteenth Century England* (Cambridge, 1994); J. Vernon, *Politics and the People: A Study in English Political Culture c.1815–1867* (Cambridge, 1993).
2. H. Jephson, *The Platform: Its Rise and Progress* (2 vols, London, 1892), ii, chs 1–3.
3. S. Inwood, *A History of London* (London, 1998), chs 19–20; S. Pennybacker, *A Vision for London 1889–1914: Labour, Everyday Life and the LCC Experiment* (London, 1995) and J. Walkowitz, *City of Dreadful Delight: Narratives of Sexual Danger in Late Victorian London* (1992), ch. 1.
4. K. Beckson, *London in the 1890s: A Cultural History* (London, 1992), ch. 1 and J. Schneer, *London 1900: The Imperial Metropolis* (New Haven, 1999), chs 7 and 10.
5. C. Driver, *Tory Radical: The Life of Richard Oastler* (New York, 1946), chs 24–27; F. Driver, *Power and Pauperism: The Workhouse System 1834–1884* (Cambridge, 1993), ch. 7.
6. N. McCord, *The Anti-Corn Law League 1838–1846* (London, 1958), pp. 75–7.
7. D. J. Rowe, 'The Failure of London Chartism', *HJ*, 11 (1968), 472–87 and D. Large, 'London in the Year of Revolutions', in J. Stevenson (ed.) *London in the Age of Reform* (London, 1977) pp. 177–211.

8. D. Goodway, *London Chartism, 1838–1848* (Cambridge, 1982), p. 13.
9. J. Saville, *1848: The British State and the Chartist Movement* (Cambridge, 1987), ch. 1.
10. A. Taylor, 'Modes of Political Expression and Working-Class Radicalism: The London and Manchester Examples', unpublished PhD thesis (University of Manchester, 1992), ch. 1.
11. J. Belchem, 'Chartism and the Trades, 1848–1850', *EHR*, 98 (1983), 558–87.
12. Goodway, *London Chartism*, p. 13.
13. *Northern Star*, 26 August 1848, p. 8.
14. I. Prothero, *Radical Artisans in England and France 1830–1870* (Cambridge, 1997), ch. 11.
15. *The Bee-Hive*, 27 March 1875, pp. 1–2.
16. Taylor, 'Modes of Political Expression and Working-Class Radicalism', ch. 2.
17. H. J. Hanham, *Dod's Electoral Facts 1832–1852* (Brighton, 1972), pp. 316–17.
18. T. Wright, *Some Customs and Habits of the Working-Classes* (London, 1867), pp. 262–76.
19. M. Baer, 'The Politics of London 1852–1868: Parties, Voters and Representation', unpublished PhD thesis (University of Iowa, 1976), p. 368.
20. R. Samuel, 'Comers and Goers' in H. J. Dyos and M. Wolff (eds) *The Victorian City: Images and Realities* (2 vols, London, 1973), ii, pp. 123–60.
21. See discussions at the Manhood Suffrage League, and the Patriotic Club, Clerkenwell in the *National Reformer*, 9 April 1876, p. 236, and 10 January 1875, p. 30.
22. V. A. C. Gatrell, 'The Commercial Middle-Class in Manchester c.1820–1857', unpublished PhD thesis (Cambridge University, 1971), pp. 114–55.
23. *Hansard*, CLXXII, 1866, p. 35.
24. D. Fraser, *Urban Politics in Victorian England: The Structure of Politics in Victorian Cities* (Leicester, 1976), chs 8, 10.
25. K. S. Inglis, 'Patterns of Religious Worship in 1851', *J Ecc Hist*, 2 (1960), 80.
26. H. McCleod, *Class and Religion in the Late Victorian City* (London, 1974), pp. 104–6.
27. H. Pelling, *Social Geography of British Elections, 1885–1910* (London, 1967), pp. 54–8; J. S. Reid, ' "Ritualism Rampant in East London": Anglo-Catholicism and the Urban Poor', *VS*, 31 (1988), 375–403.
28. J. Coffey, 'Democracy and Popular Religion: Moody and Sankey's Mission to Britain, 1873–1875', in E. Biagini (ed.) *Citizenship and Community: Liberals, Radicals and Collective Identities in the British Isles, 1865–1931* (Cambridge, 1996), pp. 93–119; V. Bailey, 'In Darkest England and the Way Out: The Salvation Army, Social Reform and the Labour Movement 1890–1910', *IRSH*, 29 (1984), 133–71.
29. For Irish and Catholic politics in Clerkenwell, T. A. Jackson, *Solo Trumpet: Some Memories of Socialist Agitation and Propaganda* (London, 1953), pp. 32–9.
30. Fraser, *Urban Politics in Victorian England*, ch. 12.
31. Taylor, 'Modes of Political Expression', ch. 2.
32. *Select Committee of the House of Lords*, 1860, p. 355.
33. H. Cunningham, 'Jingoism in 1877–78', *VS*, 14 (1971), 429–53.
34. Taylor, 'Modes of Political Expression', ch. 2.
35. G. Hill, *The Electoral History of the Borough of Lambeth* (London, 1879), pp. 178, 185.

36. S. Squire Sprigge, *The Life and Times of Thomas Wakley* (London, 1897), pp. 310–16.
37. A. Taylor, 'Palmerston and Radicalism 1847–1865', *JBS*, 33 (1994), 157–79.
38. Hill, *Lambeth*, pp. 106–13.
39. J. Parry, *The Rise and Fall of Liberal Government in Victorian Britain* (New Haven 1993), p. 230.
40. B. Harrison, *Dictionary of British Temperance Biography* (Coventry, 1973), pp. 131–2.
41. *Select Committee of the House of Lords*, 1860, p. 357.
42. For contrasts between London and Manchester: A. Taylor, ' "The Best Way to Get What He Wanted": Ernest Jones and the Boundaries of Liberalism in the Manchester Election of 1868', *PH*, 16 (1997), 185–204.
43. *The Leader*, 6 March 1852, pp. 214–15; *People's Paper*, 24 March 1855, p. 4.
44. *Cabinet Newspaper*, 23 April 1859, p. 6.
45. *Hansard*, CLXXII, 1866, p. 35.
46. E. T. Cook, *Highways and Byways in London* (London, 1902), pp. 403–5. Hyde Park provided the most well-known 'Sunday Right'; here some orators achieved 'high rank among the dialecticians of the Marble Arch'. Quoted in R. Whiteing, *No 5 John Street* (London, 1899), p. 75.
47. H. Bradlaugh Bonner, *Penalties Upon Opinion* (London, 1934 edn.), pp. 118–19.
48. B. Webb, *My Apprenticeship* (2 vols, London, 1938), ii, p. 348.
49. *Freedom*, 13 February 1888, p. 72.
50. Goodway, *London Chartism*, p. 13; *The Commonwealth*, 12 January 1867, p. 5.
51. *Lansbury's Labour Weekly*, 5 September 1925, p. 6.
52. A. Taylor, ' "Commons-Stealers", "Land-Grabbers" and "Jerry-Builders": Space, Popular Radicalism and the Politics of Public Access in London, 1848–1880', *IRSH*, 40 (1995), 383–407.
53. For the 'chaining' of the River Thames and threats to the dock-working trades, D. H. Porter, *The Thames Embankment* (Michigan, 1998), ch. 1.
54. *National Reformer*, 5 October 1879, pp. 650–1; *The Anarchist*, 1 December 1885, p. 1. Parks promoted by urban Tories became regulated spaces: Vernon, *Politics and the People*, p. 316.
55. E. Belford Bax (ed.), *Harry Quelch: Literary Remains* (London, 1914), p. 14; R. Mace, *Trafalgar Square: Emblem of Empire* (London, 1976), chs 6, 7; D. C. Richter, *Riotous Victorians* (Athens, 1981), pp. 133–62.
56. I. McCalman, 'Ultra-Radicalism and Convivial Debating Clubs in London, 1795–1838', *EHR*, 102 (1987), 309–33.
57. W. E. Adams, *Memoirs of a Social Atom* (2 vols, London, 1903), ii, pp. 314–17; C. M. Davies, *Heterodox London or Phases of Free Thought in the Metropolis* (2 vols, London, 1875), ii, pp. 264–6; and J. Ewing Ritchie,*The Night Side of London* (London, 1858), pp. 85–91.
58. H. Barton Baker, *Stories of the Streets of London* (London, 1899), pp. 123–5; A. Taylor, ' "A Melancholy Odyssey among London Public Houses": Radical Club Life and the Unrespectable in Mid-Nineteenth Century London', *HR*, 78 (2005), 74–95.
59. G. Howell, 'Autobiography of a Toiler', ms autobiography (3 vols, n.d.), Howell Collection, Bishopsgate Institute, ii, p. 44.
60. A. Fried and R. Elman (eds), *Charles Booth's London* (London, 1969), pp. 296–7; for the Eleusis Club, S. Gwynn and T. M. Tuckwell, *The Life of the*

Rt. Hon. Sir Charles Dilke (2 vols 1917), i, p. 144. *National Reformer*, 24 August 1879, p. 558.
61. J. Greenwood, *In Strange Company* (London, 1874), p. 106.
62. J. K. Walton, *Lancashire: A Social History 1558–1939* (Manchester, 1987), pp. 244–5.
63. M. Purvis, 'The Development of Co-operative Retailing in England and Wales 1851–1901: A Geographical Study', *J Hist Geog*, 3 (1990), 314–31.
64. *Co-operator*, 1 April 1861, p. 159; P. Redfern, *The New History of the C.W.S.* (London, 1938), p. 31.
65. B. Harrison, 'The Sunday Trading Riots of 1855', *HJ*, 8 (1965), 129–30.
66. H. Solly, *These Eighty Years* (2 vols, London,1893), i. pp. 379–99.
67. B. Harrison, 'Pubs', in Dyos and Wolff (eds) *The Victorian City*, i, pp. 162–80.
68. S. Shipley, *Club Life and Socialism in Mid-Victorian London* (History Workshop, 1971), pp. 51–3.
69. *National Reformer*, 15 January 1871, p. 34.
70. D. Thompson, *The Chartists: Popular Politics in the Industrial Revolution* (Aldershot, 1984), p. 333.
71. A. Howe, *The Cotton Masters 1830–1860* (Oxford, 1987), pp. 216–27.
72. Taylor, 'Modes of Political Expression and Working-Class Radicalism', ch. 3.
73. M. Steinberg, ' "The Great End of All Government": Working-People's Construction of Citizenship Claims in Early Nineteenth Century England, and the Question of Class', *IRSH*, 40 (1999), 19–50.
74. Taylor, 'Modes of Political Expression and Working-Class Radicalism', ch. 3.
75. Harrison, 'The Sunday Trading Riots of 1855', 129–30.
76. G. Stedman Jones, *Outcast London: A Study in the Relationship Between Classes in Victorian Society* (Oxford, 1971), ch. 9; V. Kiernan, 'Victorian London: Unending Purgatory', *New Left Review*, 76 (1972), 73–90.
77. H. M. Hyndman, *The Record of an Adventurous Life* (London, 1911), pp. 400–3.
78. C. Masterman (ed.) *The Condition of England* (London, 1911), pp. 7–8.

5
Secularism in the City: Geographies of Dissidence and the Importance of Radical Culture in the Metropolis

David Nash

Background to metropolitan freethought

The city of London has, since the Reformation, proved especially fertile ground for both religious dissidence and the incendiary blending of religion with politics. As a centre of the print trade it produced prodigious quantities of the very raw material that fuelled the debates that were the lifeblood of the Reformation. This print culture gave individuals the capacity to originate their own thoughts about the universe and their place within it. Marian and Elizabethan London, as Patrick Collinson has demonstrated, hosted a number of advanced religious congregations whose Protestantism outstripped the religious thinking of even the more progressive clerics associated with the Elizabethan settlement. Periodically Elizabethan London would also play host to religious radicals and the unorthodox, fleeing unfavourable circumstances or persecution on the European continent.[1]

The English revolution unleashed a kaleidoscope of religious views which permeated the Cromwellian New Model Army and the London trades. Many of these arguments informed the Putney debates and the link between the nature of government and its ordination by God came under particular scrutiny within these discussions. Many of the more extreme religious groups produced by this situation had an especial association with the capital. The Ranters, a group who indulged in divinely inspired provocative displays of swearing, smoking and promiscuous behaviour had a number of important enclaves in and around the capital.[2] Arguably their culture of divinely inspired human interaction could only flourish in an urban or metropolitan setting. Gerrard Winstanley's Diggers advocated systematic seizure of agricultural property arguing it had been misappropriated by man in defiance of God's wishes and should be held in common.[3] Winstanley's group established an illegal settlement at St. George's Hill, Kingston near the capital and actively sought to practice the communal living they had preached. Here politics blended seamlessly with religion since Winstanley's Diggers argued that private property had been a direct consequence of the Fall and that their own appointed task was to return man and his relationships to a perfect state.[4] This ideological position represented a dialogue with Hobbes who argued private property had become man's only guaranteed protection against the avarice of his fellow man.

One especially notable sect that attained particular longevity in and around the capital was the sect known to contemporaries as the Muggletonians. With a series of arcane and obscure beliefs they perambulated the city in the years straddling the Restoration emitting curses upon those who ridiculed or opposed them. Historians in the 1980s were astonished to discover that such a sect had transcended its obscure origins to survive in a relatively benign and quietist state into the contemporary period.[5] Similarly a group like the Quakers had a series of celebrated and alarming impacts upon the social peace of many late seventeenth-century cities. Perhaps the most disturbing group to bring religious politics on the streets of Restoration London was the sect known as the Fifth Monarchy Men. This group saw active violent intervention as a legitimate and laudable method of hastening the arrival of Christ's kingdom upon earth.[6] When the Fifth Monarchy Men staged an abortive millenarian rising just outside the capital the government retaliated with the arrest and subsequent execution of several members of the group. Samuel Pepys recalled in his diary witnessing the resulting execution of the Civil War hero, turned Fifth Monarchist, Major-General Harrison.[7]

The end of the eighteenth century witnessed the growth of similar millennial preoccupations which again persuaded groups and individuals that politics and religion were yoked together. The immanent coming of a new century, just as the late 1990s influenced our own age, was a period in which conventional society and its hierarchies seemed fragile. The distinct possibility that such old orders would be swept aside was confirmed by the onset of the French Revolution which placed ideas of hierarchy, kingship and their justification by Christianity firmly on trial.[8] However throughout these years religious dissidents and those who considered themselves, or were considered to be, unorthodox, were at the mercy of the so-called Church and King mobs who would regularly attack the property and persons of such individuals.[9] The Gordon riots targeted Catholics and their property whilst the Unitarian, Joseph Priestley, whose religious beliefs contradicted the Thirty Nine Articles of the Church of England, found his own laboratory besieged and destroyed by an angry intolerant mob.

Some in London took comfort and refuge in beliefs that the French revolution heralded the second coming foretold in the Book of Revelation. Only this can explain the popularity of a sequence of millennial prophets in the very early years of the nineteenth century. One of these, Richard Brothers, argued he was the nephew of the almighty and had a significant following before the authorities declared him to be insane. Of still greater significance was the prophetess Joanna Southcott whose campaign of enlisting (or 'sealing') followers became something of a popular and society turn in the latter half of the 1810s.[10] The poet William Blake's memories of London in the 1790s indicates a city of considerable danger and turbulence. On one occasion he found himself caught up in millennial events when forced into a prominent part in the riot which attempted to burn down Newgate prison in 1793 in imitation of the storming of the Bastille.[11] Such events indicated that groups believing themselves to be living in the last days could find religious justification for revolutionary activity, but this also suggested just how easy it was to find oneself caught up in such fervour. Nonetheless Blake's activities also demonstrate the longevity of religious radicalism in the city and its connections with sectaries of the past. E. P. Thompson's investigations into the radical religious milieu of late eighteenth-century London unearthed a vibrant subculture of Christianity which distrusted and turned its back upon centralising religious authority. Within this Thompson discovered evidence that Blake's mother may have been a Muggletonian and was thus responsible for the religiously libertarian views her son exhibited as a central part of the radical artisan's legacy in the early years of the nineteenth century.[12] Such a legacy was forged for Blake by reading and re-reading the staples of the artisan's library of the period – Milton, Bunyan and Shakespeare. All carried messages which were tinged with religion authoritatively informing political activity.

However, Blake was prepared to take his libertarianism over the religious edge and was notable for his tacit support for the religious views which benefited most significantly from the French Revolution. Blake is believed at one time to have protected and hidden the most fervent English advocate of revolution in the name of reason, Thomas Paine. Whilst anti-Christian, or as contemporaries called them 'infidel', views had existed in isolated pockets during the eighteenth century the overthrow of the monarchy and the priesthood in France gave renewed impetus to the ideal of revolution in the name of reason. Such views had also been inspired by the growing popularity of religious views which undermined the supremacy of religious structures without necessarily destroying the outright belief in a creator. Such views, generally described by historians as 'deist', attained a significant degree of respectability through some influential advocates who termed it 'natural religion'.

The metropolis was ideally suited to the spread and growth of this range of radical religious and irreligious ideas. The staggering growth of eighteenth-century London meant that, as elsewhere, religious provision had scarcely kept pace with the changing size and nature of the population. Outlying areas were left to struggle on with the remnants of the medieval parish system whilst city congregations remained a reasonable and prosperous size. Yet even here the anachronism of rural population patterns and deference continued with excessive provision of box pews for the rich at the expense of the mass of churchgoers.[13] Although dissent, as always, plugged the gaps in unwieldy and inflexible established provision even this could not keep pace with the explosive growth of London's population. Increasingly London appeared to the fearful prelate and the hopeful infidel as a landscape populated with the ruins of belief.

Those wishing to forward or merely consume infidel ideas within the city had regular access to the trappings of print culture such as newspapers, pamphlets and books. The impact of this access could further stimulate such arguments, since the close proximity to publishers with the material power and means to publish further encouraged individuals to add their own views to the circulation of opinion. Arguments and pamphlets could quickly be qualified or answered by counter pamphlets, all further nurtured by the availability of venues in which ideas could be shared and circulated. Many historians point rightly to the radical potential inherent in the coffee house culture of Regency England which allowed a certain degree of liberty of opinion and encouraged intellectual debate amid avaricious consumption of newspapers.[14] But it is also worth noting that the trade structure and organisation of economic production in London was especially conducive to the fostering and spread of radical ideas. Small workshop and small industrial units were, throughout the first third of the nineteenth century, considered synonymous with radical and infidel ideas. These could be discussed whilst work was underway in tailoring and printing shops, ultimately giving birth to the archetype of the radical infidel shoemaker.

Such people were portrayed as isolated individuals who held religious opinions that were quite out of sympathy with the vast majority of the population. Their inherently alien nature led most commentators to pronounce these people 'infidels' – the term medieval society had used to indicate those whose cultural preoccupations and instincts lay outside Christendom. People like Jacob Ilive who was pilloried three times in the capital for writing against divine revelation and Peter Annet personified this trend through careers in publishing and the spread of materialist ideas from the early seventeenth century onwards.[15]

The late seventeenth and early eighteenth centuries witnessed a number of campaigns which aimed to regulate the morals and manners of the population of London. This had become necessary as social problems stemming from a perceived collapse of discipline were threatening to run out of control. Campaigns against vice, immorality, profanity and drunken behaviour became the preoccupation of numerous societies for the Reformation of Manners.[16] By the end of the eighteenth century it is no surprise that infidel opinions came specifically to the mind of government and the populace through the medium of publishing. Deistical and materialist writing were one thing, but the tide of criticism the French Revolution had unleashed spread to encompass the state, the church and the close relationship they shared. Such criticisms were seen as potentially dangerous sources of disaffection and were liable to persuade the population at large to discard their loyalty to the crown, the church and the English constitution. Thus a host of government sponsored and private agencies began scrutinising and policing the vast wave of publications that emanated from the growing number of printing outlets springing up in the metropolis. Some, such as Hannah More, counteracted this tide of criticism through her own publications which substituted homespun god fearing loyalism for the seditious and the inflammatory works of the deists, infidels and revolutionaries. It is often suggested that the conservative response to such criticism should be regarded as reactionary – that is, merely seeking to safeguard the vested interests of property and land. However it is worth remembering that individuals like Hannah More genuinely believed in the benevolence of their cause and that those whose sole thoughts were to undermine it were committing pernicious crimes of the very worst kind. Indeed Hannah More and the Society for the Suppression of Vice saw such godless ideas as robbing the poor and destitute of their hope of a better life in the next world.

However, significant numbers of infidels and vocal critics saw this argument as little more than fraud and many were prepared to say so in print. One of the most prolific of these was Richard Carlile who can be said to have been radicalised by his arrival in London in 1813. From his shop in Fleet Street he commenced a protracted metropolitan war in print and from the platform which was to last for nearly 20 years. His numerous London newspapers (*Republican*, the *Lion* and latterly *The Prompter*) brought his message of continental style anti-clericalism to new audiences. Carlile and his network of printers, shopmen and street sellers of these papers were systematically targeted by the government and, through the systematic campaigns of the Society for the Suppression of Vice, many were prosecuted for blasphemy in the early 1820s. However these trials were by and large counterproductive and had the dual effect of eliciting sympathy for the accused and providing unwarranted publicity for their views and the works that contained them.[17]

Government in particular was especially slow to learn this lesson and only became guarded about its actions towards the blasphemous as late as the last quarter of the nineteenth century.[18] However early heavy handedness in meting out prison sentences against Carlile and his supporters made heroes of them all in progressive circles. Carlile himself endured an almost intolerable record of lengthy prison sentences during which he was joined variously by his wife and sister as he continued to write and publish from his prison cell. Some historians doubt the lasting or significant impact of Carlile's own campaigns.[19] but it is scarcely in doubt that he established his credentials as the leading ideologue of nineteenth-century freethought to be set alongside Thomas Paine in the creation of what historians of radicalism have come to call the Paine/Carlile tradition. This tradition had an emphasis on both outdoor and indoor speaking often tailored to different audiences. Anna Davin has noted that the impetus behind the volume and popularity of outdoor speaking was a function of growing population levels within the metropolis in the first half of the nineteenth century. Audiences were driven into areas where preaching and oratory occurred by the pressures of concentrated urban living. Open spaces were predominantly free from financial cost and generally from the watchful eye of censorious authority[20] (see Figure 6).

The impact and ideological sway of Carlile is manifest in the deference and respect paid to him and his memory by the capital's (and nation's) subsequent heir to this tradition, Charles Bradlaugh. Carlile had been a veteran of outdoor debate in Bonner's Fields (later Victoria Park) and it was precisely this world which captured the mind of the young and impressionable Charles Bradlaugh.[21] Subsequently when Bradlaugh was converted to secularism and became a stump orator, advocates and detractors alike made considerable capital of his visible youth. After service in the army and estrangement from his family Bradlaugh had taken shelter in the house of Eliza Sharples the former common law partner of Carlile before commencing a prolific career as freethought leader, lecturer and writer. In this he was joined for most of the subsequent 40 years by George Jacob Holyoake, a veteran of the previous generation who surprisingly outlived Bradlaugh. The relationship between these two men was, as we shall see, problematic and on occasions considerably hostile. For our purposes the differences between them contained the essence of many of the unresolved issues that inhibited the secular movement's progress and ultimate success.

Frequently it could appear to outsiders as a collection of entrenched ideological positions that sometimes defied full comprehension. Arguably the secular movement briefly 'tasted power' through the election of Charles Bradlaugh to parliament and the subsequent success of his struggle to take his seat. Nonetheless the apparent peak of its potential was over by the time the twentieth century commenced and it has appeared to most historians of the subject to be largely a spent force by the outbreak of the First World War.[22]

However we should immediately be wary of the temptation to use the yardsticks of success we would potentially use with other radical and working-class movements. In doing so we should remember that for the bulk of the nineteenth-century, Secularism, or some closely allied version of it, was the ideological position of choice for most of London's radical working men's clubs.[23] Judged as an orthodox political movement Secularism comes off rather badly. When we widen our scope and look more creatively at its cultural achievements then our conclusions start to alter somewhat. Whilst these conclusions in this chapter pertain to one ideological movement they also inform and elaborate upon wider historiographical questions which have forced themselves onto the agenda of those who write about class and about radicalism. The linguistic and populist turns have focused attention upon the power and immediacy of mass movement and mass communication as the medium (and indeed sometimes the message) of radicalism.[24] The ability of individuals to appropriate a broad concept from a platform speaker has been transformed by this analysis to highlight the strategies radicals employed to 'achieve' popularity and immediacy. This has downgraded the enduring power of ideology, so beloved of the subject's previous generation of historians, but it has also sidelined the gradual, the thoughtful and the cultural – to greater or lesser extents. Investigation of radical ideas that were embedded in, and drew strength from, living and flourishing cultures can give us back a more rational and central role for ideology and its trappings.

Secularism and cultural dissent

In its earliest century manifestations unbelief, shaped as infidelity, may very clearly have had a significant part to play in creating the impression of ideology linked to isolation. If viewed from a hostile perspective those who espoused unbelief and infidel ideas in the first third of the nineteenth century seemed dangerous and self-marginalising from a society which itself was scared and reticent. Where such individuals did congregate it seemed solely for the purpose of defying authority whether temporal or spiritual. We have already met Carlile's blasphemous defiance, but we should also bring to mind the considerable London network of less obviously committed publishers of infidel books and pornography uncovered by Ian McCalman.[25] More focused and troubling publishers also displayed infidel ideological leanings. Henry Hetherington, the London proprietor of the Unstamped Press's most troublesome paper *The Poor Man's Guardian*, regularly resorted to anti-clerical copy and on his deathbed trumped potential recantation stories through a last will and testament which was widely publicised.[26] In his last years, and indeed within this document, Hetherington cited the progressive influence of Robert Owen's rationalism as the most benign method of ensuring the happiness of man and woman. Owen's Rational Society of the early 1840s resembled an evangelical crusade with its missionaries and millenialist message which offered both enlightenment and prosperity the day after tomorrow. This message was preached to the capital and taken to the provinces by a number of gifted individuals who had refined their anti-clerical instincts into a more positive alternative. To hostile eyes, however, Owen's missionaries appeared as opportunists especially when quite so many of them were prepared to take out the licenses required of dissenting ministers in order to carry on their work. As with much evangelising the problems came with maintaining the impetus amongst an evangelised population, a situation rendered almost impossible when the financial and ideological infrastructure which supported Owenism collapsed amid recriminations towards the very end of the 1840s.[27] From the perspective of this period of lamentation godless radicals might well have drawn some fairly jaundiced conclusions. Whilst some radical organisations and individuals had provided hope and inspiration for a time, their long-term impact upon society at large had been disappointingly minimal. For unbelief and rationalism, marginality and self-enforced isolation seemed the order of the day for the foreseeable future.

One individual determined to resist this less than optimistic future was the former Owenite George Jacob Holyoake. Already a veteran radical with impressive credentials he was determined to ensure the crusade against the power of religion commenced by Owen would be continued. But to achieve this Holyoake had to make it possible for unbelievers to appear central to society rather than marginalised by it. In this he wanted to provide an ideological shield that would make such unbelievers appear so much less threatening and so much more acceptable. Holyoake dissented from the Jacobin scowling of a Carlile, the explosive wit of Hetherington or the rationalist dreaming of Owen. Instead Holyoake offered plausible forms of defence and protection which served to cast religious and state authority as the aggressor. Initially he formed an Anti-Persecution Union to provide moral and financial support for those imprisoned or prosecuted for religious opinions. On occasions this cleverly invoked the spectre of European despotism to create sympathy for British citizens facing prosecution abroad.[28] Although this organisation faltered in the provinces it remained successful in the capital and was behind the formation of the London Atheistical Society which sought to campaign against all laws which restricted the profession and expression of opinion. This organisation provided a link of personnel with the unstamped days of Hetherington through its first secretary Thomas Powell.[29]

However of greatest lasting value was to be Holyoake's creation of a new ideological position around the issue of religious belief and its role for both the individual and society at large. This he labelled 'Secularism' which constituted a deliberate escape from the treacherous connotations of the term infidel. This expression, which some mistook for a species of agnosticism, tried to shelve damaging discussion with opponents of the existence of a deity, preferring systematic and meaningful discussion of the knowable universe – namely the material and philosophical world. Behind this fortress built against religious aggression all species of opinion could flourish from mild Unitarianism to virulent anti-clerical atheism. In time the word 'discussion' was to loom large as this protective environment nurtured forms of Millite liberalism as well as eventually, socialism and anarchism.

The appeal of Secularism was that it offered the chance for umbrella organisations to adopt its stance and thus to provide the infrastructure religious congregations regularly took for granted. It offered plausible forms of defence against local Christian opponents without wholly closing the door to opportunities for dispute and fruitful exchange. This formula proved popular in both the capital and provinces whilst the extensive networks of secular clubs and institutes which provide the local organisation for this process flourished to varying degrees from the early 1860s onwards. Where the various movements which grouped under the secularist banner really scored was in their ability to provide premises for virtually every conceivable radical activity. Thus premises under secular ownership, or at least stewardship, provided throughout the second half of the nineteenth century a long, if occasionally episodic, record of service as lecture halls, theatres, clubs and reading rooms. It has long been recognised that radicalism in the capital could be a 'fair weather' activity as metropolitan radicals frequently resorted to the parks, greens and fields of London as venues for political meetings. For many even the hire, never mind the maintenance, of indoor venues was prohibitive. Infidels were really the first to buck this trend in the capital. This was because speakers and practitioners so frequently saw themselves engaged in a form of ministry (or indeed counter ministry) that it was inevitable for such activity to be associated with a chapel or meeting hall. Thus, almost by default, infidels and freethinkers became a recognised focal point of London's radical topography. Although some individuals, like Robert Wedderburn, acquired their own preaching licenses and access to chapel premises, it was buildings like Richard Carlile's Rotunda which hosted the sensational lectures of the 'Devils Chaplain' Robert Taylor, which became a more obvious focus. Halls and premises also provided an inspiration for infidel and later secularist ideas to have an obvious indoor presence. After the 1850s the informed disputation between the street secularist and his or her orthodox opponent or heckler became formalised to the advantage of both. Holyoake and subsequently Bradlaugh took such disputes indoors to the various public venues of the capital and the provinces. These charged admission, could last several nights and often provided significant profit for both parties. Although outdoor preaching still had an allure the dynamism of both Christian and Secularist exponents of it were ultimately challenged by urban London's encroachment upon open spaces in and around the capital. Ironically both were anxious to defend the spontaneity and chance for conversion and contact that open space preaching had allowed. Larger parks, such as Victoria and Hyde Park, persisted as venues but the marginal and less frequently peopled open spaces fell out of use.[30] Nonetheless the capacity for the thoroughfares of

London to become contested territory once again was always present once religion and infidelity mutated into new forms. By the end of the 1870s the Salvation Army (itself a response to the spiritual and philanthropic inadequacies of the capital) had become a presence upon London's streets which angered secularists.[31] What ultimately sounded the death knell for radical outdoor activity on any scale was the noise and changed street pattern created by the coming of the motor car.[32]

The later secularist movement, or we might call it a tendency, took root especially where light industry was the norm – notably in Lancashire, South and West Yorkshire as well as in the East Midlands. Although there were notable outposts in the West Midlands and urban lowland Scotland these never eclipsed the primacy of the aforementioned areas and would only sporadically spring to life. Nonetheless taken together they formed a network of congregation style groups which provided support for their members and constituted a lecture circuit for provincial and metropolitan speakers alike. What, however, always seemed troubling for such a movement or tendency was the fact that it had turned its back upon engaging with society at large. This tension seemed very near for those who thought for any length of time about the Paine/Carlile tradition they had inherited. These two individuals and their lasting ideological shadows strongly argued that cant and error should be attacked and exposed not conciliated or tolerated.

It was the dangers provoked by such ideological ambivalence that arguably gave birth to new departures and brought individuals other than Holyoake to the fore. The atmosphere changed significantly when Charles Bradlaugh appeared on the metropolitan scene in the early 1860s. Whether by accident or design Bradlaugh had become Richard Carlile's obvious ideological heir. More obviously an atheist than practically all others in the contemporary movement Bradlaugh and his acolytes would readily attack the Holyoake style tendency for its quietist tolerance. On occasions (especially if the historian pays too much attention to the views of biased contemporaries) it is tempting to see this as a battle between stridency and tolerance or even courage and timidity. Such judgements ignore the context and many of the crucial facts. The generation represented by Bradlaugh had seen Liberalism become coherent and viable and thus thought modern progressivism had a duty to attack and to overturn the spurious and the outmoded – especially in the area of religious belief. For Bradlaugh's generation this was best achieved through high profile campaigning on the metropolitan stage about issues (such as the right for atheists to give evidence in court and to enter parliament) rather than abstract ideas. However

Bradlaugh's generation had not witnessed and survived the turbulent years of the 1830s and 1840s nor had they experienced the ignominy of coming away from them comparatively empty handed.

For the metropolitan secularists it was possible to experience the advantages and pitfalls of living with these twin emphases on the doorstep and even to experience a hybrid of both. Outlying parts of London regularly looked to the network of suburban clubs and societies which, whilst reflecting both ideological persuasions, still placed a Holyoake style premium upon movement culture and support network functions. In doing so they could look to the manifestations of Bradlaugh's new organisation the National Secular Society (NSS) in the centre of the capital for an occasional national impetus. The title of Bradlaugh's movement strongly conveyed its intention to both speak for the whole of secular thought and to bestride the metropolitan and national stage. There was also a half-way house solution in which what we might call 'district' societies became the focus for a number of smaller localities. These were named after specific districts and some of these had their own satellite branches. Organisations like the London Secular Society (formed in 1853) were augmented by similar structures covering North East, West and South London.[33]

Although there were moments when a degree of success was potentially within its grasp local Secularism ebbed and flowed throughout the outlying parts of the capital and to an extent mirrored the climate for radicalism that prevailed in the years after 1850. Years of obvious nationally visible activity led to a more prosperous local scene, but for the historian this also means that smaller attendances and a less obvious profile kept the radically minded and radically inclined ready for action in leaner years. Certainly for secular activity the years before 1860 appear lean indeed with organisation patchy, variable and meetings more episodic than was healthy for a movement that required its culture to be thriving. However Edward Royle's survey of Secularist activity estimated that the 1860s and 1870s witnessed on average a dozen active clubs and societies in and around the metropolis. Clubs existed in the West End of London in Chelsea and further outlying areas such as Kingston and Brentford whilst the East End had a more concentrated and more significant cluster.[34]

It is important here to place the secular club life of the capital in its wider historical and historiographical context. Antony Taylor has strongly challenged the notion that metropolitan club life was a mirror of constitutional forms and an agent of self and mass working-class improvement. In particular he denies the link between club life and late century apolitical leisure patterns is as obvious or complete as others have argued.[35] Certainly the picture offered by secular clubs in the capital extends and widens this analysis still further. Whilst Taylor suggests the radical political clubs demonstrated continuity with Chartism it is also clear that secular clubs exhibited a degree of continuity with aspects of Owenite socialism. Personnel transferred allegiance after Owenism folded and secular clubs constituted an independent presence in club-land, which like the political clubs were full of ex-Chartists. Many secular clubs offered a small slice of rationalism if only for an evening a week. Similarly, far from falling into line with a species of commercialised leisure, both secular clubs and secularists themselves could actively demonstrate highly effective forms of opposition to them. Secularists often asserted that the world of leisure was populated with choices and clubs were duty bound to offer the uplifting and rational as antidote to the capital's counter attractions such as the music hall. Within secular clubs and societies theatrical performances would demonstrate rationalist principles – the *Merchant of Venice* as an exposé of Christian anti-Semitism was a favourite. Thus more mundane concessions to the world of leisure such as billiard tables, skittle alleys and alcohol could be given sufferance whilst the more charged potential for anti-sabbatarian activity offered by Clarion style cycling clubs would be embraced enthusiastically. This resembled how Owenites had sparred with the old immoral world yet the end of the century would revive this critique in the ethicist desire to socialise through uplifting activities.[36] Certainly none of these attitudes could be labelled compliant nor indeed a component of mainstream Liberalism. Indeed the role clubs played in organising and communicating support for Charles Bradlaugh's numerous campaigns for citizenship rights proved a succession of embarrassments for the centre ground of Liberal politics.

Local club life with an insular outlook should be contrasted with the provision that Charles Bradlaugh and the national movement made for its own activities. By the end of the 1860s the NSS had located its headquarters in Finsbury, in succession to myriad earlier temporary premises, by funding an impressive hall which could contain audiences of over 1,200. This was obviously a major radical metropolitan centre rather than a local congregation since secularists journeyed from all parts of London to attend lectures.[37] Although the Holyoake style wing of the movement would occasionally attempt to produce a rival it was never able to challenge Charles Bradlaugh's possession of the national agenda. Holyoake had once argued for an Atheon (in contrast to a Pantheon) which was to centralise like-minded organisations and functions into a single building.[38] This was arguably trumped by Bradlaugh's own plans which, unlike Holyoake's, came to fruition. Thus the Finsbury Park 'Hall of Science' was the headquarters for Bradlaugh during the crucial years of his campaigning through which he turned Secularism and secularists into at least minor players on the national political stage.

How, then, did this species of radicalism and an accompanying critique of religious versions of the universe function satisfactorily for those who followed it? Moreover the historian should also ask how these societies and individuals appeared to contemporaries. The second question is more easily tackled first. Freethought and Secularism were always a curiosity to contemporaries outside the movement, yet the impressions such observers gained of them were both informative and driven by interesting agendas. Thankfully we have the testament of a number of erudite and informed witnesses. In the years after the 1851 religious census the religious opinion formers of the age craved systematic information and knowledge of the religious state of the metropolis and many other cities. This was driven by a fear that the city itself was in fact a godless structure that spread and proliferated unbelief. The 1851 religious census both persuaded Christianity onto the streets and gave it real (perhaps even exaggerated) respect for its opponents. The danger that the indifferent metropolis could become the secular or infidel metropolis was a frequent spur to religious action. Missionary societies grew dramatically as a result throughout the 1850s and adopted systematic training schedules for talented recruits.[39] Training was considered essential since the oratorical style and skills of infidel preachers were frequently identified as dangerous and seductive; the failure of Christianity in the face of these was too much to countenance. The secular scene in the metropolis at mid-century was not short of observers or those spurred on by their curiosity as well as political commentators who were generally outnumbered by the clergy. Motives for such curiosity fluctuated between searching for an alleged 'cause' for the godless city or alternatively a fear about the society that might result from religion's effective neglect of its urban constituencies.

One such commentator was the clergyman Charles Maurice Davies and his works are particularly useful in providing snapshots not simply of the subject of religion but also, in this instance, of the 'photographer' and his motives. In all Davies investigated the variety of religious experiences available in the capital and some of his writings possess the genuine flavour of a guidebook, perhaps suggesting the growing issue of choice inherent in religious preference that some historians have told us about for sometime.[40] Davies painstakingly compiled and wrote works entitled *Orthodox London, Unorthodox London, Mystic London* and finally properly tackled Secularism and freethought in the two volume 1874 work *Heterodox London*. The collective, and substantial, impact of these volumes was to emphasise the metropolis as a collection of physical and psychological spaces where difference and dissidence flourished. When the reader bears this factor in mind it becomes easier to see that the works of Davies also echoed specific genres of metropolitan literature. Some of this work was socially investigative and sensationalist, pre-empting figures like Alfred Mearns, but much drew on the taste for curiosity which made Davies' work appear a more serious minded middle brow version of Egan, Dickens and Mayhew. As with most examples of the urban investigation genre fear vied with fascination and excitement in Davies' accounts of London's spiritual and freethinking variety.[41] This volume seemed a logical extension of the earlier work yet Davies also emphasised that he was in uncharted territory. As he put it he was close to having ' "stumped" to a pretty considerable extent the hemispheres of London, orthodox and unorthodoxy (he) projected a wider area still – the great unexplored wilderness of Heterodoxy. I would reconnoitre those regions which did not even abrogate to themselves the title of Orthodoxy'.[42]

Again like most social investigators Davies was an enthusiastic and prolific amateur who sandwiched his investigations between the demands of a hectic London curacy. Davies quietly and cautiously attended a number of meetings belonging to this milieui nonetheless he also did not flinch from observing everything relevant to the subject. His explorations took in services, lectures, musical entertainment as well as contact with the NSS paper the *National Reformer* and even attendance at a secular burial service. Where he could obtain them he willingly reproduced the rule books, 'prayers' and manifesto statements of the organisations he encountered and this served to further emphasise the eclecticism of some demands whilst also clearly showing their common libertarian roots.

As well as more orthodox secular societies Davies also attended the meetings of Unitarian groups and the more ritually inclined South Place Ethical Society. Although sympathetic Davies was still convinced that secularist activity should somehow be confronted and many of his visits praised the level of preaching offered – something he contrasted starkly with the quality of Christian apologists he encountered in such circumstances. One visit to the South London Secular Society on an early Spring evening in the early 1870s produced precisely this reaction.

Davies listened and noted attentively the lecture on the historical nature of Christ given by a Myles McSweeney. Whilst clearly not to his taste Davies exhibited exasperation at the poor quality answers offered by the Christian representative declaring 'Surely here, if ever, was an opportunity for the Christian Evidence Society sending one of their best men'.[43] Davies' perambulations give a clear indication of the growing anxiety to catalogue and expose the levels of eclecticism he encountered on his tour of the outer edges of metropolitan religious radicalism. He was amused by the frock coats of Voysey and Conway at South Place whilst also intrigued by the musical entertainment on offer at the same venue which went on far too long for his liking. A subsequent visit was scarcely more successful although he did particularly notice the quality of lecture offered by an experienced woman speaker (a Madame Ronniger).[44] On another occasion he attended a morning meeting of the Humanitarian Society in Islington and his overriding impression was of an organisation filling a niche in a competitive suburb which was characterised by a species of religious and anti-religious competition and bustle, even on an early Sunday morning.

Although Davies clearly convinced his readers that local secular societies in the capital had honed their creed to a degree of sophistication at least some of what his readers encountered could be dismissed as eccentric. However such readers would have sat up abruptly when Davies discussed Bradlaugh. Here all of conventional religion's multiple fears about the religious life of the capital appeared alongside this demonstration of Secularism as a challenge to the national religion. Davies encountered Bradlaugh lecturing at the Hall of Science and readily admitted that his influence and potential power as a speaker was 'simply prodigious'.[45] Davies outlined in considerable detail the events of the evening and managed to convey to his readers the essence of the freethinking and secularist presence in the capital. Upon seating himself in the Hall of Science Davies noted the variety of those who entered the premises after him. It was clearly a revelation to Davies and his potential readers that the audience contained respectable tradesmen alongside a smattering of the unskilled and members of the military. Of more pressing urgency was the inquiry about Bradlaugh's consistent and enduring level of popularity declaring 'How is it Mr. Bradlaugh can get these people to pay fourpence and listen to an abstruse subject, while we cannot "compel them to come in?" '[46] What followed was typical Bradlaugh and reminds us of his own personal power as well as demonstrating the fundamentals of what so many secularist lectures from the national movement actually contained. The essential theme of the lecture was to remind the audience of the power and trajectory of social progress lingering especially upon the ability of such progress to secure lasting benefits for mankind. In doing so it was possible to eliminate the injustices wrought by religion in the past and to remind the audience of why they had come; 'Racks and *auto-da-fes* had disappeared. Education could not be shut out. Bruno and Shelley and Voltaire and Paine had done something'.[47] The occasion of this lecture also allowed Davies to acquaint himself with the pages of the *National Reformer* and it unequivocally provided further proof of Bradlaugh's gifts, power and organisational ability.

Although he was ultimately impressed by the reasonable and respectable nature of club secularism it was Davies' encounter with Bradlaugh and his ideas that influenced some of his more forthright findings. Chief among these was that alongside the godless metropolis the work of religion's dedicated and able opponents was a matter of very serious concern. In amongst his discussion of Bradlaugh Davies looked his readers squarely in the eye and declared 'It would be the greatest mistake possible for Christians to depreciate their foe, or pretend to look down on Secularism'.[48]

Occasionally London secularists, if not Secularism itself, would cause concern to the governmental authorities in the City of London. As we have discovered Carlile and his shopmen were regularly arrested and tried for blasphemy. This same problem lay dormant until the campaigning days of Bradlaugh focused attention upon Secularism's most strident ideological and anti-clerical paper the *Freethinker*. This newspaper had exorcised both central and local metropolitan authority from its very first issue published in May 1881. Indeed the whole *Freethinker* drama was played out in the capital with provincial noises off which go some distance in explaining how metropolitan radicalism could reinvent itself as national radicalism when it 'called' upon the country at large. Foote's paper enraged influential individuals in the City and ultimately they were behind his prosecution when the Home Secretary (Sir William Harcourt) would have preferred caution. Unable to stomach Foote's blasphemy any longer the Mayor of London, Sir Thomas Nelson, plotted against the *Freethinker's* Christmas number of 1882, forcing the Home Office's hand. As the case progressed the 'national stage' was regularly invoked by Foote's histrionic appeals to justice and 'the spirit of the age' regularly reinforced by petitions which came from all over Britain.[49] What must also have caused concern for later commentators was the company that Secularism would sometimes keep in the latter years of the nineteenth century. London was a place where dangerous continental anarchists could drop out of sight and become a brooding presence. Many secular societies would become natural haunts for such individuals, a situation only exacerbated by the presence of anarchist ideologues on the platform. Chief amongst these were Peter Kropotkin and Stepniak who regularly spoke in this milieu.[50] In the Edwardian period there was arguably more tension when the militant end of the secular movement represented by Ernest Pack, William Stewart and J. W. Gott began associating with American anarchists like Melfew Seklew and Moses Harman. Ironically London played host to this slumbering colony of *émigrés* precisely because, compared to other European cities, it was welcoming, quiet and comfortable.[51]

Nonetheless for most secularists these ideas were either passing through or reflected a sequence of radical zeitgeists which enlivened their approach to the politics of the time and their vision of the universe. Thus it is Secularism which provides a link in London between the last days of Chartism and Owenite collapse and the campaigns against British militarism in the Second Boer War. Between these dates lie the coming of socialism, anarchism, extreme individualism, the Positivism of Auguste Comte and Ethicism. The secular umbrella provided a platform, audience and a viable press network for all of these without which radicalism in the capital would have constantly to fight against mundane practicalities such as the search for a venue.

Conclusion

Just as Davies sought to persuade his audience not to look down on Secularism it is important for us to remind historians not to do the same. Alongside more conventionally political movements of the nineteenth century it looks disjointed, episodic and occasionally at the mercy of the personalities of its leaders. Moreover as a cause which appeared to have two wings with separate ideas and motivations it is too easy to focus upon the splits and splinters that regularly occurred. Certainly, there was no love lost between the Holyoake and Bradlaugh families and their compatriots, and bitter wrangling lasted well into the twentieth century.[52] Nonetheless if we imagine too deep a divide between the local network of lecture halls and the national stage played out in the metropolis we too readily fall into the traps that have ensnared and created problems for the conventional historiography of class and radicalism. As many of the secularist periodicals demonstrate it was possible for individuals to be devoted and studious members of their local suburban society yet also to cheer on the popular campaigns that Charles Bradlaugh made his own on the national stage.

This, however, also starts to address the historiography of class and radicalism in some new ways that potentially move beyond the polarised arguments between the linguistic/populist turn and the more traditional views of class analysis. The study of radicalism in recent years has come under the influence of social historians who have challenged some of the fundamental assumptions about the subject made by almost three generations of scholars. First the assumption that those who involved themselves in the radical causes and battles of the period were inspired by ideology has come into question, at least as a single inviolate entity. This was replaced initially by a scepticism which doubted both the breadth and depth of ideological understanding and lasting commitment to the variety of causes which radicalism (and radical history) claimed for itself. From this scepticism there grew an assertion that radicalism turned more around messages than ideas. This was expressed as a belief: some of the central rallying messages of radicalism turned around sentiment and practice rather than understanding and psychological commitment. In other words radicalism's messages were more readily created to fit with their audience than to alter and advance opinion. This has created a reading of nineteenth-century radicalism which assumes that both popular and populist should reign in our analysis.

For both conventional class-based analysis and subsequent versions of the linguistic and populist turn the history of Secularism emphatically has something to offer. Conventional class-based analysis would see Bradlaugh's political campaigns as being located within the accepted broad definition of liberal radicalism. The large issues he addressed which included citizenship rights, species of anti-imperialism and the land question were all issues that merely used the platform provided by the secular movement. Even where Bradlaugh adopted a class-based message it seemed to speak to the artisan world that in an earlier generation had enjoyed Paine's old corruption analysis. Maintaining an assault upon aristocratic privilege whilst defending the rights of friendly societies and market traders looks arguably like petit bourgeois radicalism. Bradlaugh and Secularism itself within this version of events provides something of a staging post for this analysis and its graduation on to what it would see as more fulfilled and fulfilling ideologies. Such an analysis would argue that these themes were further amplified through the clubland of Holyoake style secularism. Once again these clubs look like the sounding board for new ideas which were to take the audience away from mid-century liberalism. This whole approach however underestimates how the local and national fed off each other's power and the logic of their separate agendas. The impetus to campaign and take national issues into the political sphere also worked downwards as later century secularists like Frederick James Gould and Arthur Moss took their ideas into the local sphere in School Board politics.[53]

However it is arguments about populism that founder more readily when held up to the secularist movement. A concentration solely upon Charles Bradlaugh would present no problems for this analysis since his campaigns were both popular and populist. The enduring power of anti-aristocratic discourses has been well demonstrated by historians of the nineteenth century and it might justifiably be suggested that Bradlaugh's ideas be systematically placed alongside these.[54] Moreover so much of his writings and speeches which drew upon the central idea of progress could be described as elaborating and radicalising the most populist idea of the whole nineteenth century. Moreover the spectacular ebb and flow of Bradlaugh's personal and political fortunes, the regular portrayal of his constant legal battles as an enduring drama should be material which reminds us of the power of the popular narrative in political form. Nonetheless such an analysis is in danger of denying that such a movement had dedicated ideological motives. If we focus merely upon Bradlaugh and neglect the impact of wider club and lecture hall life throughout the capital we miss an entire history of radicals quietly (and sometimes noisily) getting to grips with texts, discussing them and formulating fully theorised radical positions around them. Bradlaugh might lead these people from time to time but ultimately they would always go back to the books.

If we listen too readily to populist turns we also dangerously nudge Secularism and secularists into being middle brow and middle class through judging their desire to acquire knowledge and discrimination in a harshly negative manner. For those who seek populist potential secularists becoming associated with the 'elite' disciplines, robs these individuals of their popular power and identity. Thus we might consider the history of Secularism and the cheek by jowl manifestation of its two tendencies in the capital as a clear means of qualifying the ambition of populist explanations of nineteenth-century radicalism. Perhaps describing this outright as an ideological turn is to overstate this, especially since all it really asks for is a return to a more balanced view about what individual historical actors say and do as well as what they themselves think about both actions. Indeed the most recent work by Patrick Joyce investigating the interaction between Liberalism and the city seems to acknowledge this. Joyce characterises Liberalism, especially within urban contexts as ruling through the use, discussion and application of freedom. For this argument to succeed, as he openly acknowledges, this 'depended upon cultivating a certain sort of self, one that was reflexive and self-watching'.[55] Moreover the quid pro quo for the creation of this reflexive self were individuals who could 'practice freedom by constantly questioning its limits'.[56]

Nonetheless accepting a more obvious ideological turn (or perhaps less ambitiously a 'twist') might once more allow us to accept that the history of radicalism in the nineteenth century must make room for those who were ideologically motivated. There should always be room for those who saw knowledge as itself liberating and those who were prepared to think through the consequences of ideological positions, even if the last of these activities left them exhausted, hidebound and inactive as a result. It might also restore a belief that ideology was an important aspect of radicalism and many involved in it thought likewise. Such suggestions also reopen the question of how and where knowledge was actually acquired in the Victorian city. The libraries of secular club and institute allowed knowledge to be a more fluid commodity and its consumption to be much more diverse and self-fulfilling than the potentially negative panopticism Joyce has found in the regulated municipalized learning environments.[57] Ultimately exploration and discussion was central to cultures of criticism some of which survived beyond the chronology conventionally describing the process of class formation. Although this may constitute a cornerstone of liberalism and culture that is less easily explored than populism this chapter hopes to suggest that the task is still worth undertaking by future researchers. The club life of Secularism was about immersing audiences in ideas and exploring ideology whilst insisting on rational testing of theory and institution before admission to a wider culture. For some this may have been a lifestyle choice (one secularist in his old age recalled that it was a straight choice between 'Bradlaugh or the bottle') but this was also a call to seriousness. Emphatically we need to investigate further the impact of both lifestyle and the radical 'calling' individuals were seized by. These had lasting impacts upon everything from discourses about rights, the nature of education through to the nature of wider radical culture.

Notes

1. P. Collinson, *The Elizabethan Puritan Movement* (1982 edn). Cf. D. McCulloch, *The Reformation; Europe's House Divided* (London, 2003), p. 257.
2. A. L. Morton, *The World of the Ranters: Religious Radicalism in the English Revolution* (London, 1970); cf. J. C. Davies, *Fear, Myth, and History: The Ranters and the Historians* (Cambridge, 1986). C. Hill, *The World Turned Upside Down* (London,

1972); *idem*, 'Abolishing the Ranters', in C. Hill, *A Nation of Change and Novelty: Radical Politics, Religion and Literature in Seventeenth Century England* (London, 1990), pp. 152–94.
3. Sean Sheehan's analysis links defiance of authority with freethought and critiques of Christianity's power as a hierarchy. S. Sheehan, *Anarchism* (London, 2003), pp. 82–4; P. Marshall, *Demanding the Impossible: A History of Anarchism* (London, 1993), pp. 96–100.
4. F. Brockway, *Britain's First Socialists: The Levellers, Agitators and Diggers of the English Revolution* (London, 1980); D. Petergorsky, *Left-wing Democracy in the English Civil War: A Study of the Social Philosophy of Gerrard Winstanley* (London, 1940).
5. C. Hill, B. Reay and W. Lamont, *The World of the Muggletonians* (London 1983).
6. B. Capp, *The Fifth Monarchy Men: A Study in Seventeenth-Century English Millenarianism* (London, 1972).
7. Pepys diary, 13 October 1660 (various editions).
8. J. F. C. Harrison, *The Second Coming* (London, 1979); R. Porter, 'The 1790s: Visions of Unsullied Bliss', in A. Briggs and D. Snowman (eds) *Fins de Siecle: How Centuries End 1400–2000* (New Haven, 1996), pp. 125–6.
9. R. Porter, *London: A Social History* (London, 1994), p. 303.
10. For Brothers see Harrison, *The Second Coming*, ch. 4 and for Southcott see ch. 5 of the same book. F. Brown, *The Woman Clothed with the Sun* (Cambridge 2002); J. K. Hopkins, *A Woman to Deliver Her People: Joanna Southcott and English Millenarianism in an Era of Revolution* (Texas, 1982).
11. P. Ackroyd, *William Blake* (London, 1995).
12. E. P. Thompson, *Witness Against the Beast* (London, 1994).
13. Porter, *London*, p. 200.
14. Ibid., pp. 205–6.
15. E. Royle, *Victorian Infidels: The Origins of the British Secularist Movement 1791–1866* (Manchester, 1974), p. 24.
16. R. B. Shoemaker, 'Reforming the City: The Reformation of Manners Campaign in London, 1690–1738', in L. Davidson, T. Hitchcock, T. Keirn and R. B. Shoemaker (eds) *Stilling the Grumbling Hive: The Response to Social and Economic Problems in England 1689–1750* (Stroud, 1992), pp. 99–120.
17. D. S. Nash, *Blasphemy in Modern Britain* (Aldershot, 1999), ch. 3.
18. J. H. Wiener, *Radicalism and Freethought in Nineteenth-Century Britain: The Life of Richard Carlile* (Westport, 1983); Royle, *Victorian Infidels*, pp. 31–43.
19. P. Hollis, *The Pauper Press* (Oxford, 1970), p. 100; E. P. Thompson, *The Making of the English Working Class* (London, 1963), p. 839.
20. A. Davin, 'Socialist Infidels and Messengers of Light: Street Preaching and Debate in Mid-Nineteenth Century London', in T. Hitchcock and H. Shore (eds) *The Streets of London from the Great Fire to the Great Stink* (London, 2003), p. 166.
21. Ibid., pp. 169–70.
22. S. Budd, *Varieties of Unbelief: Atheists and Agnostics in English Society, 1850–1960* (London, 1977); E. Royle, *Radicals, Secularists and Republicans: Popular Freethought in Britain, 1866–1915* (Manchester, 1980).
23. S. Shipley, *Club life and Socialism in Mid-Victorian London* (Oxford, 1972). This has received little attention.

24. R. McWilliam *Popular Politics in Nineteenth-Century England* (London, 1998) offers the best introduction.
25. I. D. McCalman, 'Females, Feminism and Freelove in an Early Nineteenth-Century Radical Movement', *Labour History* (Australia) 38 (1980), pp. 1–25; idem, 'Unrespectable Radicalism: Infidels and Pornography in Early Nineteenth Century London', *P & P*, 104 (1984), pp. 74–110; idem, *Radical Underworld: Prophets, Revolutionaries, and Pornographers in London, 1795–1840* (Oxford, 1993), ch. 8.
26. D. S. Nash, ' "Look in her face and Lose thy Dread of Dying": The Ideological Importance of Death to the Secularist Movement in Victorian England', *JRH*, 18 (1995). For the original, *The Reasoner*, 7 nos 171 and 172 (1850).
27. Royle, *Victorian Infidels*, pp. 62–74.
28. *Reasoner and Anti-Persecution Gazette* nos 2, 5, 8, 17, 18, 27 (1865).
29. Royle, *Victorian Infidels*, p. 88.
30. Davin, 'Socialist infidels' p. 180. For the history of Secularist indoor places of assembly, more generally, see W. Kent, *London for Heretics* (London, 1932), ch. 3.
31. Nash, *Blasphemy in Modern Britain*, pp. 132–5, for the Salvation Army and Foote's early 1880s *Freethinker* cartoons.
32. Ibid., p. 182.
33. Royle, *Victorian Infidels*, pp. 191–2.
34. Royle, *Radicals, Secularists and Republicans*, pp. 46–7.
35. A. Taylor, ' "A Melancholy Odyssey Among London Public Houses": Radical Club Life and the Unrespectable in Mid-Nineteenth-Century London', *HR*, 78 (2004), pp. 74–95.
36. D. S. Nash, *Secularism, Art and Freedom* (Leicester, 1992) chs 8 and 10.
37. Royle, *Radicals, Secularists and Republicans*, p. 46.
38. Royle, *Victorian Infidels*, p. 88.
39. Davin, 'Socialist Infidels', p. 175.
40. S. Yeo, *Religion and Voluntary Organisations in Crisis* (London, 1976).
41. D. Englander, 'Comparisons and Contrasts: Henry Mayhew and Charles Booth as Social Investigators', in D. Englander and R. O' Day, *Retrieved Riches: Social Investigations in Britain 1840–1914* (Aldershot, 1995), pp. 105–42; M. Freeman, 'Journeys into Poverty Kingdom: Complete Participation and the British Vagrant 1866–1914', *HWJ*, 52 (2001), pp. 99–121.
42. C. Maurice Davies, *Heterodox London; Phases of Free thought in the Metropolis* (2 vols, London, 1874) i, p. 19. All subsequent references are to the reprint by Augustus Kelley (New York, 1969).
43. Ibid., p.119.
44. Ibid., pp. 88, 208.
45. Ibid., ii, p. 117.
46. Ibid., ii, p. 119.
47. Ibid., ii, p. 127.
48. Ibid., ii, p. 153.
49. Nash, *Blasphemy in Britain*, ch. 4.
50. W. J. Fishman, *East End Jewish Radicals 1875–1914* (London, 1975).
51. Porter, *London*, p. 293.
52. See D. Nash, ' "The Credulity of the Public Seems Infinite": Charles Bradlaugh, Biography and Attempts to Resacralise Fin de Siècle England', *JVC* (2002), pp. 239–62.

53. F. J. Gould, *Life Story of a Humanist* (London, 1923).
54. A. Taylor, *Lords of Misrule: Hostility to Aristocracy in Late Nineteenth and Early Twentieth Century Britain* (London, 2004), ch. 2.
55. P. Joyce, *The Rule of Freedom: Liberalism and the Modern City* (London, 2003), p. 4.
56. Ibid., ch. 2.
57. Ibid., pp. 132–3.

Figure 1 Rioters in the Strand during the West End Riots of 1886
Source: *Illustrated London News*, 12 February 1886, p. 175.

Figure 2 'The Mob' in the 1880s
Source: By permission of the People's History Museum, Manchester.

Figure 3 'A Struggle for Liberty': Anarchists arrested in a scuffle at the *Club Autonomie* in 1894

Source: *The Graphic*, 24 February 1894, p. 205.

Figure 4 Metropolitan Police raid on the *Club Autonomie* Anarchist Society in 1894
Source: *The Graphic*, 24 February 1894, p. 205.

Figure 5 Wat Tyler killing the King's poll tax inspector in 1381 (1860s)

Source: David Hume, *The History of England from the Invasion of Julius Caesar to the Revolution of 1688* (London, 1868), p. ii.

Figure 6 'The Reformer' speaking in Regent's Park in the 1900s

Source: E. T. Cook, *Highways and By-ways in London* (London, 1902), p. 403 (Thanks to Macmillan Ltd for permission to reproduce this illustration).

Figure 7 The aftermath of looting during the West End Riots of 1886
Source: *Illustrated London News*, 13 February 1886, p. 176.

Figure 8 Ducking of an unpopular speaker
Source: *Illustrated London News*, 13 February 1886, p. 176.

Figure 9 Popular disputation at a public meeting in Holborn Town Hall during the General election of 1880

Source: *Illustrated London News*, 3 April 1880, p. 316.

Figure 10 James Gillray's depiction of the candidates at the Westminster by-election of December 1806

Source: Marc Baer.

Figure 11 The Hustings at Covent Garden during the Westminster election of 1865
Source: *Illustrated London News*, 17 July 1865.

6
Transcending the Metropolis: London and Provincial Popular Radicalism, c.1860–75

Detlev Mares

Almost naturally, 'space' has long been a prominent category in urban history. Towns extend across geographical space, and they constitute the background for the cultural, social and political milieux located in particular quarters of towns or in networks of communication. Research on the social background of Victorian popular political movements has been inspired by a close analysis of residential patterns and electoral behaviour in particular towns. Although recent research has tended to dissolve any direct links between social class and political expression, in the process introducing further factors such as gender into the historian's perspective on urban politics,[1] the local dimension has remained fundamental for the understanding of popular politics ever since Asa Briggs edited a ground-breaking volume of articles on Chartism.[2] Many of the best examples of historical research in this area take their starting point from the situation in particular towns.[3]

However, less attention has been accorded to the interrelation between popular politics in single towns and the nationwide dynamics of popular campaigns. Despite invaluable comparative treatment of the structural differences between expressions of radicalism in particular towns there is still no systematic attempt at a geography of radicalism on a nationwide scale.[4] Any inroads into this field would have to consider the networks between radicals from different cities, but they would also have to include expressions of local pride and rivalries in the struggle for the leadership of popular campaigns. Perceptions about the value and legitimacy of claims for national spokesmanship often reflected understandings about the role particular towns might adopt in the political arena. Such processes of identity-building led to a kind of 'anthropomorphic' view of towns which were 'constructed' as actors in their own right on the political stage.

This chapter cannot claim to offer more than some preliminary considerations on a small, but crucial element in any geography of popular politics. It deals with the particular place of 'London' in national popular radicalism. The starting point will be a short summary of London-specific features which distinguished the political clout of the metropolis from most other British towns with strong traditions of popular politics. The second section will present areas of rivalry and local pride between London and other towns before the third section delineates attempts at overcoming the real or imagined barriers between 'London' and the 'provinces'. Ultimately, it will be argued, the failure to establish nationwide links between the metropolis and provincial towns was due less to ill-will than to the limited means of communication that fostered delays of information and related misunderstandings. Since the perspective is directed at London's role in popular radicalism, a stark dichotomy between 'metropolis' and 'provinces' will be maintained. It goes without saying that a more detailed account of the relationship between London and other towns would necessitate both a more searching enquiry into the preconditions of radicalism in different parts of the metropolis and a more sophisticated differentiation of individual provincial towns than that offered here.

The focus of the chapter will be on the period from about 1860 to 1875 when the Chartist legacy and new impulses combined in an upsurge of radical politics.[5] The emergence of the parliamentary franchise movement in this period offers a first opportunity to analyse the relationship between 'metropolis' and 'provinces' in a nation-wide campaign. As recent research has shown,[6] once franchise extension had been achieved in 1867, popular radicalism found expression in a variety of movements and campaigns – ranging from land reform and republicanism to the work of working-class electioneering bodies such as the Labour Representation League (LRL) – each trying to achieve 'national' importance. It was also in this period that the activities of the International Working Men's Association (IWMA) gained their greatest public resonance. Throughout what follows, the focus will be on institutionalised contacts between London and provincial bodies, since it was here that co-operation and conflict had their most direct impact on the dynamics of campaigns and movements.

London – a singular place for popular radicalism?

A concern for urban historians has been to define specific features or qualities of individual cities or their inhabitants, with the aim of discovering what made them distinctive. Economic historians view cities as environments favourable to certain forms of production and distribution. For the London case, Michael Ball and David Sunderland have pointed to the advantages arising from agglomeration effects in the mass market and the high density of infrastructure in the world's leading metropolis of the nineteenth century.[7] Cultural historians have tried to define the 'spirit' of individual towns, and to assess the influence of 'mentalities' on the formation of political movements – for example the role played by Vienna and Munich in the rise of Adolf Hitler and the early Nazi movement.[8] Finally, new approaches in urban studies try to relate urban space to the creation of so-called innovative milieux, which, by the accumulation of talent and the dense networks of communication, inspire new ideas and create opportunities for these ideas to be implemented in new modes of production or intellectual exchange.[9]

While not all these approaches are equally suited to the task of locating London's place within mid-Victorian popular radicalism, some do indicate major factors which put the metropolis in a singular position as the base for political activities. If communication is the cornerstone for the coherence and success of any political movement, London was the ideal breeding ground for political organisation. It was here that a huge mass of people lived who might be motivated to participate in radical politics. It was here that radical printers had a considerable reservoir of political writers and a big market for their papers, broadsheets and pamphlets. It was here that countless political associations existed, surrounded by a wealth of heterodox and free-thinking clubs.[10] By the 1860s, the improvements in infrastructure, especially the provision of public transport, made it easier to move beyond the boundaries of one's district to take part in metropolitan-wide radical politics. It was also easy to establish links of co-operation between different associations. Whenever mutual assistance became an urgent requirement, London clubs and associations were quick to send delegates to meetings and to set up funds in support of common aims.[11]

Much information about radical issues and campaigns in the metropolis went straight into the national press. Radical concerns in London could muster a national audience even if they seemed to be small, sectarian issues; for example, the activities of the so-called O'Brienites, supporters of the socialist land-reformer Bronterre O'Brien, have drawn much attention although to many contemporary observers the group seemed to be a fringe phenomenon.[12] Activities in other cities had to be much more substantial before they moved on to the level of national recognition.

In several respects radical activities and modes of expression benefited from the sheer size of the metropolis. One might argue that in cultural and political terms we see something at work similar to the agglomeration effects noted by economic historians. If you were politically active in London, you had the largest potential audience in the country on your doorstep. A campaign in London was a matter of national importance; a campaign got up in any other town only became so when it managed to transcend its town of origin. Even a mighty movement such as the Anti-Corn Law League experienced the barriers that had to be overcome before 'London' could be roused. In 1839, when the Leaguers already dominated Manchester politics, their enthusiasm did not capture London audiences. Meetings in the metropolis were poorly attended, and the League decided to return to their Manchester powerbase before launching a fresh attempt at the capital.[13] It was to take another seven years before the Anti-Corn Law Leaguers were able to celebrate the victory of their campaign. The size and variety of London radicalism also guaranteed continuity in radical politics at times when mass movements subsided and radical politics had to fall back on a smaller base of activists. If a minority, popular radicals in London were a vocal minority that might uphold the regularity of proceedings even without a high level of mass support. The same might be possible in large provincial centres, but it was hardly an option in small places. For an extreme example, consider the town of Brecon in South Wales. Here, in one of the smallest parliamentary boroughs in the United Kingdom, a mere handful of activists constituted the local movement for parliamentary reform in the 1860s: when their interest slackened, the town disappeared from the map of British radical politics.[14]

It was much easier for leaders of London radicalism to become household names across the country than for anyone launching themselves from a provincial base. The same applies to the role of London spaces in the emotional household of British radicals. London contained a large number of symbolically charged locations with a strong emotional appeal to radicals all over the country. Hyde Park, Trafalgar Square, Blackheath and, indeed, parliament are only the most obvious examples (see Figures 1, 8 and 9). Other cities had their own connections between traditions of radicalism and particular public spaces. But only in a few cases – such as St. Peter's Fields in Manchester – did these symbolic connotations of space transcend local boundaries and reach a nation-wide audience.[15]

Much of what has been said so far can be related to another parameter that made London radicalism special among popular movements in Britain – London's function as the nation's capital. This undoubtedly did much to enhance the authority of London's popular leaders. It created opportunities for wielding political influence that simply did not exist in provincial towns. London popular radicals could carry demonstrations and processions directly to parliament's doorstep, thereby highlighting a striking dichotomy between the official people's chamber in Westminster and a politics that could be presented as the 'true', most immediate expression of the people's wishes. Besides this very public display of the people's claims, there also were networks of communication and co-operation with MPs. Several of London's radical leaders seem to have been well known in the lobbies of the House of Commons, and familiar with sympathetic MPs. George Odger, for example, seems to have been on rather friendly terms with Sir Charles Dilke and Henry Fawcett, whereas George Howell was closely acquainted with Anthony Mundella and Thomas Brassey. These contacts opened up direct ways of carrying popular politics into parliament.

Keeping these particular preconditions of political activity in view, London might seem to have constituted a self-contained island of radical politics, with concerns and movements distinct from those in the rest of the country. Examples can certainly be found. The battle between the National Sunday League and the Working Men's Lord's Day Rest Association over the opening of London museums and libraries on Sundays provides a case in point. The religious heterodoxy of the metropolis bred calls for less restricted opening hours of museums and art galleries while many towns in the 'provinces' were ruled by much stricter sabbatarian tendencies. Advocates of more flexible opening hours had the impression that this question hardly caught on with fellow radicals outside the metropolis. The moderate radical and trade union leader, George Howell, noted that 'London stands alone in this matter'.[16] The Royal Parks agitation of 1872–73 provides another example. When, in February 1872, A. S. Ayrton, the Liberal Chief Commissioner of Works, announced a bill regulating access to the London royal parks, he unleashed a storm of protest from popular radicals defending the right of public access. Despite the intensity of protest, the radical campaign remained a London-induced and London-based affair.

In this respect, it seems to confirm the image of isolation and self-sufficiency of London radicalism. However, this campaign also provides an example of a radical campaign moving beyond the boundaries of the metropolis. When the popular outcry had failed to prevent Ayrton from issuing regulations restricting political meetings in parks, London radicals decided to test the authorities' resolve to act on the new measures. A huge gathering nominally calling for the release of Fenians in English prisons became the test case for the defence of the unrestricted right of public meeting in royal parks. The demonstration itself was conducted without any disruptions, but on the following day, 4 November 1872, the speakers from the meeting were summoned before the magistrates of Marlborough Street Police Court. Among the defendants were the well-known radical and republican George Odger, the republican and internationalist John de Morgan and J. P. McDonnell, the Irish secretary of the International Working Men's Association.[17]

With this summons, the character of the agitation abruptly changed. Now it seemed to be a question of defending the right of free speech, one of the core liberties cherished by British radicals.[18] The issue quickly spread beyond metropolitan concerns and was taken up by radicals across the country. A defence fund for the speakers was established which drew contributions from all over the country. The issue of free speech ensured that the question did not remain the sole preserve of any political group or association; as a fundamental concern of radicalism the campaign managed to unite radical reformers from the more 'extreme' internationalist and republican wings of radicalism as well as more conciliatory 'moderates' from quasi-Liberal associations such as the Labour Representation League. Radical MPs also contributed to the fund. The speed with which the campaign spread shows the extent of the networks of communication that existed between London and the provinces. Thus, the parks campaign – which ended with a government climb-down – shows that under certain circumstances London radicalism could transcend the borders of the metropolis.

There is, however, no denying the rivalries between radicals from the 'metropolis' and the 'provinces' – the very terms indicate a kind of hierarchy firmly inscribed in contemporary discourse.[19] Therefore 'provincial' pride and differences of interest between 'London' and the rest of the country provide the logical next step in our analysis. Only by giving due attention to this aspect, can the characteristics of the relationship be understood.

Provincial pride and metropolitan dominance

Many radical campaigns that claimed to speak for 'the nation' emerged from local or regional initiatives. Yet the limited possibilities of communication often left them confined to their regional base, eroding the claim to 'national' importance. Setbacks and failures to succeed in the metropolis were enough to cause visible indications of tension between 'London' and the 'provinces'.

A groundswell of geographical rivalry was no specific feature of radical politics. It was ingrained in the very constitution of the United Kingdom. The political structures preserved the memory of national independence in Scotland and Wales,[20] and in many places local interests and identities competed with political initiatives emerging from London. In many towns in the north of England, religious nonconformity and industrialisation had created social and economic structures notably different from the metropolis. Attempts at centralisation emanating from the London-based government often only served to engender claims for local and regional independence.[21]

At the local level, radical activities frequently merged with anti-centralising initiatives that rejected incursions from the capital into local affairs.[22] Occasionally, democratic ideals of republican federation joined with liberal attempts at strengthening local against central government.[23] The emphasis of locality did not necessarily preclude participation in national initiatives. Rather it allowed for a specific local interpretation of wider political concerns.[24] 'Local' and 'national' politics need not compete, but might support and complement each other.[25]

The localising or regionalising tendencies of political campaigns reflected geographically grounded identities; but they also resulted from the organisational preconditions of extra-parliamentary politics. It took considerable effort to transcend the local background of campaigns that had started outside London. Apart from the Manchester Anti-Corn Law League mentioned earlier, the education reform movement starting from Birmingham in the 1870s is another famous example of a successful campaign.[26] In both cases, one element of nationwide recognition and success was the emergence of able politicians whose names could be associated with the respective cause, often via local government – such as the 'Manchester men' Richard Cobden und John Bright in the 1830s and 1840s and the Birmingham manufacturer Joseph Chamberlain in the 1870s.

The trade union movement also proceeded from local starting points, attempts at national union notwithstanding. With the Trades Union Congress, a national umbrella organisation was established in 1868 but the local and regional differences in working conditions, salaries and working time secured the survival of a localised organisation of labour.[27]

Similar processes of regional concentration characterised the nationwide collaboration of popular radicals. Even in the case of Chartism, the best-known working-class agitation in the Victorian era, a clear regional focus can be discerned. Chartists were most strongly organised in regions such as the West Riding of Yorkshire and South Lancashire, while their impact on London proved disappointing.[28]

When a vocal republican movement emerged in the late 1860s,[29] it was in Birmingham that the first republican club in England was founded.[30] Its definition of the term 'republic' and its statutes became the model for similar clubs in many other parts of the country.[31] Only a couple of months later the first Republican Club in London was established by the well-known freethinker and republican Charles Bradlaugh.[32]

The Birmingham republicans are just one example of the numerous political initiatives that were firmly grounded in local traditions of popular radicalism. In the years after the decline of Chartism, activists from Sheffield and Newcastle acted as an inspiration to demotivated London radicals. In 1859 Benjamin Lucraft, a veteran Chartist from Holborn, drew on experiences from the Newcastle-based Northern Reform Union when trying to establish a North London Political Union to agitate for parliamentary reform. This first of all meant rousing an audience 'in a great measure new to politics'.[33] Lucraft assured the secretary of the Newcastle association that he was 'happy to receive any Suggestion from you whereby we may be enabled to act in the same direction as the Northern Reform Union'.[34]

Lucraft's initiative was one of the impulses leading to the formation of the Reform League (1865), the major London-based association agitating for manhood suffrage. The early contacts with the Northern Reform Union survived the transformations of the reform campaign in the next decade. In the mid-1860s, two associations led the movement for parliamentary reform – the Reform League and the National Reform Union. Usually historians argue that there were strong tensions between the associations due to the differences in programme and social composition. The National Reform Union is presented as a movement organised by Liberal Radicals to campaign for household suffrage, while the Reform League is seen as working-class based and eager for manhood suffrage.[35]

Yet the dividing lines between the associations were anything but clear. In both, the precise shape of their respective political demands remained contentious. Moreover, both were far from homogenous in their social and political composition. There were former Chartists in both associations,[36] and the Reform League was only marginally less successful than the Reform Union in securing financial support from middle-class sympathisers.[37] Some sections of the Reform League cooperated with local Liberal associations.[38] Programmatic differences between working-class and middle-class radicals in the formation process of the National Reform Union cannot be denied;[39] there was some competition for the leadership of the national reform campaign[40] – and yet the divisions between the two organisations also featured a rather different dimension; they were based on an informal agreement to organise the reform agitation according to the needs of different parts of the country. When both associations met in Manchester for a common reform conference in May 1865, they decided to move along different lines. In the north of England, the Manchester-based National Reform Union was meant to campaign for a limited suffrage since electors in the north did not seem to be willing to support a universal extension of the franchise; the Reform League on the other hand was convinced that its activities in London would be doomed to failure if it did not go for universal suffrage.[41] A reader of the *Commonwealth* newspaper insisted that in view of the fight '*against the common enemy*' any differences in the programmes seemed to be 'really very trifling'.[42] Significantly, when Howard Evans recalled the reform agitation in old age, it was the geographical division that stuck to his mind: 'The agitation in the Provinces was led by the National Reform Union; the Reform League worked mainly in the London district.'[43] In the course of the campaign, many radicals simply seem to have joined the organisation that happened to be active in their town or region. This might explain why a couple of years later members of the (allegedly) 'liberal' Reform Union reappear in the (allegedly) 'extreme' republican movement.[44] Thus, while the relationship between the associations showed some signs of strain, there also seems to have been a sense of a geographical division of labour that offered a pragmatic solution to the conflicts of interest.

At least partly, this solution must be seen as the result of competition rather than premeditated arrangement. The Reform League never really stopped trying to make advances into Reform Union-territory. But even within the Reform League, regionalisation set in. When it was founded in 1865, the organisation consisted of two layers – a central executive office in London and local sections. After a couple of years, a third layer of organisation had emerged – the district level. Some local sections had combined into regional *departments* that were focused on urban centres. By 1867, there were a Midland Department (centred on Birmingham), a Northern Department (Manchester), a Yorkshire Department (Leeds), the North-Eastern League (Newcastle-upon-Tyne) and the Scottish National Reform League (Glasgow).[45] These departments were most successful in those regions outside London where the National Reform Union only showed a weak presence. Significantly, the Northern Department did not manage to make much headway on the home turf of the National

Reform Union,[46] while attempts at the establishment of a Welsh Department simply failed for lack of support.[47] Some departments became almost independent from the London executive of the Reform League. When the Reform League tried to organise working-class candidacies in the general elections of 1868, John Stuart Mill observed that the London office had 'little influence' on the departments.[48] Thus, any signs of competition between the London and provincial reform campaign cannot be reduced to the relationship of Reform League and Reform Union: even within the Reform League, London activists had to take the pride and assertiveness of the 'provinces' into account when shaping their policies.

In the republican movement of the late 1860s and early 1870s, divergent regional approaches caused centrifugal tendencies that eventually thwarted any chances of success English republicans might have hoped for. Although George Odger in 1871 had expressed his hope that provincial radicals would follow the 'appeal of the metropolis'[49] in the formation of a republican movement, in the subsequent year London republicans failed to take the lead. In this situation, Yorkshire republicans gathered at Mexborough in October 1872 to organise their 'district'.[50] Influenced by John de Morgan, an agitator active in the north of England, they decided to move a crucial step further and, given London's default, establish a national republican body.[51] At a conference in Sheffield on 1 December 1872, the National Republican Brotherhood (NRB) was founded as the central body of English republicanism.[52]

The conference at Sheffield was not confined to delegates from the north of England. One of the most prominent participants was Charles Christopher Cattell, the founder of the Birmingham Republican Club, and well-known London republicans, such as Charles Bradlaugh, Charles Watts and G. H. Reddalls, were nominated to the executive committee of the new association.[53] Despite such conciliatory moves the NRB had little real chance of success. Even before the founding conference, Bradlaugh had refused to co-operate with the northern initiative.[54] Other London republicans expressed their worries about John de Morgan's collaboration with the IWMA,[55] an organisation founded in 1864 and which achieved notoriety in 1871 when it came out in defence of the Paris Commune, the relevant statements being written by a German agitator in London named Karl Marx.[56] Now John de Morgan's membership of the International served as a welcome excuse for refusing co-operation with the NRB.[57]

The London republicans' reservations about de Morgan and Internationalism must not be underrated; yet they do not fully explain the icy relationship between the NRB and the Bradlaugh republicans, who – incidentally – met in Birmingham in May 1873 to form yet another national body, the National Republican League.[58] From the very start, London republicans had rejected the northeners' claim to represent all republicans. One argument mustered was that John de Morgan was 'too little known' to lead a nation-wide movement.[59] This statement appealed to London radicals who had not yet heard much of a campaigner already well known in the north of the country. Thus, among the mix of motives shaping the relationship between the associations, geographical factors must not be neglected. The fate of the NRB again demonstrates a fundamental lopsidedness of influence within popular radicalism: without support from 'London', no campaign claiming to represent 'the nation' was able to gain legitimacy and succeed.

This did not, of course, stop provincial radicals from asserting their regional pride and associated claims for leadership. London was not granted pre-eminence without an argument. Regional pride came to the fore during a congress of the IWMA in 1872. This body had its head office in London. Whereas many countries around the globe had their own national councils that reported to the London office, the local sections in England were administered directly from the General Council in London. Only in 1872 was an English Federal Council established as an intermediary 'national' layer between local sections and the London-based General Council.[60] When it met for its first congress at Nottingham in July 1872, delegates from the north of England moved to transfer the permanent office of the English Federal Council from London to Manchester. They emphasised Manchester's importance as 'the great centre of the Provincial Trades Unions'[61] and pointed out that 'the greatest political movements had emanated from the north of England'.[62] Such claims were based on the history of Chartism, but they could also be substantiated with reference to the Nine-Hours-Movement of the early 1870s. In addition, they were the outgrowth of a more general feeling; to many activists from the 'provinces' it might seem that London radicals tended to usurp the right to speak in the name of 'the people' or the 'working classes' of the whole country. In 1870, a worker from Yorkshire complained: 'It appears to some of us "men in the country" that the leading men amongst the working classes in London occasionally forget our existence and political activity, and speak and act as if *they* solely are "the working classes of England".'[63]

In the end, pragmatic arguments usually carried the day. In the 'provinces' there were voices who accepted the need for 'London' to take the organisation of radical activities in hand. This was the case with popular radicals from Nottingham where, even in the 1860s, the memory of Chartism was still very much alive. When the Reform League officially dissolved in 1869, the leaders of the so-called Nottingham Chartist Association called for further pressure to carry the six points of the original charter. In order to do so, they suggested 'that a new association will be formed in London, and that the country will once more join in one great and grand organisation for the accomplishment of the people's charter'.[64] Similarly, when a republican club was founded in Dundee, one member suggested 'that London be made a centre to which all other clubs should become united as branches'.[65]

Even at the above-mentioned debate at the Nottingham congress of the English Federal Council of the International, the arguments of the London faction were hard to refute. John Hales, the most prominent London delegate, pointed out that 'London was the life and soul of English thought, and they might as well propose to remove the Imperial Parliament. The means of information were greater in London than elsewhere, and the London press was the best supplied in the world'.[66] Another delegate succinctly called London 'the most advantageous place'.[67] The final vote went 14–7 in London's favour.

Linking metropolitan and provincial radicalism

The role of London as 'the centre of thought and action' may have tempted London popular radicals into easy claims of being the natural representatives of 'the people'.[68] Yet, in general, the relevance of provincial initiatives was duly acknowledged in the metropolis. When Edmond Beales, president to the Reform League, attended a Birmingham reform demonstration in 1866, he alluded to the role played by the Birmingham Political Union in the run-up to the Reform Act of 1832: 'Now your fathers, the men of Birmingham, wrested from the oligarchy of 1832 the enfranchisement of the middle classes. You will complete the work which your fathers began – you will assist us Londoners, we ask you to do so – to wrest the enfranchisement of the working classes from the parliamentary oligarchy of the present day.'[69] George Howell, secretary to the Reform League, also knew how to pander to the pride of the local sections outside London. After the Second Reform Act was passed, he informed a Leicester correspondent that it was 'a source of gratification to us that we have the confidence of our Provincial Branches, for were it not for this confidence and cooperation our failure would have been certain'.[70] In more general terms, Charles Bradlaugh assured a

Newcastle meeting of Northumberland miners in 1873: 'They knew in the South they could neither fight nor win the battle without the aid and countenance of the North; they knew it was impossible to gain a fair victory without each man worked with them in the struggle in which they were engaged.'[71]

When the Reform League encouraged the formation of local electoral associations after the passing of the Second Reform Act, its London leaders accepted provincial calls for independence from the London executive 'as they always know best their own affairs'.[72] Howell explained that the new associations should be 'as local as possible but always in communication with us'.[73] Obviously, what London popular radicals tried to achieve was not dominance over provincial radicalism; they rather seem to have insisted on London institutions acting as the centre of communication for nation-wide radical activities.

Consequently they showed great zeal in establishing interregional networks of activity. Apart from the radical press and correspondence by letter, one means towards this goal was travelling. The major London bodies, such as the Reform League, established lecturing funds to support itinerant lecturers who visited different parts of the country to agitate for reform and to initiate the establishment of local sections of the London bodies.[74] Frequently, well-known London radicals went on lecture tours, giving public speeches or appearing in radical clubs in places across the country. Lecture tours were crucial in securing Charles Bradlaugh's leading role in the republican movement, for example, and his reputation was bolstered by the favourable coverage given to his lectures in the columns of his own newspaper, *The National Reformer*.

The impact a lecturer made thus arose with the reports of his activities in the press, the geographical range of his operations and the frequency of his returns to places he had visited before. An early biographical pamphlet claims that John de Morgan (admittedly an agitator at first based outside the metropolis) 'lectured eight times and travelled 800 miles every week for three years'.[75] The republican and secularist Charles Watts travelled 1400 miles within 24 days in 1871, appearing for 29 lectures and discussion panels in 12 cities.[76] For many small places in the country, as the London radical press never tired of relating, the visiting lecturer offered the 'natives' their first contact with radical politics. When Charles Watts visited Farnborough, for example, the village doctor was supposed to chair the meeting at which Watts spoke. But when the honourable physician noticed the lecturer's political opinions, he stormed from the room, 'exclaiming that Mr. Watts was a Red Republican, and ought to be burnt'![77]

Apart from gaining visibility and personal contacts through travelling lecturers, the London bodies tried to achieve nation-wide legitimacy by supporting the establishment of local sections in other towns. George Odger strategically used his parliamentary candidatures to encourage such moves in the boroughs he contested. The radical associations founded in connection with his candidacies in Bristol and Southwark long survived the limited objective of their establishment.[78] It was with such models in view that a correspondent of the *Republican* expected 'a glorious day for the democracy of England' as soon as 'a hundred paid lecturers' travelled the country in order to propagate 'the cause of the people'.[79]

Odger's activities were part of the strategy pursued by the LRL, an electioneering association founded from the remnants of the Reform League in 1869. Its main purpose was to organise working-class candidacies in promising constituencies all over the country. For all its historiographical reputation as having been, 'to all intents and purposes a London body',[80] the League tried hard to transcend its metropolitan origins. From the outset, the Executive Committee believed that 'the action of the League was looked for with considerable eagerness in several of the large manufacturing towns of the kingdom',[81] and by March 1870, 17 applications for the formation of local branches had been supplied.[82] Within a year, preparations had been reported from Sheffield, Bristol,[83] Birmingham, Maidstone,[84] Derby, Plymouth, Great Bridge,[85] and Exeter.[86] By the summer of 1871, it could present individual supporters' names from 34 different places,[87] and in 1873 the London executive decided to invite a number 'of Influential Working Men of the Provinces' to join the General Council.[88] By this time, a London and Provincial Council had already been in existence for two years although it probably did not ever get down to proper work.[89] All this made for the creation of a nation-wide network of contacts that facilitated the exchange of information. When the General Council of the LRL decided in 1871 to issue statements on the much-discussed question of secret balloting, it must have felt justified in its expectation that the material would circulate 'in all popular constituencies, and amongst the various working-men's organizations throughout the kingdom'.[90]

Despite promising tendencies, the results of the LRL's efforts proved rather disappointing. Apparently many sections remained suspicious of London interference. From Birmingham, the LRL was accused of having damaged the election prospects of David Kirkwood, the working man candidate for the local School Board.[91] Radicals from Bristol claimed that the League had forced Odger out of the parliamentary contest in the borough in 1869. The argument over this question resulted in Odger's withdrawal from the LRL – an example of how London conflicts were exported to the 'provinces' when metropolitan bodies became active there.[92] Many local sections, such as Maidstone, seem to have been rather short-lived,[93] and the League never managed to coax the provincial trades councils into wholehearted support of its activities.[94]

The history of the LRL demonstrates the barriers that had to be surmounted before a nation-wide network of contacts resulted in tangible political rewards. But the attempts to move beyond the London base are beyond doubt, and despite the meagre results, London radicals continued to woo the country. Another body trying to do so was the Land Tenure Reform Association (LTRA). Established by John Stuart Mill in 1869 to unite middle-class and working-class land reformers on a platform of 'free trade in land', the LTRA remained a predominantly London affair.[95] But even this association experienced some expansion beyond the metropolis, with sections being established in Oldham and Derby.[96] In this respect the LTRA was slightly more successful than a rival London body, the Land and Labour League, which agitated for a more comprehensive land reform scheme, many of its members calling for the nationalisation of the land. In this case, the existence of sections outside the metropolis cannot be proven, but there were statements of support from provincial cities and lecturers of the association tried to mobilise support in the big cities.[97] Even a short-lived precursor of the Land and Labour League, the Working Men's National Reform League, had claimed to have contacts with 'important manufacturing districts'.[98]

A hitherto unexpected opportunity to foster co-operation between 'town' and 'country' seemed to open up in 1872 when the agricultural labourers in Warwickshire combined for strike action. The strike quickly spread and encouraged the establishment of independent unions, the most famous of them being the National Agricultural Labourers' Union. It was based in Leamington and led by Joseph Arch, a hedge-cutter and locally respected Methodist preacher.[99] For the first time, the formation of an agricultural labourers' movement promised a viable chance to propagate radical ideas among the rural population.[100] High expectations moved London radicals and trade union leaders to become involved in the rural movement.[101] Yet once more, the results were disappointing. Although single London radicals, such as Howard Evans, became deeply committed to the agricultural labourers' initiative,[102] the movement soon split into two rival bodies. Several unions disagreed with the National Agricultural Labourers' Union over the distribution of funds that had been established in the metropolis and the rest of the country in support of the striking agricultural labourers. These unions combined to form the Federal Union of Agricultural and General Labourers in November 1873.[103] Some London radicals, among them George Odger, were involved in the founding of the Federal Union. Relations between metropolitan radicalism and the National Union cooled, while the Federal Union never really reached a critical level of mass support.[104] Although not a complete disaster, the new links between town and country failed to grow into an example of substantial co-operation between metropolitan and rural radicalism.

Limitations to nation-wide communication

The preceding sections of this chapter have traced the initiatives emanating from London radicals in their attempts to integrate the provinces into nation-wide campaigns. They have also shown, though, that these efforts remained relatively fruitless. London presumption and provincial pride resulted in often uneasy relationships that also suffered from structural problems. If London radicals pushed too hard for pre-eminence, they often failed to reach provincial audiences; where provincial initiatives tried to organise nation-wide movements, they in turn frequently met with recalcitrance from the capital.

But even in cases of mutual goodwill, success was far from guaranteed. Limited mobility hampered the execution of everyday business, causing delay and misunderstandings. The national bodies of radical associations were concentrated in the metropolis. If there were weekly meetings of the central bodies, sections from outside London had little chance to send representatives for regular attendance. Some associations solved this problem by naming London-based correspondents for particular regions or towns. They were supposed to keep a regular exchange of letters going, inform 'their' sections about the proceedings in London and introduce ideas from the sections into the capital.

This procedure was adopted by the English Federal Council of the International. For every 100 members, sections in the country could nominate a delegate resident in London who would be their representative on the council.[105] But even this solution did not effectively bridge the gap between metropolis and local sections. Frequently, the available London delegates were not well known in the provinces, as occurred in both Nottingham and Salford during 1873.[106] In such cases, it was not easy for provincial sections and London representatives to establish a relationship of trust and mutual respect. This became evident when metropolitan rivalries and conflicts emerged within the Federal Council and affected its relations with the General Council of the IWMA.[107] The provinces felt helplessly exposed to the whims of the Londoners, and often did not entirely understand what was going on in the metropolis. The Manchester Central Section complained that the 'unfortunate quarrel' in London had 'a very detrimental effect on our work'[108] just when it seemed on the verge of success. Its secretary, Edward Jones, was 'awfully bitter'. In his opinion the London quarrels were nothing but petty jealousies which destroyed 'the Harmony of our Sections'.[109] The Liverpool section also blamed its notable decline in membership on the 'unseemly squabbles' in London.[110] The sale of the *International Herald*, the official press organ of the International in England, was also affected. The Liverpool branch secretary reported to London that 'the sale of the *Herald* in L[iver]pool was going on very well, up to a certain date, now it is Nil'.[111] While power games were played out in the London organs of the IWMA, the sections preferred 'to defer all disputes until the next congress' when there would be the opportunity for face-to-face encounters.[112]

This example shows that disparities between 'London' and the 'provinces' were hard to overcome. All attempts to find ways of co-operation paled in the face of London's structural advantages which resulted from the agglomeration of political capital and the means of communication at the disposal of metropolitan initiatives. On the other hand, metropolitan preponderance was not 'preordained' and had not to be taken for granted. Consequently, the task of finding a balance between provincial independence and London centrality was a constant challenge for radical movements, a challenge that could never be solved definitively but had to be tackled afresh at each new approach to nation-wide action. The issue remained a thorn in the flesh of popular radicalism. Its democratic ideals did not tolerate any preference for London, and yet realities did not allow equality in carrying through radical politics. In the end, one structural feature of nation-wide campaigns could not be overcome: a radical platform lacked legitimacy if 'London' was not with it. However, although some attempts by London radicals to transcend the boundaries of the metropolis carry the touch of petty interference in local affairs, the general impression is that London radicals eagerly sought to co-operate with their provincial counterparts.

Thus any attempt to map the geography of popular radicalism would show regional networks of activity around the more important towns of the United Kingdom, but also reveal many connections linking regional activities to the capital and vice versa. Regional distinctiveness remained important, however. Different traditions of radicalism in certain parts of the country were frequently associated with the names of particular towns, and rivalries that, grounded in issues of ideology or power-struggles, often found their short-hand expression in an opposition of the names of different cities. 'London' or 'Manchester' came to be seen as actors in their own right, with such artificial constructions blurring the manifold lines of argument within each place. 'London' in particular was blamed for arrogance, praised for leadership and needed to transform radical campaigns into nationwide concerns. Despite numerous instances of provincial self-assertion, the capital was invested with all the characteristics of a 'natural' centre of radical activity. It was the failure of popular radicals to overcome communicative disruptions between the metropolis and other towns more successfully that eventually spelt doom for many popular radical campaigns.

Acknowledgement

I am grateful to Martina Heßler for helpful comments and suggestions on an earlier draft of this chapter.

Notes

1. D. Cannadine, 'Residential Differentiation in Nineteenth-Century Towns: From Shapes on the Ground to Shapes in Society', in J. H. Johnson and C. G. Pooley (eds) *The Structure of Nineteenth Century Cities* (London, 1982), pp. 235–51; M. Savage, 'Space, Networks and Class Formation', in N. Kirk (ed.) *Social Class and Marxism. Defences and Challenges* (Aldershot, 1996), pp. 58–86; J. Lawrence, 'The Dynamics of Urban Politics, 1867–1914', in J. Lawrence and M. Taylor (eds) *Party, State and Society. Electoral Behaviour in Britain since 1820* (Aldershot, 1997), pp. 79–105; J. Lawrence, 'Class and Gender in the Making of Urban Toryism, 1880–1914', *EHR*, 108 (1993), 629–52.
2. A. Briggs (ed.), *Chartist Studies* (London, 1959); J. C. Belchem, 'Beyond *Chartist Studies*: Class, Community and Party in Early Victorian Populist Politics', in D. Fraser (ed.) *Cities, Class and Communication. Essays in Honour of Asa Briggs* (Hemel Hempstead, 1990), pp. 105–26.
3. P. A. Pickering, *Chartism and the Chartists in Manchester and Salford* (London, 1995); M. Hewitt, *The Emergence of Stability in the Industrial City: Manchester, 1832–67* (Aldershot, 1996).
4. A. Taylor, 'Modes of Political Expression and Working-Class Radicalism 1848–1874: The London and Manchester Examples', unpublished PhD thesis (Manchester University, 1992).
5. J. Belchem, *Popular Radicalism in Nineteenth-century Britain* (New York, 1996), pp. 102–27.
6. A. Taylor, *'Down with the Crown'. British Anti-monarchism and Debates about Royalty since 1790* (London, 1999), pp. 52–79; E. Biagini, *Liberty, Retrenchment*

and Reform. Popular Liberalism in the Age of Gladstone, 1860–1880 (Cambridge, 1992).
7. M. Ball and D. Sunderland, *An Economic History of London 1800–1914* (London, New York, 2001).
8. B. Hamann, *Hitler's Vienna. A Dictator's Apprenticeship* (Oxford, 1999); D. C. Large, *Where Ghosts Walked. Munich's Road to the Third Reich* (New York, 1997).
9. M. Heßler, 'Technopolis and Metropolises: Science, Technology and the City. A Literature Overview', in M. Hard and T. J. Misa (eds) *The Urban Machine: Recent Literature on European Cities in the 20th Century*, http://www.iit.edu/~misa/toe20/urban-machine/hessler_review-1.pdf (a printed German language edition in *Neue Politische Literatur*, 47 (2002), 193–223).
10. C. M. Davies, *Heterodox London: or, Phases of Free Thought in the Metropolis*, 2 vols (London, 1874); W. S. Smith, *The London Heretics 1870–1914* (London, 1967).
11. A. Taylor, ' "A Melancholy Odyssey among London Public Houses": Radical Club Life and the Unrespectable in Mid-Nineteenth-Century London', *HR*, 78 (2005), 74–95.
12. M. Bevir, 'The British Social Democratic Federation 1880–1885. From O'Brienism to Marxism', *IRSH*, 37 (1992), 207–29; S. Shipley, *Club Life and Socialism in Mid-Victorian London* (Oxford, 1971).
13. N. C. Edsall, *Richard Cobden. Independent Radical* (Cambridge/London, 1986), pp. 73–4, 126, 206, 311.
14. D. Mares, 'A Radical in Wales. Alfred A. Walton and Mid-Victorian Welsh Popular Radicalism', *Welsh Hist Rev*, 21 (2002), 271–91.
15. M. Finn, *After Chartism. Class and Nation in English Radical Politics 1848–1874* (Cambridge, 1993), pp. 121–41.
16. Bishopsgate Institute, London, Howell Collection, Letter Book 5, p. 88, George Howell to A. S. Spurgeon (Maldon), 14 April 1869. On Sunday trading: G. R. Searle, *Morality and the Market in Victorian Britain* (Oxford, 1998), pp. 233–40.
17. D. Mares, *Auf der Suche nach dem 'wahren' Liberalismus. Demokratische Bewegung und liberale Politik im viktorianischen England* (Berlin, 2002), pp. 213–20.
18. A. Taylor, ' "Commons-Stealers", "Land-Grabbers" and "Jerry-Builders": Space, Popular Radicalism and the Politics of Public Access in London, 1848–1880', *IRSH*, 40 (1995), 383–407.
19. D. Read, *The English Provinces c.1760–1960. A Study in Influence* (London, 1964), pp. 1–4; I. Dyck, 'The Town and Country Divide in English History', in M. Chase and I. Dyck (eds), *Living and Learning. Essays in Honour of J. F. C. Harrison* (Aldershot, 1996), pp. 81–102.
20. K. G. Robbins, *Nineteenth-Century Britain. England, Scotland, and Wales. The Making of a Nation* (Oxford/New York, 1989), pp. 63–161.
21. K. T. Hoppen, *The Mid-Victorian Generation, 1846–1886* (Oxford, 1998), pp. 104–08. D. Russell, *Looking North. Northern England and the National Imagination* (Manchester, 2004).
22. M. Taylor, *The Decline of British Radicalism, 1847–1860* (Oxford, 1995), pp. 87–92.
23. J. Prest, *Liberty and Locality. Parliament, Permissive Legislation, and Ratepayers' Democracies in the Nineteenth Century* (Oxford, 1990), pp. 1–6, 12, 208–20.

24. J. Lawrence, *Speaking for the People. Party, Language and Popular Politics in England, 1867–1918* (Cambridge, 1998), pp. 73–160; J. Vernon, *Politics and the People. A Study in English Political Culture, c.1815–1867* (Cambridge, 1993), pp. 159–60.
25. Lawrence, *Speaking for the People*, p. 63.
26. Read, *The English Provinces*, pp. 131–51, 165–73.
27. Robbins, *Nineteenth-Century Britain*, pp. 114–17, 120–2.
28. Briggs (ed.), *Chartist Studies*; J. Epstein and D. Thompson (eds), *The Chartist Experience. Studies in Working-Class Radicalism and Culture, 1830–1860* (London, 1982). D. Thompson, *The Chartists* (London, 1984), pp. 341–68; for cultural differences between Chartism in the north and in London, H. Weisser, *British Working-Class Movements and Europe 1815–1848* (Manchester, 1975), pp. 164–6.
29. A. D. Taylor, ' "The Nauseating Cult of the Crown": Republicanism, Anti-Monarchism and Post-Chartist Politics 1870–5', in D. Nash and A. Taylor (eds) *Republicanism in Victorian Society* (Stroud, 2000), pp. 51–70.
30. *National Reformer*, 22 January 1871, p. 61; ibid., 26 February 1871, p. 139.
31. *International Herald (IH)*, 16 March 1872, 8: objects and rules of the Newcastle and Gateshead Republican club.
32. *National Reformer*, 2 April 1871, pp. 222–3.
33. Tyne and Wear Archives, Newcastle-upon-Tyne, Cowen Papers, C 818, Benjamin Lucraft to R. B. Reed, 31 October 1859.
34. Cowan Papers, C 768, Benjamin Lucraft to R. B. Reed, 29 September 1859; N. Todd, *The Militant Democracy. Joseph Cowen and Victorian Radicalism* (Whitley Bay, 1991), pp. 42–8.
35. F. Leventhal, *Respectable Radical. George Howell and Victorian Working Class Politics* (London, 1971), pp. 63, 64. Taylor, *Decline of British Radicalism*, p. 56.
36. Howell Collection, Parliamentary Reform Envelope, NRU prospectus, c.1866, names former Chartists (J. R. Cooper, Robert Cooper, Henry Vincent, R. M. Carter, William Chadwick) and trade union leaders (Thomas Halliday, John Kane) among its members. *National Reformer*, 26 July 1868, p. 54.
37. A. D. Bell, 'Administration and Finance of the Reform League, 1865–1867', *IRSH*, 10 (1965), 385–409; Leventhal, *Respectable Radical*, pp. 64–6, 84–6, 106–8.
38. M. Milne, 'Survival of the Fittest? Sunderland Newspapers in the Nineteenth Century', in J. Shattock and M. Wolff (eds) *The Victorian Periodical Press: Samplings and Soundings* (Leicester/Toronto, 1982), p. 196.
39. Hewitt, *The Emergence of Stability in the Industrial City*, pp. 253–6; Miles Taylor, *Ernest Jones, Chartism, and the Romance of Politics 1819–1869* (Oxford, 2003), pp. 215–20.
40. A. Wilson, 'The Suffrage Movement', in Patricia Hollis (ed.) *Pressure from Without in Early Victorian England* (London, 1974), p. 101.
41. *Parliamentary Reform. Report of Proceedings at the National Reform Conference, held in the Free Trade Hall, Manchester, May 15th and 16th, 1865* (Manchester, [1865]), p. 78.
42. *Commonwealth*, 5 January 1867, p. 1, letter of S. C. Kell (italics in the original).
43. H. Evans, *Radical Fights of Forty Years* (London, [1913]), p. 20.
44. For the Bolton radicals, Bramwell and Warburton: *Parliamentary Reform*, p. 5; *Republican*, 1 July 1871, p. 7; *Reynolds' Newspaper*, 18 August 1872, p. 2; *IH*, 27 April 1872, p. 5.

45. A. D. Bell, 'The Reform League, from its Origins to the Passing into Law of the Reform Act of 1867', unpublished D.Phil. thesis (Oxford, 1960), pp. 175, 238–96.
46. *Commonwealth*, 27 October 1866, p. 5; Hewitt, *Emergence of Stability*, p. 256.
47. R. Wallace, *Organise! Organise! Organise! A Study of Reform Agitations in Wales, 1840–1886* (Cardiff, 1991), pp. 112–13; Todd, *Militant Democracy*, pp. 80–2; I. G. C. Hutchison, 'Glasgow Working-Class Politics', in R. A. Cage (ed.) *The Working Class in Glasgow 1750–1914* (London/Sydney, 1987), pp. 108–12.
48. J. S. Mill to Edwin Chadwick, 30 October 1868, in J. M. Robson (ed.) *Collected Works of John Stuart Mill* (Toronto/London, 1963–90), vol. 16, no. 1311, p. 1470. See also R. Harrison, *Before the Socialists. Studies in Labour and Politics 1861–1881* (London/Toronto, 1965), pp. 174–83.
49. *Bee-Hive*, 25 March 1871, p. 4.
50. IH, 19 October 1872, p. 6.
51. Ibid., 9 November 1872, p. 3.
52. Ibid., 14 December 1872, pp. 2–3.
53. Ibid., 21 December 1872, p. 2.
54. *National Reformer*, 1 December 1872, pp. 345–6.
55. Ibid., 15 December 1872, p. 373.
56. H. Collins and C. Abramsky, *Karl Marx and the British Labour Movement. Years of the First International* (London, 1965).
57. D. Mares, 'Die englischen Publikationsorgane der IAA. Zum Kontext der politischen Tätigkeit von Karl Marx', *MEGA-Studien* 1998/2, 24–48.
58. *National Reformer*, 18 May 1873, pp. 306–11, 314–20.
59. Ibid., 15 December 1872, p. 373.
60. H. Collins, 'The English Branches of the First International', in A. Briggs and J. Saville (eds) *Essays in Labour History. In memory of G. D. H. Cole* (London, 1967), pp. 242–75.
61. *IH*, 27 July 1872, p. 4 (Heys).
62. Ibid., 27 July 1872, p. 5 (Parker).
63. *Bee-Hive*, 15 October 1870, p. 548, letter of John Oliver.
64. Ibid., 10 April 1869, p. 6, letter of W. Buxton and W. Vardy.
65. *Reynolds' Newspaper*, 14 May 1871, p. 2.
66. *IH*, 27 July 1872, p. 5.
67. Ibid., 27 July 1872, p. 5 (Clarke).
68. Ibid., 27 July1872, p. 5 (Clarke).
69. Birmingham reform demonstration, 27 August 1866, in J. Breuilly, G. Niedhart and A. Taylor (eds), *The Era of the Reform League: English Labour and Radical Politics 1857–1872. Documents Selected by Gustav Mayer* (Mannheim, 1995), p. 193.
70. Howell Collection, Letter Book 4, p. 14, G. Howell to A. Sythall, 9 October 1867.
71. *Miners' Advocate and Record*, 19 July 1873, 5–7, quote 7.
72. Howell Collection, Letter Book 5, p. 4, G. Howell to W. J. Shea, 8 January 1869.
73. Howell Collection, Letter Book 5, p. 4, G. Howell to H. F. Tammage, 8 January 1869.
74. Bell, *The Reform League*, pp. 212–31. P. Howell, 'Diffusing the Light of Liberty': The Geography of Political Lecturing in the Chartist Movement, *J Hist Geog*, 21 (1995), 23–38.

75. S. St. Clair, *Sketch of the Life and Labours of Jno. De Morgan, Orator, Elocutionist, and Tribune of the People* (Leeds, 1880), p. 1.
76. E. Royle, *Radicals, Secularists and Republicans. Popular Freethought in Britain, 1866–1915* (Manchester, 1980), p. 151.
77. *National Reformer*, 30 October 1870, p. 285.
78. *Bee-Hive*, 26 March 1870, p. 5; *Republican*, 1 June 1871, p. 7, letter of 'A Bristol Radical'.
79. *Republican*, 19 August 1871, p. 6, letter of Robert Reid.
80. G. D. H. Cole, *British Working Class Politics 1832–1914* (London, 1941), p. 51.
81. *Bee-Hive*, 18 August 1869, p. 1.
82. *Times*, 14 March 1870, p. 9.
83. Ibid., 14 February 1870, p. 11.
84. *Bee-Hive*, 23 April 1870, p. 148.
85. Ibid., 22 April 1871, p. 3.
86. Ibid., 30 November 1872, p. 11; 13 December 1873, p. 9.
87. Ibid., 17 June 1871, p. 16.
88. British Library for Political and Economic Science, London, Broadhurst Collection, Labour Representation League, Minute Book, p. 53 (24 October 1873).
89. W. Lamb, 'British Labour and Parliament, 1865–93', unpublished PhD thesis (University of London, 1933), p. 286.
90. *Bee-Hive*, 5 August 1871, p. 14.
91. *National Reformer*, 4 December 1870, pp. 361, 363; 11 December 1870, pp. 373–4; 18 December 1870, p. 394.
92. Lamb, *British Labour and Parliament*, p. 233.
93. Broadhurst Collection, Labour Representation League, Minute Book, p. 10 (10 May 1873).
94. Bradford Central Library, 56/D80/1/1, Bradford Trade Council, Minute Book, 2 April, 5 August, 2 September 1873, I. MacDougall (ed.) *The Minutes of the Edinburgh Trades Council 1859–1873* (Edinburgh, 1968), p. 290.
95. Finn, *After Chartism*, pp. 267–71.
96. John Rylands Library, Manchester, Stanley Papers (42), Undated circular, Oldham Working Men's Branch of the Land Tenure Reform Association; J. C. Cox and H. F. Cox, *The Rise of the Farm Labourer. A Series of Articles Illustrative of Certain Political Aspects of the Agricultural Labour Movement* (London, 1874), pp. 32–6.
97. *National Reformer*, 30 April 1871, p. 285; *National Reformer*, 24 April 1870, p. 271.
98. *Bee-Hive*, 31 July 1869, p. 6; *Bee-Hive*, 24 July 1869, p. 1.
99. J. Arch, *The Story of his Life Told by Himself. Edited with a Preface by the Countess of Warwick* (London, 1898), pp. 65–144; J. P. D. Dunbabin: 'The "Revolt of the Field": The Agricultural Labourers' Movement in the 1870s', *P & P*, 26 (1963), 68–97.
100. *Bee-Hive*, 6 April 1872, pp. 3–4; *IH*, 8 June 1872, pp. 4–5.
101. *The Federal Union of Agricultural and General Labourers. Report* [London, 1874], pp. 6–7, 24–8.
102. Evans, *Radical Fights*, pp. 37–79.
103. *Bee-Hive*, 30 March 1872, p. 5.

104. *The Federal Union of Agricultural and General Labourers. Report* [London, 1874], pp. 2–8.
105. *IH*, 17 August 1872.
106. IISG, Amsterdam, Hermann-Jung-Collection, 1001, Thomas Smith to Samuel Vickery, 3 March 1873; 576, John Darbyshire to Alfred Days, 26 June 1873.
107. Collins and Abramsky, *Karl Marx*, pp. 231–82; Collins, 'English Branches'.
108. Hermann-Jung-Collection, 529, undated letter of Manchester Central Section to Jung.
109. IISG, Amsterdam, Marx-Engels-Collection, L 2525, Edward Jones to Friedrich Engels, 2 October 1872; Hermann-Jung-Collection 707, Edward Jones to Jung, 8 October 1872.
110. *IH*, 15 March 1873, p. 6.
111. Hermann-Jung-Collection, 598, W. Dodd to Samuel Vickery, 2 March 1873.
112. Hermann-Jung-Collection, 600, W. Dodd to Samuel Vickery, 11 March 1873.

7
From 'First Constituency of the Empire' to 'Citadel of Reaction': Westminster, 1800–90

Marc Baer

In 1832, the *Spectator* declared Westminster to be the 'first constituency of the empire'.[1] Long regarded as the most radical of London's boroughs, Westminster's 9 parishes were home to almost 250,000 people by the middle of the nineteenth century. The basis of its radical reputation was two-fold. In the first place, it possessed the largest electorate in the country. Until 1832, the right to vote at parliamentary elections in the borough lay with male householders who paid scot and lot (local rates) and had been resident for at least 6 months prior to the election.[2] Perhaps 3 out of every 4 male householders possessed the suffrage, and 8000 or 9000 men, including many of plebeian origin, regularly cast their votes at election time.[3] The second factor underpinning the borough's reputation was its tradition of furnishing some of parliament's most radical members: Charles James Fox and Sir Francis Burdett, for example, both won the suffrages of the Westminster electorate. Both owed much to the work of Westminster 'Committees'. The first of these organizations, founded in 1780, was originally dominated by town-based aristocrats connected with the Marquis of Rockingham, and, headed by Fox, adopted a six-point programme for parliamentary reform. By the early nineteenth century, however, it had been superseded by a second Westminster Committee dominated by radical shopkeepers and merchants; their ability to appeal directly to the large plebeian elements within the electorate ensured that the Committee played a defining role in Westminster politics.

So strong was popular support for Liberalism in Westminster that as late as 1859 the Tories did not bother to contest the seat. Yet within a matter of 25 years, Westminster's political character had undergone a fundamental realignment. From having been the safest of Liberal seats in the era of the Great Reform Act, it had become a Tory 'banker' by the time the Third Reform Act was passed in 1885.[4] Under the leadership of the ambitious London bookseller, W. H. Smith, who first stood for the Borough in 1865, and won a seat in 1868, the Conservatives constructed an organization which rendered them impregnable to all assaults from the left well into the twentieth century. Thus did the Labour Party's national agent in 1924 term the borough 'the citadel of reaction'.[5]

In this chapter, the strange death of Liberal Westminster will be examined through an examination of associational politics in the borough. While such an approach, concentrating on organization at the expense of issues, must perforce tell only half the story of politics, it will be argued that an understanding of the central role played by the associations is essential to an understanding of politics in Westminster. The chapter is arranged in two sections, the first dealing with the period of radical–liberal ascendancy, the second with their supercession by the Tories.

The making of radical Westminster

If the success of the Westminster Committee in returning Charles James Fox hinted at the radical potential of Westminster, it is arguable that this was not fully realized until 1806–07. Fox, for all his reputation as a tribune of the people, seemed to some of the borough's middle-class reformers to be hopelessly compromised by his connection with aristocratic Whiggery. The lesson was driven home at the by-election caused by his death in 1806, when his supporters eased into parliament Earl Percy, the son of the Duke of Northumberland, one of the major landholders in the borough (see Figure 10). Local reformers such as Francis Place later recalled seeing Northumberland's servants distributing bread, beer and cheese to the crowds they had collected to celebrate his son's return: 'Almost every man I knew was much offended with the whole of the proceedings and with all who were concerned in them', he recorded.[6]

In reaction to the manner of Percy's return, a strongly pro-reform, anti-oligarchic element emerged within the borough. The 'Westminster Committee' underwent a profound change of identity, and three elections – October and November 1806, May 1807 – in the space of eight months allowed the new organization to perfect its techniques.[7] The radicals' campaigning evoked two particulars. First it drew on the notion of artisanal honour, highlighting popular indignation over practices which had 'disgraced Westminster, demoralized the people, and sought to put a stamp of infamy on those who had opposed them'. The appeal of the new Westminster Committee in this respect was to the same 'well-meaning, sober, and industrious men', tradesmen, shopkeepers and mechanics, who had been the backbone of the London Corresponding Society. They were a group who, politicized as far back as the late 1780s in the agitation against Pitt's shop tax, now worried about their position in a changing economy.[8] The second set of issues activating the radical campaign were 'the principles professed by Parliamentary Reformers'.[9] Francis Place realized it was essential that the Committee find a candidate who could enshrine these aspirations, 'a man of popular manner, good character and a known parliamentary reformer'.[10] Ultimately, the role fell to Sir Francis Burdett, fifth baronet, husband of the daughter and co-heiress of the immensely wealthy London banker, Thomas Coutts. Dignified, generous and a forceful speaker, Burdett was immensely popular not only in London but throughout the kingdom, thanks to his espousal of radical causes since the 1790s. He had been approached to stand on an anti-Percy ticket in October 1806, but had then refused. In 1807, however, he answered in the affirmative: the scene was set for the birth of radical Westminster.

The election of 1807 was memorable, in Place's words, for the fact that 'obscure individuals of no importance or influence whatsoever' defeated both Whig and ministerialist nominees.[11] The sitting candidate, Hood, withdrew from the contest because his supporters sensed he could not win; the best the Perceval government could do was a local brewer, in effect ceding Westminster to their enemies. For the Whigs Sheridan, the borough's second sitting MP, lacked enthusiastic backing from his former ministerial colleagues and, though eventually deciding to stand again, did not pursue an energetic campaign. Meanwhile, another radical, Lord Cochrane, began independently from the Westminster Committee. Burdett, feeling impoverished by the enormous expenses of his previous Middlesex election campaigns refused to contribute money, or for that matter to participate personally in the contest.[12]

Burdett's campaign began disastrously, with divided ranks and a campaign less led, than suffered to exist, by a handful of petty bourgeois and professional men uncertain how to render indignation comprehensible to the electorate. Early setbacks forced the Westminster Committee to respond with a mixture of entertainment, camaraderie and ideology. On the evening of the third day of polling, with Burdett trailing badly, the Committee put onto the streets several ponies carrying boys wearing Burdett's colours and blowing bugles. On Sunday, local activists visited every known radical in Westminster and pleaded with them to gather their friends on Monday morning for a procession from the outer parishes to the Covent Garden hustings. It turned the election. 'From the noise the people made it was supposed half Westminster was coming to the poll', recorded Place. Although the number did not exceed 250, their appearance gave Burdett's campaign a popular dimension it had hitherto lacked.[13] Burdett was duly returned at the head of the poll, and Westminster's reputation as the centre of early nineteenth-century British radicalism was established.

The 1806–07 elections created a base sufficiently stable to provide continuity, forged out of resentment and political theatre. Burdett best expressed this when following the election he thanked the Committee for their confidence in him, and then in a triumphal tone linked patricians and plebeians against Old Corruption:

> Gentlemen, both parties laugh at the people, they despise the people, and those who have robbed us most, have justly the most contempt for us. ... if the corrupt & mercenary factions shall see the other inhabitants of England acting in union firmly and perseveringly like a People, they will soon acknowledge them to be such and those who now tread oppressively on their necks will be found humbled at their feet.[14]

The triumph of 1807 was commemorated with an annual dinner, and issue-oriented public meetings frequently took place in Palace Yard or Westminster Hall. Reliance on small subscriptions and frequent distribution of information to voters sustained the popular base. With the triumph of Burdett and Cochrane, Westminster Whiggery became moribund, and they declined to contest either the general election of 1812 or the by-election two years later. In 1818, however, Sir Samuel Romilly stole one seat for the Whigs, and at the by-election caused by his suicide in 1819, the Whigs held their ground. This outcome reflected internal divisions within Westminster radicalism, disillusionment with Burdett for not having quite lived up to his promise and something of a Whig revival.[15] In addition, there remained a pervasive hostility to radicalism among some parts of the Westminster electorate: despite the fact that some Whig electioneering materials linked Romilly and Burdett, Romilly and the Tory candidate shared 2334 votes.[16] Division among radicals and subsequent organizational disruption were part of a pattern that would be played out repeatedly in Westminster.

In 1819, the Westminster Committee brought forward John Cam Hobhouse, the radical eldest son of a Tory baronet. Hobhouse initially worked hard to secure the support of the Romilly's supporters, but the Whigs so vilified the radicals, and, thereafter, Place's writings and Hobhouse's public statements so offended Whig honour that, on the eve of the election the Whigs 'started' George Lamb, youngest son of Viscount Melborne.[17] The Westminster Committee struggled to overcome their divisions of the previous year. Disagreement over the reform programme and residual anger towards Burdett led to attacks on Hobhouse by Major Cartwright, Henry Hunt and other radicals. By contrast, the Whigs demonstrated both efficient organization and propaganda.[18] This, compounded by what the radicals claimed were a series of electoral irregularities committed by the high bailiff in favour of their opponent, together with residual sympathy for Romilly and Tory hatred of the radicals, saw Lamb returned at the top of the poll.[19] Tory support for Lamb stoked radical indignation and enabled them to interpret Hobhouse's defeat as the work of an unnatural coalition of Whigs, Tories and the followers of Hunt.

The election of 1820 – the third contest in three years – was the last occasion the Whigs intervened in Westminster. A war of words followed the election of 1819, with Place and Hobhouse alleging the Whigs were as corrupt as the Tories. In one pamphlet Hobhouse attacked the recently passed Six Acts, asking 'What prevents the people from walking down to the House, pulling the members out by the ears, locking up their doors, and flinging the keys into the Thames?'[20] For this sentence Hobhouse spent several months in Newgate, enabling him to share Burdett's mantle of the patrician martyr to reform. This, and the fact that Burdett also stood trial for seditious libel during the campaign, and that several others among their leaders were in prison, ensured that the radicals were, for once, united. The Whigs, by contrast, were tentative. Lamb alienated conservatives by seconding Burdett's 1819 reform motion in the House of Commons but then infuriated radicals by damning it with faint praise. Hobhouse increased his poll by 1000 votes over 1819, improving his margin in the poorer eastern parishes while reducing his deficit elsewhere. Lamb's campaign seemed as efficiently conducted as in 1819, and he polled the same number of votes. But the high bailiff's practice of disfranchising electors for having failed to pay their rates had been ruled illegal, and Lamb's unfortunate appeal to Tories for support against 'the lower classes' was effectively used against him. Whereas 84.5 per cent of Lamb's votes were plumpers, 96 per cent of Hobhouse's were split votes with Burdett, which pulled Hobhouse up, and both radicals were returned.[21]

At the next seven elections, from 1820 to his retirement from the borough in 1837, Burdett finished first or was returned unopposed. Westminster entered upon a decade of peace, for 1820 saw the last contested election before 1832. Hobhouse proclaimed a new era, while Place suggested that, with the victory of 1820, the Westminster Committee broke the back of Old Corruption. 'Our desire was to make a public', Place suggested, to create a 'school of political morality', producing a model for the rest of Britain to follow.[22] Under the Committee's influence, the old practices of treating, bribery, coercion and aristocratic and crown influence became shadows of what they had once been. Organizationally efficient, their use of armies of unpaid canvassers, broad-based subscriptions (as well as funds from friends of their patrician candidates) and massive propaganda enabled them to fight and win one or both seats for an average of just over £1550 per contested election.[23] Typical eighteenth-century campaigns had cost upwards of £30,000.

But if the Westminster Committee could claim to have redefined politics in the borough, not everything went their way. If Westminster was indeed a school of radical political morality its graduates did not live up to their letters of recommendation, for Burdett, Cochrane and Hobhouse were all to disappoint the Committee. Neither Burdett nor Cochrane were capable of leading, much less creating a radical parliamentary party. Hobhouse had the opposite problem: increasingly friendly with the leading Whigs as his appetite for office grew, he became increasingly ambivalent about radicalism as the 1820s progressed.[24] These tensions came to a head at the first election after the Great Reform Act of 1832.

Long-brewing clashes over ideology, personality and behavioural distinctions spilled over and, together with the fundamentally new concept of representation introduced by the Act, caused the Westminster Committee to fracture. Prior to the Reform Act radicals had begun discussing the establishment of a Westminster Reform Association with branches in each of the parishes.[25] By then, many had also come to believe that it was time for Burdett and Hobhouse to go. Hobhouse, who held office in Grey's Government, had caused enormous offence by refusing to drink the toast 'radical reform' at the 1822 dinner to celebrate the 1807 triumph. Words mattered, as did whether one operated in the context of high or low politics: to the Westminster plebeians *radical* was a badge of courage in the struggle against oligarchs, all of whom would sooner or later insult and degrade them; to patricians such as

Hobhouse *radical* was a banner around which well meaning reformers of all classes could rally.[26] Place was not alone in questioning the future prospects in Westminster of one who talked and acted 'as if he were a nominee of a Borough-Monger' rather than a representative of the people.[27]

Led by the Strand perfumer Thomas Prout, the Place faction, associated with the Westminster Reform Society, repudiated Hobhouse at a public meeting and brought forward the Irish army colonel George DeLacy Evans to contest the seat. Evans pledged himself to the political programme that Hobhouse had refused, advocating a scot and lot suffrage franchise nationally. This suggests another divide, between those who understood the 1832 Act as fulfilling the late Georgian reform agenda and those who saw it as merely the first stage on the road to democracy.[28] Old Westminster allies now battled each other; some in frustration quit politics altogether. In a bitterly fought contest a mob wrecked Hobhouse's headquarters; and on the hustings Hobhouse, the 'idol of the same populace' 14 years before, was jeered so loudly he could not be heard. Burdett stood by Hobhouse and in spite of a lengthy canvass Evans lost to the sitting MPs. Voting patterns suggest polarization: 85 percent of Evans' votes were plumpers, whereas virtually all of Burdett's and Hobhouse's votes were split between them.[29]

Just after the 1832 election Hobhouse recorded in his diary: 'I foresee the impossibility of holding office, Westminster, and character together. I may add conscience, for Westminster may require more than I ought to grant, even were I not in office'. Five months later, loyal to conscience, Hobhouse resigned from office and having given up his seat – suggesting the effectiveness of the demand for pledges – he stood for re-election.[30] The public issue was now repeal of the House and Window tax, but in truth the clash was the result of older conflicts. The Reform Society again supported Evans. Sensing a possible victory from the split in the radical ranks Conservatives brought forward their first candidate since 1818. Once again there was extensive violence before and after the election: Hobhouse was assaulted on the hustings and had to be guarded by policemen after the election.[31] On this occasion Evans narrowly triumphed by winning almost every district. The Reform Society now became the dominant political force in Westminster. Thus were the elections of 1832-33 a tipping point, like those of 1806-07. The radicals were emboldened – Evans was seen as emblematic of a new radical era – but so were Conservatives, who not only contributed to Hobhouse's defeat, but from 1833 contested eight straight elections, being competitive in five.

But where did this leave Burdett? Following the defeat of Hobhouse, Burdett loyalists and the Reform Society enjoyed an uneasy relationship.

The loss of his comrade may have given Burdett some idea of what lay ahead. His politics were, in any case, changing: several commentators noticed growing signs of Toryism in Burdett's conversations and correspondence. His ambiguity about Westminster was in turn amplified by realignment in the immediate post-Reform Act era at the national level combined with divisions between left and right wing reformers in the borough.[32]

The underlying conflict came into the open when Burdett refused to endorse a petition signed by all the other London Whig and radical MPs against the brief Tory ministry of 1834–35. His election address in January 1835 was hardly reassuring to his erstwhile radical supporters, and Burdett also clashed with Evans, who had caught wind of the fact that Burdett's agent had contacted Hobhouse about standing again. The net result of these tensions was that Burdett's share of the poll in 1835 dropped sharply, and the radicals began to sense their chance.[33] In 1837, first a deputation from the Reform Society, and then a public meeting, urged Burdett to resign his seat and submit his conduct to his constituents in a by-election. He accepted the challenge, and came out with open backing from the newly founded Westminster Conservative Society.[34] Remarkably, in view of the borough's radical reputation, he won. He more than recovered his position of 1832 in terms of votes, eking out small majorities in several poorer parishes but also won convincingly in wealthy St. George's and St. James's. Disraeli was later to claim Burdett's success as 'mainly attributable to myself', but it is clear that all Conservatives worked hard to secure Burdett's return, anticipating that the victory of a Tory Burdett in Westminster would presage national gains in a general election.[35]

Burdett, conscious that his chances might change if he had to fight a three-cornered general election, wisely chose to resign his Westminster seat at the election caused by the death of William IV later in 1837, and fight North Wiltshire as a Conservative. His earlier victory, however, opened up a decade of rosier prospects for Conservative candidates. Although their candidate was defeated in 1837, an invigorated Westminster Conservative party brought forward the racing enthusiast and ex-naval officer Henry Rous in 1841. Rous, aided by a surfeit of funds from the chairman of the Conservative Association and the national party, headed the poll in a very close race, thus producing the first Tory victory in the borough at a general election since 1806.[36] In 1846 Peel appointed him to a government post, necessitating a by-election. DeLacy Evans was only narrowly adopted by the Reform Society, but the free trader Rous was defeated in large measure as a result of Tory defections over the Corn Law issue. He lost every parish, an outcome which speaks once again to the expectation of reciprocity between electors and elected in the borough.[37] Thereafter, like other London seats, Westminster appeared to be permanently in the Liberal camp – reflected in the laughter that greeted John Stuart Mill's statement during the 1865 election, that 'It is tolerably well known that the majority of electors of Westminster are not Tories'.[38]

At the centre of radical Westminster stood Place's organization. Even before the mid-1840s, when its name changed to the Westminster Liberal Registration Society, and certainly afterwards, the Reform Society dictated the representation of the borough, to the consternation of commentators across the political spectrum.[39] In addition to registration work, the organization recruited candidates and demanded pledges, confirmed their choice at tightly controlled mass meetings, raised subscriptions, carried out campaigns, and used a primary ballot to avoid a surplus of reform candidates. Radical candidates were selected by a small group, which then made them the nominees of the party through the use of a public meeting. This technique deflated other campaigns by the appearance of an overwhelming base of support, which in turn was derived from the promised votes and financial aid of the Westminster electors.[40]

Yet not all were happy with this state of affairs, even on the Liberal side, as the general elections of 1847 and 1852 demonstrate. When in 1847 agreement could not be reached on a candidate, Charles Cochrane, a local philanthropist and cousin of Lord Cochrane came forward. Cochrane ran an aggressive independent campaign against both a Conservative peer and the two candidates of the Liberal Registration Society, 'of a nature to rouse the historic recollections of the borough'. In his address, he berated the governing body of local Liberalism:

> The Reform Society exercises, year after year, a power of nominating the candidates for Westminster, and of decreeing who shall or shall not be authorized to stand for our representation ... the Reform Society strikes at the very root of the cause of its own formation.[41]

In the event, he was beaten, but almost all his votes were from plumpers and he came within twelve votes of winning the second seat.[42] And in 1852, the Liberal Registration Society alienated another group of voters by selecting Sir John Villiers Shelley, a wealthy baronet, as their candidate. Disgusted with the choice, radicals led by the auctioneer and estate agent James Beal and the bookseller Charles Westerton offered an independent candidate, William Coningham, who appealed to the most radical element in the borough and attacked the sitting Liberal, DeLacy Evans, as the dependent of an unrepresentative elite. In scenes reminiscent of 1807, poorer voters and non-voters conducted his canvass and generated large crowds. It was all to no avail: Coningham was soundly beaten and the power of the Liberal Registration Society was demonstrated once again.[43]

The 1850s saw another period of deep tranquility descend upon Westminster politics. In fact, no further contest took place until 1865. Whether the lack of electoral exercise bred a sense of complacency in the Society, or whether its activities had bred so deep a hostility as to make a challenge by Beal and his colleagues inevitable, the Liberals were caught completely unprepared when, in February 1865, the 78-year-old Evans announced his intention to retire. The second Member, Shelley, tried but acquitted for indecent exposure in 1861, was pressured by other Liberals to withdraw.[44] As a consequence, for the first time since 1806 both Westminster seats were open. In haste, the Society brought forward the Hon. R. W. Grosvenor, 31-year-old nephew of the Marquis of Westminster, 'lord of the soil in Westminster'. The Society was so weak, however, that it made no attempt to start a second candidate, and this gave the new generation of reformers their opportunity. Now organized as the Westminster Liberal Electors Committee, they chose John Stuart Mill as their candidate. Having declared he would not concern himself with local business, make pledges, spend his own money or 'offer myself to the electors in any manner', Mill was approved at a meeting of Liberal electors: an aloof philosopher MP would clearly leave real power in the hands of local politicians.[45] The openness of the seat also attracted a Conservative challenge. In 1865 local Tories recruited W. H. Smith, son of the great Strand newsagent (see Figure 11). Although there was some support from national Conservatives, Smith's strategy was to straddle party lines to attract moderates.[46]

Smith's challenge forced the Society and the Committee to join forces. While Mill left the impression that an unaided electorate paid for his campaign, his victory resulted from an organization that had promised he would be returned free of expense.[47] The *Daily Telegraph*, in an enthusiastic but unhistorical leader, thought this approach a 'new and most promising electoral method', which would change the nature of parliamentary elections in urban constituencies.[48] In fact, the procedures the Liberal Electors Committee used – selection by a small group, large meetings ratifying their decisions, refusal to support other candidates, returning candidates free of expense – were those used by previous radical organizations. In practice, the exercise of power remained neo-oligarchic.[49] However, coalescence ultimately served Mill and his supporters well, since it had the happy effect of ensuring the Grosvenor campaign paid for the cabs that conveyed Liberal electors to the hustings![50]

Mill and Grosvenor were duly returned. Smith's straddling ploy apparently failed to disturb the apathy of hard-line Tories: he lost the wealthier parishes to Grosvenor and Mill while winning the poorer districts where he was best known.[51] Yet if the return of two Liberals suggested business as usual at Westminster, the borough was in fact on the verge of an historic realignment. The 1867 Reform Act enfranchised thousands of Westminster workers, many of whom shared some of the political values of bourgeois and aristocratic Conservatives. In this new environment, it would be Conservative associational politics that would come to the fore. The lessons of their failure in 1865 were quickly learned. A new, more effective Conservative organization was established in the borough the following year.[52] As the next section will show, it was to transform the political landscape of Westminster forever.

Conservatives triumphant

When he stood again in 1868 Mill faced widespread disillusionment with his role as philosopher MP, and he lost his seat, finishing third behind Smith and Grosvenor. One of his leading supporters, Thomas Beggs, believed the chief problem in 1868 was 'the want of cordial union in our own ranks'. 'Old wounds from 1865 had not healed', he added, 'and although the committees of the two Liberal candidates worked together they were still two separate campaigns, which duplication of effort meant waste and inefficiency'. It was a comment eerily reminiscent of elections in 1806, 1818, 1832, 1847 and 1852. Beggs also hinted at a lack of funds, which made disunity and organizational deficiency all the more serious, and that Mill's support of Charles Bradlaugh in Northamptonshire was also a factor.[53]

For his part, Mill did not think the Bradlaugh issue cost him his seat, refusing to acknowledge the religious offence given by Bradlaugh, whose campaign he perceived in political terms.[54] He believed, as did Beggs, that superior organization and the longer pockets of his opponents had beaten him, adding that his London Government Bill had engendered 'the hostility of nearly all the vestrymen and other local notables who are the customary leaders of political action in the local districts'.[55] Walter Bagehot observed about Mill that his 'practice would negate his principle and defeat his aim', an insight evident in the 1868 collision between personal and associational ideologies.[56] Allowing for inflation, the Liberals of 1868 spent about what the radicals of 1807 had, but whereas in 1807 the Westminster Committee had compensated for lack of funds with a massive volunteer canvass, apparently in 1868 the organizational thrust failed.

Yet organization and the expenditure of raw money tell only part of the story. If a broad view of elections in the borough between the first and third reform acts[57] is taken (Table 8.1), it immediately becomes apparent that high turnouts correlated with Conservative success. In the 1837 by-election and the general election of 1841, the Tories took one of the Westminster seats: both campaigns produced a turnout about 50 per cent higher than the previous election. In 1865 and 1868, a strong relationship again emerged between turnout and Conservative success: Smith received more votes in 1865 than any Tory, Burdett included, had ever obtained in Westminster; while in 1868, when the turnout was double that of some previous elections, Smith was victorious. Two forces were intertwined. First, a motivated electorate produced higher turnout: thus Burdett's victory in 1837 is explicable in terms of his anti-Catholic and nationalist rhetoric. Second, effective party organization increased the numbers who voted for the Conservatives. When the

Table 8.1 Turnout at Westminster elections between the First and Third Reform Acts

Election	Electorate	Turnout (voters who polled/eligible electors) in %
1832	11,576	38.5
1833 (by)	11,576	38.3 (approximation)
1835	13,628	32.3
1837 (by)	15,254	48.1
1837	15,745	40.5
1841	14,254	46.4
1846 (by)		45.7
1847	14,125	50.6
1852	14,883	48.7
1857	13,182	no contest
1859	12,826	no contest
1865	12,386	67.3
1868	18,879	71.9
1874	19,241	70.2 (approximation)
1880	21,081	68.3 (approximation)

Tories mounted a vigorous campaign, as they did for Burdett in 1837, Rous in 1841 and Smith in the 1860s, the party did exceptionally well.

In a major and very expensive commitment between 1865 and 1868, Smith built a powerful political machine aimed, simultaneously, at both middle- and working-class electors. The revitalized Westminster Conservative Association (WCA) assaulted the lists of Liberal electors via the registration courts.[58] The enfranchisement of lodgers under the Second Reform Act prompted the WCA to engage in a wholesale attack on the claims of all new voters 'who would not declare their politics, explaining that if not holding the principles we profess they had better apply for assistance elsewhere'.[59] The intensive canvass for Smith five months before polling took place in 1868 could be accomplished because alongside several major donors hundreds of others contributed a guinea per year.[60] If the discovery of one Tory in 1865 can be generalized, that two-thirds of the middle-class electors he canvassed were pro-Smith or leaning that way, there need not be a sociological explanation for the predominance of the party after 1868.[61] The London and Westminster Working Men's Constitutional Association (LWWMCA) was founded to attract working-class voters to the Tory party, to keep them on the register and to get them to poll, but like so many Conservative organizations in this period, the project was about more than simply politics, appealing also to principles of nationalism, religion and sociability.[62] The Association sought to unite rich and poor 'in defence of Conservative and Constitutional principles' which they deemed to be under assault by 'Democratic and Republican opinions'. Like Smith, however, the LWWMCA also had a vision of societal progress, seeking to improve the lives of the proletarian membership by improving their dwellings, encouraging thrift and saving for emergencies, and promoting improved education for their children and better accommodation in local churches.[63] The role of Conservative organizations in Westminster then was less to woo Liberals than to solidify traditional middle-class support and to encourage working-class Tories to vote according to their conscience. In this they succeeded spectacularly.

Westminster Conservatives appealed to voters as members of classes and simultaneously denounced their opponents for setting class against class.[64] The borough's Liberals, on the other hand, relied on the same supra-class approach that had won for them in the past. Until the 1870s there was no separate working-class Liberal organization in Westminster. In sharp contrast to the Tories, who, under Smith's direction, had developed a clearly articulated appeal to workers *as* workers, conflicts between middle- and working-class Liberals in Westminster and elsewhere in London sapped the party's vitality, helping produce the Labour Representation League.[65]

That the days of Liberal domination had ended was painfully realized in 1874 when Smith was able to bring in a second Tory. This came after Smith turned down a Liberal proposal to split the representation, and the Westminster Working Men's Liberal Association tried and failed to start its own candidates.[66] On this occasion the contest was not even close: 5000 votes separated the second Tory candidate from the leading Liberal. As in 1865 and 1868, the two Liberals ran separate campaigns which some thought encouraged an undue amount of plumping among Liberal supporters.[67] The Liberals, in Westminster as elsewhere, had hoped that the introduction of secret voting in 1872 would work in their favour. Yet the party's chief London agent was ultimately persuaded that it was the Tories who had benefited most.[68] Throughout the 1870s Westminster Liberals continued to be plagued by competing class-based associations, the middle-class Registration Society and the Working Men's Liberal Association, later called the Westminster Liberal Union.[69]

The situation for the Liberals improved somewhat at the election of 1880 when they reduced the margin of defeat to 2000 votes. By then, however, the parties had exchanged positions. Westminster, once the most radical constituency in the kingdom, was now permanently Conservative, and a bellwether for urban Toryism. What was most telling was the comparative strength of the parties' political organizations. By 1877 the Westminster Conservatives were able to employ two full-time agents between elections, carrying out crucial registration work.[70] Both of the defeated Liberals at the 1880 election commented on the ideologically and organizationally fragmented state in which they found the Westminster party, comments remarkably like those made in 1868 and 1874.[71] Both candidates were sanguine about future success, but such a sentiment was out of place: in 1882 the Westminster Liberals could not even mount a token effort in a by-election and the Conservative came in unopposed, while the subsequent decision of the Registration Society and the Westminster Liberal Union to end their feuding and merge came too late.[72]

The Redistribution Act of 1884 divided the borough into three single member seats. Political boundaries no longer reflected historic communities, for equal electoral districts, while democratic, were artificial. In 1885 Smith chose to stand for the new Strand seat in which his firm was located. Curiously, he was not sanguine about his prospects. 'I am in rather low spirits about my own seat', he confided to the Earl of Harrowby:

> I deliberately selected the least promising of the three but I have two serious dangers to contend with ... the first – the universal belief of the 'Party' that I am safe, because everyone whom one meets in Pall Mall, Piccadilly and the Clubs is 'all right' and therefore think that there is no need for any exertion; and the second is the extreme radicalism of the working tailors, shoemakers and their like who swarm in St. James' and St. Anne's, but I am doing my best.[73]

In the event, he defeated his Liberal rival by over 3000 votes in a poll of 8000 in what was subsequently termed one of the 'best fortified strongholds the Tories have in all the country'.[74] The future proved the claim true: on Smith's death in 1891 his son won the by-election, and after one feeble attempt the Liberals hardly bothered to fight what now looked like a family borough. In St. George and Westminster the story was the same: a Percy sat for the former through 1886, while W. A. B. Burdett-Coutts, the husband of Burdett's daughter sat for the latter and then a successor seat until 1921. In despair, E. S. Beesly, the Liberal who in 1885 won only 30 per cent of the vote for Westminster remarked, 'there is not a more hopeless seat in England'.[75] Even when the Liberals did everything right and presented a united face, they now struggled in Westminster. Thus when two Liberals were suggested for a vacancy in St. George in 1887, and the constituency's Liberal Association chose one and enforced its will, the Conservative crushed his opponent.

The *fin de siècle* saw the emergence of party domination throughout Britain, nowhere truer than in safe seats like St. George, Strand and Westminster. In contrast to eighteenth-century Old Corruption, 'demotic oligarchy' may be the best label for late Victorian British political culture, which allowed parties to force men off the register and in 1918 still recognized over half a million plural votes. And consider the language used during the 1885 Westminster election. The victor, Burdett-Coutts acknowledged his triumph thus: 'I thank you in my own name and the name of the Baroness Burdett-Coutts, on whom you have laid a debt of gratitude this night that she will not forget throughout the rest of her life.' After reporting the speech, one local newspaper commented:

> The name of Coutts carried everything before it, while the name of Percy [in St. George] was equally powerful. Making money and

enjoying it absorbs the West-end mind. Between the shopkeepers and the aristocracy the bonds are many and strong. ... Wisdom may cry aloud in their streets, but the rolling of aristocratic chariots effectually drowns that voice.[76]

Such sentiments would not have been out of place in pre-radical Westminster.

Conclusion

The ultimate success of the Conservative Party in the Borough of Westminster can be attributed to a range of factors. Some were outside the realm of the ability of politicians to control, such as the long-term demographic patterns that undoubtedly favoured the Tories. W. H. Smith need not have feared the swarms of radical tailors in the Strand in 1885. The small retailers and lesser professionals in the eastern parishes who had been the backbone of radical Westminster, as well as their patrician allies, had moved elsewhere by the late Victorian era. The line between interests and constituencies, already blurring, became virtually impossible to discern after the Redistribution Act.[77] The 1867 Reform Act had called a new electorate into existence, with half the voters now workingmen. In competition with the increasingly crotchet-ridden and fissiparous middle-class Liberals, working-class activists failed to realize power within the local Liberal parties commensurate with their voting strength. Over time this drained vitality and numbers from the London Liberals, and would build a case for the establishment of a separate working-class party. Sidney Smith, the Liberal party's chief agent in London both understood the problem and by his personal actions exacerbated it. Writing to William Gladstone after the debacle of 1874, Sidney Smith cynically urged his party's leader to stem the democratic tide.

> Anyone who watched the Chartists, and who examines the present action of the labouring people, may satisfy himself that their powers of organization, their discipline, and their determined self-sacrifice in support of their opinions, are far more perfect than the public spirit of all other classes. ... The practical veto of each class upon the predominance of one, is the only security for our equal rights, and for the stability of social order.[78]

W. H. Smith used the same spectre to make the case for integration, his rhetoric and organizations appealing to the variety of working-class outlooks which had emerged in late nineteenth-century London.[79]

Yet other factors within the control of local politicians can be identified. The enduring power of personality in the borough's politics provides one example. Burdett and Mill were galvanizing personalities critical to the success of radical political campaigns. It may be paradoxical that to emancipate themselves from the clutches of the court and aristocracy the makers of Westminster radicalism – students that they were of Paine and Bentham – were forced to acknowledge the charismatic. Perhaps their successors forgot, for after Mill the Liberals were never able to discover a candidate who fitted the earlier mould; the history professor and positivist pamphleteer Beesly was a lugubrious end to Westminster radicalism. Smith's modest nature better fitted the Westminster tribune model than any candidate since Burdett.[80]

If an absence of star personalities provides one locally explicable cause of Liberal decline, another factor is that following the late 1830s Westminster Liberals failed to replicate the elements of political theatre that had been so successfully applied in the early nineteenth century. Such corporate celebration had been and remained a critical part of the process of political socialization. More than other political figures in the late nineteenth-century metropolis, W. H. Smith understood there remained a need for good political theatre, a calculated adoption for political purposes of ritual forms to which working-class voters responded.[81] In contrast, the professional men who dominated Liberal politics in late Victorian Westminster, while fond of speaking about the workingman's world, were cut off from it and were incapable of producing political language or ritual that were not dry and lifeless. John Morley, Professor Beesly and Frederick Harrison felt uncomfortable in that world and had no connections to the neighbourhood politics and values of such men.[82] In a letter to the prime minister after his defeat in 1880, Morley himself expressed this sentiment.

> I have always felt that the scientific specialist is most likely of all men to lose the useful and human point of view. His mind is inevitably narrowed, I fear, by the narrowness or minuteness of the specialist's conception of Truth; and this narrow view of Truth chokes his care for Freedom and Humanity.[83]

Perhaps their most serious failure, however, lay in the sphere that had once been their greatest strength: associational politics. Comparing the experiences of Hobhouse, Burdett, Rous and Mill reveals that conflict with an important segment of the local political elite was the root cause of the MPs' difficulties with the Westminster electorate. Whereas specific concerns motivated electors – Hobhouse holding office, Burdett's tacit approval of a Tory ministry, Rous's conversion on the Corn Laws or Mill's support for an atheist – reciprocity was the underlying issue. Westminster political activists might accept deviations if these could be adequately justified, but they expected that at appropriate moments their representative should defer to his most loyal supporters, whose personal sacrifices produced his election victory. As Place put it in 1816:

> It is ... evident that to a body of people who do their own business the person to be elected must be made familiar, he must see and be seen by them on all proper occasions, he must speak to them, that they may judge him, and he must convince them, as well by his actions as his words, that he will maintain the principles they espouse, and that he has NO RESERVE.[84]

To a certain extent this chapter neglects ideologies in favour of an associational reading of continuity and change in nineteenth-century Westminster's political culture. It has been the argument of this chapter that the power of issues of the moment must be understood contextually, in this case within long-term associational developments. Thus when we ask who the electors of Westminster were, how they came to be and remain electors, and what motivated them, the extent to which Westminster political organizations worked strenuously to mould the electorate in their own images becomes clear. Once the registration clauses of the 1832 Reform Act became institutionalized it seemed less important to convince voters than to get one's own supporters to the polls and object to those of an opponent. It was however possible, indeed in the long run critical, to combine these concerns. Francis Place understood that in 1807. The radicals who followed him did not. It was the late nineteenth-century Westminster Conservatives who put the two back together, and in so doing constructed urban Toryism, a key component of politically modern Britain.

Acknowledgements

I am grateful to Patricia Baer, Matthew Sterenberg and Matthew Cragoe for their comments on earlier drafts of this essay. Many of the issues covered here will be examined at greater length in my forthcoming study, *Workshop of Democracy: The Rise and Fall of Radical Westminster, 1780–1890*, where more extensive references can be found.

Notes

1. *Spectator*, 24 November 1832.
2. British Library, London, Place Papers, BL Add. MS (hereafter Place) 27843, fos 63–5, for the complexities of the borough franchise.
3. E. Green 'Social Structure and Political Allegiance in Westminster, 1774–1820', unpublished PhD thesis (University of London, 1992), p. 233.
4. Details of the impact of the nineteenth-century Reform Acts on Westminster can be found in the Introductory chapter to this volume.
5. National Museum of Labour History, Labour History Archives and Study Centre, Labour Party National Executive Committee, LP/GS/NEC.
6. *Courier*, 8 October 1806; Place 27850, fos 12, 19–20.
7. *Cobbett's Weekly Political Register*, 29 November 1806; J. Paull, *A Refutation of the Calumnies of John Horne Tooke* (1807), pp. 17–19, 69–71.
8. T. Hardy, *Memoirs of Thomas Hardy* (1832), pp. 89–90, 107, 109; I. Prothero, *Radical Artisans in England and France, 1830–1870* (Cambridge, 1997), pp. 16, 19.
9. Place 27838, f. 3; *Westminster Election, 1807* [1807], 2.
10. Place 27838, f. 18.
11. Place 27836, f. 18.
12. Bodleian Library, Oxford [Bod. Lib.], Burdett Papers (hereafter BP), MS Eng. lett. c. 64, f. 72.
13. Place 27838, fos 20–1; 27850, f. 79; *Independent Whig*, 10 May 1807.
14. BP, MS Eng. hist. d. 216, f. 324; *MC*, 30 June 1807.
15. *Cobbett's Weekly Political Register*, 26 July, 13 September, 11 October, 20 December 1817, 3 and 24 January, 11 April 1818; *The Life and Correspondence of Major Cartwright*, ed. F. D. Cartwright (1826), ii, p. 126; *Memoirs of the Life of Sir Samuel Romilly*, ed. his sons, 3rd edn (1842), ii, pp. 506–07; HMC, *Manuscripts of J. B. Fortescue Preserved at Dropmore* (1915), x. 429; *MC*, 6 July 1818; Place 27849, fos 3, 36v–37.
16. Place 27841, fos 188, 260, 389; 27842, f. 36; 27849, fos 25–7; *MC*, 18, 23–24 June, 30 June, 1 July 1818; Holland House Papers, BL Add. MS 51678, f. 96v.; *Dropmore Papers*, x. 440; *Cobbett's Weekly Political Register*, 14 March 1818; Romilly, *Life*, ii, p. 508; *Morning Post*, 15, 19 June 1818; *Evening Star*, 9 July 1818.
17. *MC*, 5 November 1818, 13 January, 22, 24 February 1819; Hertfordshire Archives and Local Studies, Cowper Papers, D/ED F427, f.12; Broughton Papers [Broughton], BL Add. MSS 47224, fos 57, 60 and 47226, fol. 32; Holland House Papers, BL Add. MS 51667, f. 39; Lord Brougham, *Life and Times* (Edinburgh, 1871), ii, pp. 340–1; Elector of Westminster [Francis Place], *Reply to Lord Erskine By An Elector of Westminster* (London, 1819), p. 3.
18. Place 27843, fos 9, 19 and 27838, f. 4; *MC*, 23, 30 June 1818; City of Westminster Archives Centre (hereafter WAC), E3349/3–5.
19. Place 27843, f. 29; *Authentic Narrative of the Events of the Westminster Election ... 1819* (1819), p. 326.
20. *A Trifling Mistake of Lord Erskine Corrected* (London, 1819), p. 49.
21. BP, MS Eng. lett. d. 96, f. 6; Place 27843, fos 9 ff.; A. Aspinall, *Lord Brougham and the Whig Party* (Manchester, 1927), p. 279; *Courier*, 27 March 1820; *Correspondence of Jeremy Bentham*, ed. S. Conway (Oxford, 1968), ix, p. 413; R. Zegger, *John Cam Hobhouse: A Political Life, 1819–1852* (Columbia,

MO, 1973), p. 79; W. Thomas, 'Whigs and Radicals in Westminster: The Election of 1819,' *Guildhall Miscellany* 3 (October 1970), 212.
22. *MC*, 27 March 1820; Place 27838, fos 4, 20; *Westminster Election of 1819*, 49.
23. Place 27838, f. 4, 27841, fos 18, 131, 243; 27842, fos 135, 348; 27843, fos 63, 219, 224–5, 228, 375; 27847, fos 10–11.
24. J. C. Hobhouse, *Recollections of a Long Life*, ed. Lady Dorchester (New York, 1909–11), iii, pp. 173, 260 and iv, p. 28; J. M. Main, 'Radical Westminster, 1807–20', *Historical Studies (Australia and New Zealand)* 12 (April 1966), 203; Zegger, *Hobhouse*, pp. 96–100, 105, 187.
25. Broughton, Add. MS 47226, f. 142; BP, MS Eng. hist. b. 200, f. 228.
26. Place, *Letter to Independent Electors of Westminster*, 15; Place 27844, fos 47, 49 and 54v; Zegger, *Hobhouse*, pp. 92–7, 204–6, 286–8.
27. Place 35146, fos 102, 115; 35148, f. 369; 27843, fos 348–9 and 35146, f. 84v; Broughton, *Recollections*, iii. 229; Zegger, *Hobhouse*, pp. 92–4, 150 ff., 199–200.
28. *MC*, 20 November 1832; *Times*, 13 December 1832; cf. BP, MS Eng. lett. c. 64, f. 40.
29. BP, MS Eng. hist. b. 200, fos 180, 183; *MC*, 20 November 1832 *Spectator*, 24 November 1832; *Evening Mail*, 7 December 1832; A. Aspinall, *Three Early Nineteenth Century Diaries* (London, 1952), p. 286; M. W. Patterson, *Sir Francis Burdett and his Times (1770–1844)* (London, 1931), ii, p. 615; Zegger, *Hobhouse*, pp. 200–2; E. M. Spiers, *Radical General: Sir George de Lacy Evans, 1787–1870* (Manchester, 1983), pp. 50–2.
30. Broughton, *Recollections*, iv, pp. 264, 268, 271, 305–7; BP, MS Eng. lett. d. 96, fos 42–3; *Times*, 15 February and 1 May 1833.
31. *Morning Post*, 6 May 1833; *The Croker Papers*, ed. Louis L. Jennings, 3 vols (London, 1884–85), ii, p. 210; Broughton, Add. MS 56557, fos 147–51; Aspinall, *Three Diaries*, pp. 327–8.
32. Patterson, *Burdett*, ii, pp. 627–8.
33. Patterson, *Burdett*, ii, p. 626; BP, MS. Eng. hist. b. 200, fos 218–19; d. 95, f. 115.
34. *MC*, 20 November 1832; Place 35150, f. 140v; T. Raikes, *A Portion of the Journal kept by T. Raikes, Esq., 1831–47* (London, 1856–57), ii, p. 27; *The Holland House Diaries, 1831–1840*, ed. A. Kriegel (1977), p. 361.
35. W. F. Monypenny and G. E. Buckle, *Life of Benjamin Disraeli* (1910–20), i, pp. 367, 370; *John Bull*, 30 April 1837; *St. James's Chronicle*, 13 May 1837; W. Thomas, *The Philosophic Radicals* (Oxford, 1979), p. 298; Charles Greville, *The Greville Memoirs: A Journal of the Reign of Queen Victoria, from 1837 to 1852*, 5 vols (London, 1885–87), iii, p. 406.
36. *MC*, 14, 19, 22, 26, 29, 30 June 1841; *Times*, 26, 29 July 1841; N. Gash, *Politics in the Age of Peel* (London, 1953), p. 366.
37. Peel Papers, BL Add. MS 40583, f. 229; C. S. Parker (ed.) *Sir Robert Peel from His Private Papers* (London, 1899; 1970), iii, p. 334; *MC*, 12 February 1846; *Times*, 20 February 1846; *Illustrated London News*, 21 February 1846; T. H. Bird, *Admiral Rous and the English Turf, 1795–1877* (London, 1939), p. 54.
38. Mill, *Public and Parliamentary Speeches, Collected Works* (Toronto, 1963–91; hereafter *CW*), xxviii, p. 25.
39. *Morning Post*, 6 May 1833; *Times*, 11 May 1837; *MC*, 1 July 1841; Westminster Elector [Charles Cochrane], *Address to the Business-like Men of Westminster* (1847), 5; *Morning Herald*, 12 July 1865.

40. BP, MS. Eng. lett. d. 96, f. 195; Place 35150, fos 147–8; *Examiner*, 2, 16 July 1837; broadsides, *Westminster Reform Society* [*c*. late 1830s] and *Westminster Reform Society* [*c*.1846], Bodl. Oxf., John Johnson Collection, Elections. London Folder.
41. [Cochrane], *Address to Westminster*, 5.
42. *MC*, 26 July, *Morning Advertiser*, 31 July 1847; *Times* 24, 31 July 1847; Peel Papers, BL Add. MS 40599, f. 81.
43. *Guardian*, 10 March 1852; *Morning Advertiser*, 24 June 1852; *Times* 3, 8 July 1852; P.P. 1860, *Election Expenses*, lvi. 167.
44. 'Committee Meeting held ... February 24, 1865', Bod. Oxf., John Johnson Collection, Elections. London Folder; *Times*, 7 October 1891; W. H. Smith Archive, Swindon, Hambledon Papers (hereafter HP), B, f. 56.
45. Mill, *CW*, xvi, pp. 1005–6; *Times*, 14 February 1865; *Mr. J. S. Mill: The Story of the Westminster Election* (1865), p. 3.
46. HP, PS1, fos 11, 56.
47. Mill, *Autobiography, CW*, i, pp. 273–5; British Library of Political and Economic Science, Mill-Taylor Collection, I/88, f. 212; Hanham, *Elections and Party Management*, p. 96.
48. *Daily Telegraph*, 24 March 1865.
49. *Times*, 14 February, 4 March 1865; Mill, *Later Letters, CW*, xvi, 1035, 1038.
50. Mill, *Later Letters, CW*, xvi, pp. 1059, n. 6, 1073; S. M. Ellis (ed.), *The Hardman Papers* (New York, 1930), p. 33.
51. *John Bull*, 15 July 1865; H. E. Maxwell, *Life and Times of the Right Honourable W. H. Smith, M. P.*, 2 vols (Edinburgh, 1893), i, p. 118; *Story of the Westminster Election*, pp. 19–20.
52. HP, PS1, f. 46; PS2, fos 2, 6; Hanham, *Elections and Party Management*, pp. 107–8.
53. *Morning Star*, 21 November 1868.
54. Mill, *Later Letters, CW*, xvi, p. 1487; *Observer*, 15 November 1868; *Tomahawk*, 7 November 1867; Bod. Lib. John Johnson Collection, London Folder, broadside, *Mr. John Stuart Mill and Mr. Bradlaugh* [1868].
55. Mill, *Later Letters, CW*, xvi, pp. 1495–6, 1501–2, 1512–13, 1518–19; xvii, p. 1541.
56. *Economist*, 29 April 1865.
57. Sources: *St. James's Chronicle*, 9 May 1837; P.P. 1836, *Electors Registered*, xliii, 373; P.P. 1843, *Election Expenses*, xliv, 117; P.P. 1852, *County Electors*, xlii, 303; P.P 1859, sess. 1, *Poor Rates*, xxiii, 203; P.P. 1860, *Elective Franchise*, xii, 1; P.P. 1861, *Registered Electors of Middlesex and Cheshire*, l, 791; P.P. 1866, *Population and Electors*, lvii, 215; P.P. 1866, *Working Class Electors*, lvii, 747; P.P. 1868–69, *Election Expenses*, l, 109; P.P. 1880, lvii, 53; F. McCalmont, *The Parliamentary Poll Book* ... (1910).
58. Westminster Conservative Association Annual Report, November 1867, HP, PS2, f. 57.
59. HP, PS2, f. 88.
60. WAC, Records of the Westminster Conservative Association, MS 487, f. 4.
61. HP, PS1, fos 15–15A; Hanham, *Elections and Party Management*, 225–6, R. Blake, *The Conservative Party from Peel to Churchill* (New York, 1970), p. 111.
62. LWWMCA, *Prospectus* [1867?]; HP, PS2, fos 29–47, 66, 70; *Times*, 9 November 1869; Maxwell, *Smith*, i, p. 70; Viscount Chilston, *W. H. Smith* (1965), p. 33; J. Lawrence, 'Class and Gender in the Making of Urban Toryism, 1880–1914', *EHR*, 108, July (1993), 638–9.

63. Metropolitan Working-Men's Conservative Association, *Prospectus* (1867); LWWMCA, *First Annual Report* (1868); HP, PS2, f. 111; *Times*, 29 January 1874, 7 October 1891.
64. Metropolitan Working-Men's Conservative Association, *First Annual Report* [1868].
65. BL, Gladstone Papers, Add. MS 44413, fos 79–81; HP, PS2, f. 70; Bishopsgate Institute, Howell Collection [Howell], Letterbook 1868, fos 29–30; *Spectator*, 7 November 1868; Labour Representation League Minutes, 24 November 1873 and 27 January 1874, British Library of Political and Economic Science, Broadhurst Collection, B/LRL, fos 64, 72–3.
66. HP, PS3, fos 1, 117; Maxwell, *Smith*, i, 248; *Times*, 29 January 1874; *Chelsea Times*, 31 January, 7 February 1874.
67. P.P. 1874, *Election Charges*, liii, 1; P.P. 1877, *Parliamentary and Municipal Elections*, xv, 1, ques. 913.
68. Ibid., ques. 798; Maxwell, *Smith*, i, 247; BL, Gladstone Papers, Add. MS 44446, fos 75v–76.
69. *Times*, 2 December 1872; Howell, Political Parties Envelope, *Resolutions Adopted at Inaugural Meeting of the Westminster Working Men's Liberal Association* [1872].
70. WAC, Westminster Conservative Association, MS 487, f. 14.
71. BL, Gladstone Papers, Add. MS 44255, f. 13; L. T. Hobhouse and J. L. L. Hammond, *Lord Hobhouse: A Memoir* (London, 1905), pp. 122–3, 159–60; *Times*, 6 February, 16 December 1882.
72. *Times*, 16 March 1880, 8 February, 16 December 1882, 12 January 1883; *Liberal and Radical Yearbook* (1887), p. 46.
73. Harrowby MSS Trust, Sandon Hall, series ii, vol. liv.
74. *Pall Mall Gazette*, 1 July 1886.
75. M. Millgate (ed.), *Life and Work of Thomas Hardy* (London, 1984), p. 175.
76. *Westminster and Lambeth Gazette*, 28 November 1885.
77. P.P. 1877, *Parliamentary and Municipal Elections*, xv, 1, ques. 1026; Paul Thompson, *Socialists, Liberals and Labour: the struggle for London 1885–1914* (1967), p. 93, n. 2.
78. BL, Gladstone Papers, Add. MS 44446, fos 77–8.
79. *Pall Mall Gazette*, 16 November 1868; cf. G. S. Jones, *Languages of Class: Studies in English Working Class History, 1832–1982* (1983), ch. 4.
80. C. L. Graves, *Mr. Punch's History of Modern England*, 4 vols (London, 1921–22), iii, p. 377.
81. Bod. Lib. John Johnson Collection, *The Successful Candidate*, 21 November 1868 Elections. London Folder; F. Harrison, 'The Conservative Reaction', *Fortnightly Review* 21 (March 1874), 297–309; Lawrence, 'Making of Urban Toryism', p. 631; Patrick Joyce, *Work, Society and Politics: The Culture of the Factory in Later Victorian England* (Brighton, 1980), p. 276.
82. F. Harrison, *Autobiographic Memoirs*, 2 vols (London, 1911), ii, p. 219; D. A. Hamer, *John Morley: Liberal Intellectual in Politics* (Oxford, 1968), pp. 124–5; cf. Viscount Gladstone Papers, BL Add. MS 46508, f. 196.
83. F. W. Hirst, *Early Life and Letters of John Morley* (1927), iii, p. 89.
84. Place 27809, f. 31.

8
Late Victorian and Edwardian 'Slum Conservatism': How Different were the Politics of the London Poor?

Marc Brodie

Henry Pelling established the modern model for describing the politics of the late Victorian and Edwardian London working class. In his 1960s study of elections in this period, he said of the city:

> There was little heavy industry in the metropolitan area, and large factories were rare. The working class was divided, more sharply than elsewhere, into the skilled artisans and the comparatively unskilled, depressed and often casual workers to be found generally in East London ... So far as working-class Conservatism is concerned ... the anti-alien sentiments of those living in areas of alien [Jewish] immigration led to a long period of Conservative voting on their part ... the independent labour movement was so weak in London.[1]

In summary, this was a city generally whose poor were poorer, and whose workforce more fragmented than elsewhere. Less able to see their true (class) interests, as a consequence, its working class was more responsive to the sectional, racist or other populist appeals, most commonly drawn upon by the Conservatives.

Such apparent political irrationality was re-emphasised by Gareth Stedman Jones, for the poorest parts of the city, particularly its East End (where, he explained, workers were often engaged in dock or other forms of casualised labouring work). In perhaps the most influential statement on this issue, he wrote:

> At a political level, the most striking characteristic of the casual poor was neither their adherence to the left, nor yet to the right, but rather their rootless volatility ... those who had participated in the great Dock Strike of 1889, fell with little resistance under the spell of protectionists and anti-alien propaganda in the 1890s ... [East End] Constituencies like Limehouse, Mile End, St. George's-in-the-East, and Stepney, generally voted Conservative in the period 1885–1906.[2]

The connection again made here was that the poor were easy prey to the populist appeals used by Conservatives, and that London had greater concentrations than elsewhere of the very poor within its working class. The hopes of progressive working-class politics in London were largely ruined by a 'Conservatism of the slums'.

And similar views have continued to dominate scholarship on London politics.[3] Duncan Tanner, for example, argues that there were 'two Londons':

> The political/electoral problems which the Liberal party faced were most acute in East End seats, and to a lesser extent in the sink holes of poverty which littered West London. Voters worked in an enormous variety of ill-paid, casual or sporadic occupations. Tory success was built ... on cultural affinities with working-class social activities, on attendance to ethnic tensions, and, allied to this, on support for the protection of British values, British jobs and British international prestige. The attraction of this appeal was far less apparent in the socially mixed and more affluent artisan and lower middle-class settlements in North and South-West London.[4]

Such imagery parallels the earlier description of division by Pelling: 'it was the more prosperous workers who were the more politically militant and radical, while the lower ranks displayed either apathy or conservatism'.[5]

In this chapter it will be argued that this view is unduly limiting. Studies of working class Conservatism in other parts of England suggest a much greater sense of agency on the part of voters than has been allowed by historians such as Pelling, Stedman Jones and Tanner. This revisionist literature is reviewed in the following section; the next two sections examine the socio-cultural environment of London in an attempt to ascertain whether a re-reading of working-class politics in the metropolis is sustainable.[6]

Working-class Conservatism revisited

Apart from London, apparent working-class Conservatism in this period has also been most widely identified and studied in Lancashire, the West Midlands, and, to some extent, the dock areas of the South coast.[7] Explanations in all of these regions initially concentrated upon similar themes to those noted above for London, although the metropolis continued to be seen to present in more extreme forms the 'problems' that inhibited the growth of a politicised working-class consciousness before 1900.[8] The impact of poverty was often emphasised by historians. In F. M. L. Thompson's description,

> The uneducated, the unwashed, the casual labourers, the slum-dwellers ... did not easily lift their eyes above their own small world of the immediate neighbourhood to identify with any wider community or class; but they formed fiery material whose primitive religious and nationalist prejudices were easily fanned into the ugly eruptions of the 'Church and King' mobs of the 1790s, the no-Popery demonstrations of 1850 against the 'papal aggression' of re-establishing Catholic bishoprics in England, or the notably savage Murphy riots of 1867–8 in Lancashire when the Orange demagogue Murphy roused the rabble against the Irish. These groups were preordained by their own traditions to become Conservative working-class cannon fodder when some of them, as householders of a sort, acquired the vote either in 1867 or 1885 ... their identity as a subclass ... was already firmly shaped by their destitution, insecurity, and hopelessness.[9]

Placed on top of such explanations was also often a perceived stronger Conservative identification with 'traditional' working-class pleasures based on the pub and club (and mixed with a measure of deference to local community elites). Martin Pugh argues that there was a 'boisterous working-class culture that made Lancashire a bastion of Toryism'.[10]

Yet such explanations also began to evolve in a way which provided, over time, a difference between how working-class politics was described in London and elsewhere. Studies began to appear which placed these earlier issues and explanations more firmly within the framework of rational 'identity' politics, suggesting that, rather than simply deviant in class terms, even Conservatism amongst the working-class could be based upon a true political identity formed around other than economic position.

As Jon Lawrence and Jane Elliott write, a number of historical studies appearing by the 1990s began to suggest that rather than simply being the result of 'easily fanned' responses to populist causes, 'urban Toryism may have been a more dynamic, genuine popular force outside the metropolis'.[11]

Some sense amongst working-class Conservatives had begun to be identified, reflected in Mike Savage's description of a 'rational choice' explanation in Preston in Lancashire: 'Conservative support ... did not rely on deferential workers or people who for some reason were acting irrationally against their own interests. Rather it relied on workers pursuing their interests in a particular economistic way ... Toryism made no bones about accepting the reality of class, simply emphasising that working-class interests were served by local employers able to provide employment ... Working-class Conservatism was not based on the denial of the salience of class, and it placed no great emphasis on appealing to people as members of ethnic groups or religious blocs'.[12]

But most other new studies concentrated upon the way in which the political identity, and so party allegiance, of an individual was formed. Important in this formation could be religion, or gender (encompassing now, as a rational identity, the 'traditional working-class man' and his pleasures),[13] or identification of oneself within one of the various constructions of the 'people', as examined by Patrick Joyce.[14] Within the 'linguistic turn' in political history, the focus also became the ability of politicians, as Lawrence puts it, 'actively to shape political identities (i.e. create partisanship), not only by engaging with and appealing to pre-existing identities, but also by using both political language and government policy to *create* identities'.[15] Such identities and also the methods of their construction have become more important in explaining political support than objective class position or 'rootless volatility' amongst the poor.

Trevor Griffiths, in his recent study of the Lancashire working classes, notes that historians now entertain a 'fundamental doubt' regarding the emergence of both 'a more homogenous working class' and a 'unionised workplace culture'; their relationship to the rise of the Labour Party, in turn, has become problematic.[16] 'From the workplace to the ballot box', he writes, 'class, as an influence affecting the choices made, appears to have been secondary, at best. Alternative sources of identity, including religion ... proved altogether more robust in shaping the social and political dynamic'. Importantly, these other identities often clashed with and weakened existing 'solidarities of work and neighbourhood'.[17]

Even where aspects of the classic 'slum conservatism' of fatalistic poverty are found, such as in John Boughton's study of Birmingham, he also finds this form of working-class politics built there upon 'the major institutional and ideological pillars of the local community: the pub (itself a significant target of Unionist propaganda), and a strong sense of civic identity (stressed within the Chamberlainite Tradition)'.[18] Once again, there is a greater emphasis upon community and identity than usually considered to be the case in London.

London has been largely left behind in this rehabilitation of the 'identity politics' of the working-class Tory, partly because such ideas have not been applied to London's situation, but also because of a continuing perception that the metropolis had more deep-seated economic 'problems' than most. As Andrew August noted recently, 'apathy and fatalism, along with political passivity' amongst the poorer working class, and a resultant rejection of labour politics in favour of short-term populist solutions, even if noticed elsewhere has been accepted on a continuing basis by historians 'particularly as it relates to late Victorian and Edwardian London'.[19] At its base continues to be seen the existence of the much poorer, and larger, 'sink holes' of poverty in the city.

But exactly how did London compare with elsewhere in Britain in this regard?

The economic context of London politics

It has been argued by historians that casualisation and underemployment in London, particularly amongst manual workers such as those on the docks, was more extreme and widespread than elsewhere in Britain and that this resulted in both exceptional poverty and political irrationality. Stedman Jones argues that amongst those suffering from the effects of irregular work and income, the 'ever-pressing demands of the stomach ... the arbitrary sentence of destitution ... provided no focus for any lasting growth of collective loyalty upon which a stable class-consciousness could be based ... It was for such reasons that the poorest areas of South and East London were to remain easy targets for corrupt Conservative electioneering between the 1880s and 1914'.[20]

As Peter Hennock notes, Stedman Jones in *Outcast London*, the most comprehensive examination of casual labour and its problems in London, drew largely, as others have done, upon the work of Charles Booth's massive study of the lives and fortunes of the people of late

Victorian London, which included the first true attempted statistical measurement of poverty in the city.[21] But, as Hennock suggests, Stedman Jones not only used much of Booth's massive store of evidence, but in many ways continued to confer unique importance upon Booth's study, similar to that it had been accorded in the late nineteenth century. The social and political fears and debates that surrounded the problems of the metropolis, and particularly fears of the poverty-stricken 'dangerous classes' in the East End at the end of the century, meant that Booth's statistical results, especially regarding the poor, were seen as nationally significant and exceptional to an extent they probably did not deserve. Both the original anxious response to Booth's work, and Stedman Jones's later work, suggested that 'London's poverty was far from typical, and that it responded to factors peculiar to itself'.[22] Yet Rowntree's later survey of York, and other works, suggested that the level of poverty (defined as below an income of approximately one pound a week) that Booth had found across London, around 30 per cent, was not unusual in the large cities of England. Even the much-feared East End seems less an atypical 'sink hole', with the average level of poverty across its central Tower Hamlets section at 38 per cent hardly surprising in a contemporary working-class concentration.[23] It is clear that at times Stedman Jones overstates the existence of casualisation of the workforce even from Booth's investigators' own words.[24] Casual employment was not nearly as widespread, even in the East End, and employment there was much more varied, with even strongly middle-class pockets, as we will see later. As Michael Ball and David Sunderland, in the most detailed recent study of nineteenth-century London economics and living standards, suggest, 'hypotheses about the immiserisation of the metropolitan workforce during the nineteenth century are wide of the mark'.[25]

Working-class London was not as poor as assumed, and neither, it seems, were its voters.[26] The most striking result of a detailed study of voters in a range of areas in the East End of London is the extent to which the sub-letting of properties – extremely common in London – combined with the complexities of the 'compounding' of rates (assumed to be paid as part of the rent) to allow *some* tenant householders to be counted as ratepayers and so registered as voters.[27] In sub-let accommodation, it was generally the 'principal tenant', who most usually had the direct relationship with the landlord, who was entered onto the local government rate book and could become a 'householder' voter,[28] a category which covered approximately 85–90 per cent of those with the vote in the East End constituencies in this period. Other sub-letting tenants had smaller holdings in each property, and the 'principal tenants' were to an overwhelming extent only from amongst the more regularly employed and better-off across all East End occupations (including 'permanently' employed dock workers, for example).

Across all the areas studied, based on the number of rooms they rented and using Booth's statistics, the average weekly rent paid by a non-voter with a family would have been around 3s to 3s 6d. For those who were householder voters it was approximately double that – 6s to 7s. Six shillings or above represented the top 30 per cent of all rents paid by the 6000 working-class men surveyed in the East End in 1887, and those paying that much in rent were generally those regularly earning in the range 25 to 30 shillings per week, around the average London wage of a policeman or clerk, and well into the range of 'working class comfort' defined by Booth.[29] It was such 'principal tenants' who made up the vast majority of voters across the East End, and interestingly, voters possessed broadly similar social characteristics across all the areas examined.

There were four central East End constituencies – Limehouse, Mile End, St. George's-in-the-East and Stepney – named above by Stedman Jones as regularly returning a Conservative in the parliamentary elections between 1885 and 1906. In the six general elections 1885–1906, the relative Conservative and Liberal success in these seats was Limehouse 4 : 2; Mile End 5 : 1; St. George's 4 : 2; Stepney 5 : 1. The idea of a London 'slum Conservatism', at least in the East End, comes in large measure from the results in these seats. In the other 7 East End constituencies directly surrounding these 4 there were 42 general election contests in total in this period. The Liberals were successful in 33 of these polls, a marked contrast to the results in the central 4 constituencies.

In turning to examine these four 'Conservative' constituencies in detail, it is clear that the district of Mile End Old Town, which encompassed both the Stepney and Mile End constituencies, was the wealthiest of the areas in East London. Nearly 75 per cent of the residents of that district were deemed to be 'in comfort' by Booth, far higher than any other East End area.[30]

The Times considered that the Mile End seat 'remained impervious to Liberal attacks' because of its largely comfortable nature as the 'principal residential district of East London'.[31] The *East London Observer* reported in 1895 that Conservative success there was at least partly due to their greater organisational ability to cope with getting their supporters to the polls as 'Between six and eight the greatest rush was experienced as the [commuting] residents returned from the City'.[32]

The Stepney seat also included a similar central core of more prosperous voters. Of the major areas of the Stepney Centre and South wards,

Booth said, respectively, that the 'majority of these people belong to a fairly comfortable class of artisans, shopmen and clerks' and the 'majority of the people are in regular steady work: artisans, postmen, policemen, clerks, shop assistants'.[33]

Even superficially, much of this evidence, both of individual better-off working class and more prosperous voters, and of constituencies, can be seen to begin to directly reverse the general argument as to the likely class geography of Conservative success in these areas of London.

But if Conservative victories here were not the result of the 'split' working-class city suggested by Tanner, and so not based upon poverty and short-term responses to desperation, what drove this success? Were the cultural and identity factors identified for other working-class Conservative areas in Britain of importance?

Religion and identity in London

Working-class Conservative identities have often been seen to have had a religious or ethnic base. Ewen Green emphasises the central importance of the ability of the Conservatives to link themselves to a 'popular Anglicanism' identity. This was partly exhibited in 'ethnic prejudices' against outsiders in these areas, as will be discussed later, but

> Popular Anglicanism was also directed at British Nonconformists, and especially at militant Nonconformity ... an emphasis on the 'regulatory' politics of Nonconformity in the spheres of, for example, gaming and licensing, allowed Conservatives to portray Nonconformists, and by association Liberals, as a group of puritanical killjoys who wished to interfere with working-men's pleasures. In contrast the social life of the Conservative clubs and associations presented almost an anti-politics of 'beer and bonhomie' as a defence against any threat from a new Parliament of the Saints.[34]

In this case the particular type of 'identity' drawn upon by the Conservatives was that of the 'traditional working class man', with his drinking and other pleasures, as noted earlier. Tanner suggests, in a related way, that the appeal of Toryism 'was far less apparent in the socially mixed and more affluent artisan and lower middle-class settlements in North and South-West London', where, according to Paul Thompson, both Nonconformity and Liberalism benefited from a 'back bone' of support from these groups.[35] But this oppositional imagery of popular Conservatism up against Nonconformist principle and 'faddism'[36] seems not to hold for London, at least its East End. This can be seen most clearly in the central 'Conservative' seat of Stepney.

Contemporary political analysts commonly noted that the 'Nonconformist character of Stepney is a most important consideration', but as a reporter asked the local Liberal election agent in 1892, 'Stepney has always been regarded as a Nonconformist stronghold. How was it the Liberal party lost in 1886?'.[37] Indeed, it continued to lose it. Stepney had been won by the Liberals in 1885, but then was held by the Conservatives in all seven general elections from 1886 to January 1910, falling to the Liberals only in a by-election in 1898, and then again in the second election of 1910.

The Stepney constituency, which was relatively wealthy in East End terms, had at least a dozen Nonconformist chapels and missions operating within or on its boundary streets. Nearby vast evangelical and Nonconformist centres also had extraordinarily large attendances, with many coming from within Stepney. But, politically, Stepney seems to have exemplified the model of London Nonconformist drift away from the Liberals from the mid-1880s onwards, described by David Bebbington and Stephen Koss. Many Nonconformists, they argue, already unhappy with Liberal actions such as the 1870 Education Act, moved to the Liberal Unionists in response to Gladstone's Home Rule proposals in 1886. While some later moved back towards Liberalism, others drifted closer to the Conservatives. The Boer War splits again pushed a number, particularly Wesleyans, away from the Liberals, and despite a coming together against the Conservatives' 1902 Education Act, the tie of religion and politics was dissipated.[38] This pattern captures well the shifting loyalties of Nonconformity in Stepney in the years following the Liberal victory of 1885, save that the drift seems not even to have been temporarily reversed by the Education Act alliance after 1902.

In Stepney South ward, a Nonconformist stronghold,[39] Booth's detailed investigations showed that both the membership of local Nonconformist churches and the local population generally was 'in regular steady work; artisans, postmen, policemen, clerks, shop assistants, and many others engaged in one branch or another of the shipping trade'.[40] This ward was where the 'Temperance Party' – based heavily upon Nonconformist support – was 'particularly strong'. In the South Ward in 1898 the temperance 'party' was able to deliver approximately one-third of the total vote (on a 50 per cent turnout) to its independent candidates in local elections, against the combined and determined strength of both major parties, when the temperance group objected to a political compromise which would have seen a publican elected to the vestry.[41]

The Stepney South ward, apart from this one occasion, was also an absolute stronghold for the Conservative party. After 1900 in the local borough elections, the ward elected only Conservative councillors, with the party's support peaking at 78 per cent, and averaging two-thirds of the total vote. Before that, the ward had also been well 'known for its moderate [Conservative] propensities'.[42]

In the Centre ward of Stepney, where at least six Nonconformist churches were located, the only non-Conservative candidate elected at the five borough council elections 1900–12 was again an independent Temperance candidate, the Rev. W. G. Boyd of St. Faith's mission church. Boyd's nomination was thought at the time to be 'calculated to injure the Moderate cause' and was bitterly resented by the Moderates, 'for it was felt that this splitting of the votes would cause the loss of a seat', which it did[43] – by splitting away from Conservatism the temperance vote which normally ensured its success. The Temperance movement in this ward was based mainly on Nonconformist organisations. Yet in relatively wealthy East End areas, such as Stepney, Nonconformist adherence in no way ensured a Liberal vote.

'Ethnic prejudice', as mentioned by Green, has also been seen as central to East End Conservatism through its identification with populist opposition to the significant Jewish immigration into the area from the 1880s. But a 'dynamic' connection of this reaction with popular Anglicanism has not been usually made in London, largely because of a perceived lack of religious feeling or affiliation amongst the London poor. Nevertheless, an examination of the general claim for the importance of 'ethnic prejudice', or 'anti-alienism', in the politics of the London working class is worth undertaking. Somewhat surprisingly, after the Rev. Boyd's 'temperance' victory in Stepney Centre ward, noted earlier, the *Jewish Chronicle* claimed that Boyd won largely 'through the votes of Jews and the instrumentality of Jewish canvassers'.[44] That a temperance campaigner who clearly won by splitting the Conservative vote should have relied significantly on Jewish support seems a bizarre possibility, but it is one that ties in closely with other similar evidence.

After 1900 Stepney was the constituency of Major William Evans-Gordon. Evans-Gordon was a principal force behind the anti-immigration Aliens Act of 1905, and it has been often claimed that he held Stepney for the Conservatives against the general Liberal swing of 1906 largely on the basis of popular support for his restrictionist activities.[45] Indeed, the one voting ward with an overwhelmingly large Jewish population in the constituency – the West ward – was considered to be 'a hotbed of Toryism'.[46] If its politics was seen as a reaction to the immigration issue this might confirm the standard interpretations of the importance of race. Yet it is noticeable that reports of meetings of Stepney West Ward Conservative Club were dominated by members with Jewish names. The chairman of this Club for a significant period was the area's previous Conservative Jewish MP, Wooton Isaacson, who with his background was unlikely to have attracted a strong 'popular Anglican' vote. The teachers of the Stepney Jewish Schools were said to have 'put in an immense amount of hard work' for Isaacson in 1895. In fact it is clear that until well into the Edwardian period, as John Garrard and Geoffrey Alderman have shown, those Jews who possessed the vote in the East End and elsewhere often used it in support of Conservative candidates, and the Jewish vote was often significant in deciding results in some of the East End seats.[47]

Across the East End constituencies, observers, including Jews and Liberals, noted the often strong support of Jewish voters for the Tories. In St. George's in 1886, it was said 'the English Jews ... were almost unanimous in favour of Mr. Ritchie [Conservative]'. In Mile End in 1895, meanwhile, the Jewish vote apparently 'went solid' for the Conservatives, with the *Jewish Chronicle* noting in 1905 that the 'majority of Jewish electors' had been Conservative in that seat. In Stepney in 1889, it was recorded that 'a large percentage of the aliens voted for the Conservative candidate', and in 1898 the Jewish vote again 'formed a great bulk of the Unionist poll'. David Dainow found generally 'a large amount of Tory opinion amongst Jews in East London'.[48]

It is also apparent that the mere fact of a candidate being Jewish certainly did not guarantee support from Jewish voters. Bertram Straus was the Jewish Liberal candidate for St. George's in 1900. His Conservative opponent was T. R. Dewar, who made his 'speciality' for the election his promise to 'do everything in his power to restrict the immigration of foreign aliens ... the canker that is eating out the life blood of St. George's'.[49] Yet a witness at a meeting of Jewish voters in that election recalled later that

> it was the Jewish vote and Jewish influence that secured the seats of St. George's and Stepney for their present occupants [Conservatives]. I still remember with shame and disgust the proceedings of a meeting of Jewish voters called together in support of Mr. Dewar's candidature. The principal speaker of the evening ... [who] was stated to be

the private secretary and right hand of Lord Rothschild, enlarged upon the friendship and goodwill of the Conservative Party for the Jewish people ... it was the cherished wish of 'our Lord' that the Jews should return the Conservative candidate. This had the desired effect and the Jewish vote, with few single exceptions, went solid for Mr. Dewar. Similar things happened in Stepney.[50]

The extent to which influential members of a community could 'work' on voters, or reinforce, their economically based political preferences, was perhaps one key to political alignments. In Whitechapel, also with a very high Jewish population but, by comparison, always won by the Liberals, the local Jewish community was swayed politically to a large extent, as David Feldman suggests, by the 'network of influence which circulated around [local Liberal M.P.] Samuel Montagu and the Federation of Synagogues' (of which Montagu was President).[51] Tied to this was the fact that the Federation of Synagogues was more closely linked to more recent Jewish immigrants, in contrast to other more established sections of the London Anglo-Jewish community. In other parts of the East End for most of this period the majority of Jewish voters were those who had been in the country longer and were not necessarily opposed to new restrictions on immigration. In St. George's in 1886, claimed the *East London Advertiser*, the 'English Jews, who may be called the party of order, were almost unanimous in favour of Mr. Ritchie [Conservative]'.[52]

This could in some instances have had a decisive effect on election results, particularly in very tightly fought seats such as St. George's, where a few hundred votes changing sides could have swung most elections. A detailed case could easily be made, that without the Jewish vote, St. George's, and perhaps even Stepney, would have been won by the Liberals in nearly every election from 1892 to 1910, a result which would have turned much of the assumed political impact of 'ethnic prejudice' in the East End completely on its head.

Both these examples are cases where specific religious 'identities' were not operating politically in these areas of London in the way that has normally been assumed. This is in fact one general theme in understanding working-class Conservatism in the city in this period – that, broadly defined, religious identities were important, but had perhaps an unexpected impact.

But a concurrent 'lack' of both religion and politics has often been argued to have existed amongst workers in London. Hugh McLeod suggests that feelings of economic desperation or vulnerability inhibited reflective thought in either sphere:

> The secularism and parochialism that pervaded working-class London ... was a typical proletarian response to a world in which most decisions were made by other people ... only the most intent parochialism could save the individual and those who depended on him from disaster ... little neighbourly encouragement was likely to be offered to those who concerned themselves with matters of abstract principle or world interpretation ... In politics, the result was an ad hoc approach, consisting of the use of direct action to remove particular grievances, together with the lack of any long-term commitment.[53]

Yet, in Limehouse, another of the 'classic' London slum Conservatism seats, the defeated Liberal candidate in 1895 attributed his loss directly to the influence of 'The spread of electioneering lies, such as that I was an "Atheist"... [and the] hostility of the established clergy'.[54]

Of importance here seems to have been a combination of a form of religious attachment, not normally recognised in relation to the London working class, with the particular social structures in these areas. This combination seems to have been particularly significant in both St. George's and Limehouse, the least well-off of the four central Conservative seats in the East End. In these seats, the most apparently politically Conservative areas were undoubtedly the local areas of Shadwell and Wapping respectively. The borough wards they were in both had average local government Conservative votes of around 60 per cent. Both these areas were also dominated by block 'model' workmen's dwellings, built by local authorities and philanthropic trusts to replace slum areas, and which were increasingly common in London from the 1880s. As Stedman Jones notes, the result of the strict rules of the dwelling companies regarding both the prohibition of arrears and the payment of rent in advance put this type of accommodation 'out of the reach of the casual poor. Such dwellings were in effect confined to a relatively more prosperous and more secure section of the working class'.[55] Booth calculated that even in the poorest block dwelling in Shadwell, 60 per cent were within his definition of 'in comfort'.[56]

Model dwellings housed a total of perhaps 3500 people, between 40 and 50 per cent of the population, in the Shadwell ward by 1901. Of Wapping, also, it was said that it 'was peculiar in that the best of its inhabitants have gone to live in Buildings rather than in the small houses'.[57] Shadwell and Wapping had easily the highest percentage of rated households of any identifiable area in the East End, and, flowing from that, the highest level of enfranchisement of any ward in the district. Both of these were the result of the compounding of rates in the model dwellings (due to the individual relationship of the tenant with the dwelling company, rather than sub-letting arrangements). Even in 1891 around one-quarter of the electors in the relatively small Wapping polling district lived in just two blocks of dwellings, and of the flats in these blocks, 80 per cent had a registered voter.[58] Thus it is clear that voters from these dwellings possessed a presence out of proportion to their numbers in the community at large. These block dwellers were the most important single voting group in many wards.

Both Shadwell and Wapping were apparently significantly more 'Conservative' than the other, perhaps 'poverty sink-hole', riverside wards. But the Conservatives only won, it seems, because of their opponents not being able to turn out the vote. Although there are some problems with comparing local to parliamentary voting patterns, similar themes can usefully be identified. In four contested local borough elections across 1900–12, in Shadwell ward the broadly defined 'progressive' vote could *double* (or halve) from one election to another, while the number of Conservative voters only varied by a tiny 14 per cent below and 6 per cent above the average number across the 12 years. At the time of their maximum vote, in 1912, the 'progressives' swept all positions in the ward. Significantly, however, the Conservative vote did not fall at all in that election from the previous contested poll. This suggests that Conservative dominance in this model dwelling dominated ward was the result of a general weakness in allegiance of its progressive voters, but that an 'underlying' majority was perhaps for the progressives. This parallels the situation with many Conservative parliamentary victories in the East End.

In the Mile End constituency, for example, there was an extremely stable Conservative vote. The average Conservative vote across the 8 parliamentary elections in the years 1885–1906 was 2239. The lowest Conservative vote in this period was 2091 (in 1885) and the highest 2440 (in 1900). So the variation from the average was only −7 per cent and +9 per cent. This was a rock solid vote. The Liberal vote in this seat, on the other hand, fluctuated dramatically, going as low as 1280, and being maximised in 1906 at 2295. It varied each side of the average by −30 per cent and +26 per cent. The situation in Limehouse was similar, with the Conservative vote varying around the average by only +12 per cent and −15 per cent, while in comparison, the Liberal vote in 1906 was more than double that of 1886. The figures in St. George's and Stepney, for example, are harder to calculate, due to the declining size of their total electorates as a result of immigration, but broadly the patterns are the same. Conservative parliamentary victories in these areas were to a significant extent based upon abstention from voting by supporters of their opponents.

An examination of detailed geographic patterns of fluctuation in the progressive vote in some parts of the East End shows that in fact vote variation was highest, and so Conservative victories more common, not only in the most 'respectable' working-class neighbourhoods, like those dominated by the model dwellings, but also, to return to the issue of religion, in the areas where the strongest attachment, even if only 'marginal' attachment, to the Church of England was apparent.[59]

To see the connection here, we can begin by looking at the detailed descriptions Octavia Hill and others provided for Booth on life in model dwellings. Here there was a limited level of community spirit and contact. Generally Hill described the 'large groups of blocks where the tenants are the quiet, respectable, working-class families, who, to use a phrase common in London, "keep themselves to themselves"'. The 'friendlessness' of women in block dwellings, compared to those in poorer street settings, was often emphasised, and seen as resulting from the desire to establish a social distance from the neighbours to distinguish one's family from the 'rough' working class and their habits.[60] Beatrice Potter noted also of such buildings that the 'respectable tenants keep rigidly to themselves. To isolate yourself from your surroundings seems to be here the acme of social morality ... Do not meddle with your neighbours is perforce the burden of one's advice to newcomers.'[61]

Sarah Williams notes the existence of a 'public opinion' within poorer working-class neighbourhoods which operated to reinforce 'shared values and identities', but argues that in areas such as the model dwellings a 'public opinion' did not develop.[62] There was little neighbourhood identity or solidarity, even one of male 'beer and bonhomie'. In 1887 the Liberal MP Thorold Rogers made a comment which drew together the social structure and politics of areas such as these model dwellings. Of the London voter, he said, who 'does not know who his neighbour is ... [and who] is commendably indifferent to his neighbour's private affairs', with 'comparatively few exceptions politics have a loose hold on him. He has no alacrity in voting, a great alacrity in abstaining', and, Rogers continued,

> by far the largest part of the [London] working classes, though not particularly sectarian, is religious. The Tory party is perfectly aware of

how useful a canvasser is who can boldly state that the Radical candidate is an atheist or a freethinker.[63]

These characteristics can be seen to be intimately connected.

First, as Rogers suggests, while attendance at church may not have been high in working-class areas such as East London, a number of clergy interviewed by Booth and his associates reinforced the general point concerning the importance ascribed to religion by local inhabitants. 'Altogether the East End is much more alive [spiritually]' than most of South London, said one, adding that the people in their parish 'were the most religious in London'. Another remarked that the 'influence of the church in the district is strong', and another that 'people are no more irreligious than they were but that there is a greater neglect of church-going'. Others believed that 'Most would call themselves Christians: however, if asked to attend church, people would say, "I can read my Bible just as well at home".' A missionary noted that 'Nearly all the working people in my district who are in comfortable circumstances are more or less under religious influence'. Margaret Loane, a visiting nurse, commented upon the 'strong religious faith' of her patients, although their 'views on doctrinal questions could scarcely have been considered orthodox by the instructed members of any church or sect'.[64]

Visiting work by women from London bible societies and similar organisations was extremely common in this period. In the block dwellings they found many who were most willing to listen to them. In Mile End, one biblewoman said of one such area, that the

> people there [in the blocks] seem so friendless ... Over and over again in this one block the Biblewoman had been told how glad the people are to realise that she cares enough for them to make an effort to overcome their reluctance to admit her and to manage to get on friendly terms with them.

The isolation of those living in these dwellings, combined with a broad religious belief, gave their visitors enormous potential influence. As Loane noted, social isolation was

> often practised more strictly with regard to near neighbours than with regard to educated visitors. With no further desire than to enjoy a little of human intercourse and sympathy of which they voluntarily stint themselves, men and women alike will reveal many things which they fondly hope are not even dimly suspected by the 'keerless [sic] common sort of neighbours'.[65]

These educated visitors were often from the church, and would either regularly visit with the couple, or quite often in the East End could encourage a 'friendless' woman, or occasionally her husband, to attend one of the parish's groups. Another told of her success in reaching some new mothers with advice: 'her practical guidance is of untold value to one who perhaps has no other respectable woman friend in the world, or had not until she was induced to come to the Mothers' Meeting'.[66] Marginal attachment to the church was held to some extent by the ritual attendances of post-birth 'churching', baptism, funerals and weddings, as well as visits by church activists, but it went further than this. As an example of widespread connection to the church, in the respectable East End working-class parish of St. Mary's, Bromley, the vicar claimed that his church was 'in touch', in one way or another, with 'quite 3/4 of the parish', and in addition to the normal services the church ran 17 bible classes and other clubs, with a total attendance of around 2500 people – or 6 times the Anglican church service attendance.[67]

The political influence of this connection and the visiting of these homes by biblewomen and others was significant. The Conservative Party's Primrose League election campaigners believed that in working-class areas women were politically 'the best canvassers, in as much as they are used to district visiting', and that 'advice or opinion given concerning the social or parochial matters ... often have a greater influence than political considerations in deciding votes'.[68] A working-class woman told a Liberal canvasser that

> if she had ten thousand votes she would give them to Mr.——, naming the Conservative candidate. I told her his party wanted to tax the tea ... 'Well, he ought not to do that; but you know he is such a good man, he attends church regularly, and helps the poor. I couldn't help voting for such a man as he'.[69]

Another candidate, in local elections when some women had the vote, complained that

> One woman whom I asked to vote for me replied that the 'lady' [visitor] had not yet told her which way to vote. So you see ... the mothers' meetings are a factor in the election.[70]

Patricia Hollis says that women who did have the vote in local elections 'were known to show more independence than men by preferring moral character over party loyalty in their candidates'.[71] But politicians, such as Rogers, evidently believed that a canvasser (who was perhaps also a local church visitor) could influence the votes of both men and women at home in this way, even if only indirectly through the influence of the wife on her husband.[72] This is clearly suggested by the fact that candidates from both sides used mission workers and other female canvassers even in parliamentary elections when no women had the vote. James Vernon notes that in mid-century elections 'Candidates' wives were often used as canvassers, while the candidates themselves were always appealing to women to use their influence as wives, sisters, or daughters over the male voters'.[73] The wife of the Liberal candidate in the 1908 Haggerston (East End) parliamentary by-election made a point of making 'friends ... among the working women' as she went from street to street on foot.[74] The Primrose League believed that 'the influence of the wives of the working men with their husbands is unbounded',[75] as one of these wives seemed to confirm to a visitor:

> She was expecting me to call – she had 'eard up at the Church that someone was coming'. She began to consult me about her children and everything else under the sun, and finished up by asking me how her husband was to vote.[76]

Yet overall it was the influence of a broadly moral, vaguely religious framework for judging political action and individuals that was importantly reinforced through these contacts. In the bible classes, mothers' meetings and home visits, and other activities associated with marginal attachment to the church, it was in the interests of the activist, or the group, to emphasise any 'scandal' or atheism, or other individual moral limitations, particularly in public life. Very importantly, as most of the 'marginal' attachment to religion was to Anglican rather than Nonconformist churches, this meant that most contact that these people had with religious issues, and the social activities associated with them, was through the perspective of this denomination and its committed activists, who were more usually Conservative in inclination.[77] The attitude of the Liberal party in London to such activists was clearly demonstrated by the fact that the St. George's party objected in 1899 to the municipal franchise registration claims of 'four philanthropic ladies working for a mission' who 'devoted most of their time to visiting'.[78] As was said regarding a young wives' club run by the church, the 'club is not primarily a place to exchange gossip, but a centre where it can be judged against a set of standards which the members feel to be superior'.[79] 'Standards' were undoubtedly applied to political candidates in discussions in the home and at such clubs, as we have seen earlier, and most usually to the benefit of the Conservatives. For working-class men in London, there is little doubt that a view of the importance of individual morality in both politics and life (and so a likelihood to react to such influences) was also reinforced by their experiences in the workplace. Corruption and bribery, amongst foremen and others at low levels in many industries did not encourage a view that their problems lay with capitalism itself; instead, the 'deeply rooted' impression of the docker, for example, was 'that he is being cheated at every turn ... [although] he knows not by whom'.[80] This was reinforced by the often religious-based socialism of many of their union leaders, such as Ben Tillett, the great Dock Strike leader who argued that the impulse for all he had done or said 'had come from the Bible and from the personality of Christ', and that the 'emancipation of the people from vile conditions, from ignoble life' would not be achieved by parliament, but lay 'at the door of the churches'.[81]

A lack of neighbourhood identity or 'public opinion' in these respectable working-class areas provided little encouragement for progressive voters to get out to vote. But this was compounded by relatively widespread moral or broadly religious beliefs, and a greater isolation from the surrounding community may have led to a much greater effectiveness of 'electioneering lies' and similar messages spread in favour of the Church of England and Conservatives amongst this group. But when such moral/religious comments were in conflict with their political leanings, as Rogers stated directly on this point:

> it does not follow that electors to whom these statements are made and reiterated are made hostile to a candidate, but they are rendered indifferent, and think that, after all, they had better abstain from voting.[82]

As abstention seems to have been so much more common amongst potential progressive voters in these areas, it seems likely that it was partly a clash of identities – perhaps that of class-based political identity with a religious or moral one reinforced by the other influences upon them – which made them thus more 'indifferent' to politics.

By itself, this perhaps might have caused relatively few voters to neglect to vote, but Rogers also noted how influences could compound. It was these same voters, he said, who when faced also with perhaps 'a schism in the party to which he has previously given his support', could become 'entirely neutral' in his politics.[83] It was a combination of such factors which clearly could have the greatest impact on the political responses of the working class. The Liberal party, without doubt, had its very public 'schisms' around the time of the disastrous elections of 1886, 1895 and 1900. Yet it may not have lost its support so quickly amongst these groups of voters if their political allegiances had not been already weakened by the type of influences suggested earlier.

Yet it is very important to note that the simple strength of the Church of England in any area did not automatically lead to this influence and response amongst the working class. In a detailed study of wards in the East End constituencies of Poplar and Bow and Bromley, as noted, it was seen that progressive vote fluctuation generally closely matched levels of working-class church attendance. Yet clear differences could be seen between socially similar (comfortable working-class) wards such as Bromley South-East and Poplar East. Despite quite high levels of working-class church attendance, in Bromley South-East the size of the progressive vote varied by only an average of a tiny 5 per cent across the period. Bromley South-East exhibited probably the most consistent overall turnout of voters in borough elections from 1900 to 1912 of any of the Poplar wards.[84] In that ward, a group of generally progressively inclined clergy from the parish church personally undertook the local 'Systematic house to house visiting' of working-class homes. In contrast, the parish church in Poplar East was quite different in this regard. It was claimed that the clergy in this parish had little time for visiting in the area, which was done mainly by 14 voluntary District Visitors, who also attended the Mothers' Meetings. Of these '5 are residents who belong to the local aristocracy, daughters or wives of doctors etc. The remaining 9 are ladies from other parts of London.'[85] This, it seems is much more likely to have been the 'face', and the influence, of the Church met by working people in that parish. In Poplar East, the number of progressive voters in the party's worst borough elections dropped to nearly half that of its best year, and Conservatives won 13 out of 15 positions contested across the period. In Bromley South-East, by contrast, where progressive support was stable, the Conservatives averaged only 42 per cent of the vote in this time.

Contact with the church in Bromley South-East with its more radical visiting clergy, unlike in Poplar East, possibly did not act to weaken, but to reinforce, working-class progressive political allegiance in the parish. Mike Savage suggests something of a similar pattern in his work on Preston. Between the 1890s and the First World War, he says, as church institutions were 'taken over' by the working class they changed from being institutions which worked to 'pacify' the working class to 'sites of neighbourhood-based capacities leading to political mobilisation'.[86]

Conclusion

Issues of identity were thus as central to political outcomes, to 'popular Conservatism', in London as they have been identified elsewhere in Britain in recent times. But it was the precise dynamics of how different influences based upon these identities acted to reinforce or clash with each other which was important. In regard to perhaps the most important of all, religion, we have seen this in relation to Nonconformist, Jewish and Anglican (or perhaps more general 'moral' or vaguely religious) identities and how particular structures and influences affected their interaction with issues of class and politics.

But in concentrating upon explanations of the apparent Conservatism amongst the East End working class, in many ways this has meant a simplified emphasis upon factors possibly acting to dilute the expression of the 'underlying' political tendencies of the working class. The progressive vote in some areas of poorer London did often fall well short of its 'potential'. But of course voter abstention by itself could not deliver a seat to an opponent. The arguments provided earlier do not deny that factors such as individual occupational concerns or the impact of a range of political issues could gather working-class support for Conservatives in the East End. But having said that, it still needs to be remembered that much of the Conservative vote in the East End potentially came from other than the working class. For example even in the very poor St. George's North ward up to a quarter of those on the electoral register were the middle class, shopkeepers and workers, or white-collar employees. In a wealthier area such as the section analysed of Mile End East, such residents comprised perhaps close to 40 per cent of the register. Given the fact that they may have been slightly more likely to actually vote than many of the working-class voters, and the fluctuations in voter turnout levels, these voters may have accounted for up to 60 per cent of votes in some elections in an area such as Mile End East.[87] This need not assume, of course, that all, or even a majority, of such voters supported the Conservatives on a 'class' basis, although, as David Bebbington suggests, it was in London that 'the process whereby the middle classes were swinging towards solidarity against Liberalism was more advanced than anywhere else in Britain'.[88]

But clearly the evidence does show on a number of occasions that voting abstention seems to have distorted an underlying majority progressivism amongst the working class in some areas. Without this distortion, the consequent progressive victories in those areas of London would have seemed unremarkable, and would probably have been ignored as a topic for study. I have to some extent been trying to counter what have become accepted explanations of a London political exceptionalism which in a sense did not exist. But the overall argument of this chapter is that in late Victorian and Edwardian London, as elsewhere in Britain, it is vital to look in very close detail at voters and their milieu. Only if we examine the influences working upon them, the range of their 'identities', and the processes by which these may have reinforced or negated each other, can we fully understand their motivations and their reception of political ideas. We have seen some of the complexities of this, and it is clear that many of the broad assumptions upon which the ideas of 'Slum Conservatism' in London were based, stand in urgent need of revision.

Notes

1. H. Pelling, *Social Geography of British Elections 1885–1910* (London, 1967), pp. 27, 57–8.
2. G. Stedman Jones, *Outcast London: A Study in the Relationship between Classes in Victorian Society* (London, 1976), p. 343 and fn. 17.
3. D. Howell, *British Workers and the Independent Labour Party* (Manchester, 1983), p. 257; K. D. Wald, *Crosses on the Ballot: Patterns of British Voter Alignment since 1885*, (Princeton, 1983), p. 104; M. Pugh, *The Tories and the People 1880–1935* (Oxford, 1985), pp. 105–6.
4. D. Tanner, *Political Change and the Labour Party, 1900–1918* (Cambridge, 1990), pp. 164–5.
5. H. Pelling, *Popular Politics and Society in Late Victorian Britain* (London, 1968), p. 56; T. Lummis, *The Labour Aristocracy 1851–1914* (Aldershot, 1994).
6. Length constraints prevent detailed discussion of the different support bases for Liberal and socialist candidates. The term 'progressive', adopted by the 'Liberal-labour' alliance on the London County Council, is used here to signify non-Conservative political groups, whether Liberal or 'Labour'.
7. Tanner, *Political Change*, chs 5, 6.
8. D. Mayfield and S. Thorne, 'Social History and its Discontents: Gareth Stedman Jones and the Politics of Language', *SH*, 17, 2 (1992), 169–73.
9. F. M. L. Thompson, *The Rise of Respectable Society: A Social History of Victorian Britain, 1830–1900* (London, 1988), pp. 317–18.
10. M. Pugh, 'The Rise of Labour and the Political Culture of Conservatism, 1890–1945', *History*, 87, 288 (2002), 517.
11. J. Lawrence and J. Elliott, 'Parliamentary Election Results Reconsidered: An Analysis of Borough Elections, 1885–1910', *PH*, 16, 1 (1997), 23.
12. M. Savage, *The Dynamics of Working-Class Politics: The Labour Movement in Preston, 1880–1940* (Cambridge, 1987), pp. 140–1.
13. See J. Lawrence, 'Class and Gender in the Making of Urban Toryism, 1880–1914', *EHR*, 108 (1993), 629–52.

14. P. Joyce, *Visions of the People: Industrial England and the Question of Class, 1848–1914* (Cambridge, 1991).
15. J. Lawrence, 'The Dynamics of Urban Politics, 1867–1914', in J. Lawrence and M. Taylor (eds) *Party, State and Society: Electoral Behaviour in Britain since 1820* (Aldershot, 1997), p. 90.
16. T. Griffiths, *The Lancashire Working Classes c.1880–1930* (Oxford, 2001), p. 268.
17. Ibid., p. 331.
18. J. Boughton, 'Working-class Conservatism and the Rise of Labour: A Case Study of Birmingham in the 1920s', *Historian*, 59 (1998), p. 17.
19. A. August, 'A Culture of Consolation: Rethinking Politics in Working-class London, 1870–1914', *HR*, 74 (2001), 194.
20. Stedman Jones, *Outcast London*, p. 334.
21. C. Booth, *Life and Labour of the People in London*, 17 vols (London, 1902).
22. E. P. Hennock, 'The Measurement of Urban Poverty: From the Metropolis to the Nation, 1880–1920', *Ec Hist Rev*, 2nd series, 40, 2 (1987), 212.
23. M. Mackinnon, 'Living Standards, 1870–1914', in R. Floud and D. McCloskey (eds) *The Economic History of Britain Since 1700, Vol. 2: 1860–1939*, 2nd edn, Cambridge 1994, p. 278, and Hennock, 'The Measurement of Urban Poverty', *passim*. For East End Tower Hamlets: Booth, *Life*, 1st Series, 2, appendix, pp. 32–3 and 1, p. 36, table II; Stedman Jones, *Outcast London*, p. 132.
24. M. Ball and D. Sunderland, *An Economic History of London, 1800–1914* (London 2001), p. 104; M. Brodie, 'Artisans and Dossers: the 1886 West End Riots and the East End Casual Poor', *London Journal*, 24, 2 (1999), 39–40.
25. Ball and Sunderland, *Economic History*, p. 110.
26. M. Brodie, *The Politics of the Poor: The East End of London, 1885–1914* (Oxford, 2004), ch. 2 and *passim*.
27. Three groups of census enumeration districts, covering 18,000 people and 1400 male parliamentary voters, were examined, one from the North Ward of St. George's in the East, and two in Mile End Old Town: Brodie, *Politics of the Poor*, ch. 2. Anthony Wohl, *The Eternal Slum: Housing and Social Policy in Victorian London* (Montreal, 1977), p. 24, suggests three-quarters of all rented properties were sub-let in London in mid-century, a figure which, from a range of other evidence, seems not to have declined by its end.
28. J. Davis, 'Slums and the Vote, 1867–90', *HR*, LXIV, 155 (1991), 375–88.
29. P. P. 1887 LXXI, *Statements of Men Living in Certain Selected Districts of London*, pp. 306, 323, 423; Stedman Jones, *Outcast London*, p. 216.
30. Booth, *Life*, 1st series,1, p. 36.
31. *Times*, 3 January 1905, quoted *East London Observer*, 7 January 1905, p. 7.
32. *East London Observer*, 20 July 1895, p. 6.
33. Booth, *Life*, 1st series, 2, appendix, areas 75B and 77B.
34. E. H. H. Green, *The Crisis of Conservatism: The Politics, Economics and Ideology of the British Conservative Party, 1880–1914* (London, 1996), p. 127.
35. P. Thompson, *Socialists, Liberals and Labour: The Struggle for London 1885–1914* (London, 1967), p. 20.
36. Lawrence, 'Class and Gender'.
37. *East London Advertiser*, 2 July 1892, p. 8; 6 August 1892, p. 8.

38. D. W. Bebbington, 'Nonconformity and Electoral Sociology, 1867–1918', *HJ*, 27, 3 (1984), 644–6; S. Koss, *Nonconformity in Modern British Politics* (London, 1975).
39. For the 1902–03 *Daily News* survey of religious attendance in London: R. Mudie-Smith (ed.) *The Religious Life of London* (London, 1904).
40. Booth, *Life*, 1st series, II, appendix, area 77B. See British Library of Political and Economic Science, Charles Booth Collection, Booth MSS B184, pp. 25–9, 33.
41. *East London Advertiser*, 14 May 1898, p. 7.
42. Ibid., 27 October 1900, p. 8; 8 July 1902, p. 8. For methodological issues: D. Tanner, 'Elections, Statistics and the Rise of the Labour Party, 1906–1931', *HJ*, 34, 4 (1991), 905; Brodie, *Politics of the Poor*, introduction, ch. 3 and appendix 4.
43. *East London Advertiser*, 31 October 1903, p. 8.
44. *Jewish Chronicle*, 6 November 1903, p. 26.
45. Pelling, *Social Geography*, p. 46; C. T. Husbands, 'East End Racism 1900–1980: Geographical Continuities in Vigilantist and Extreme Right-wing Political Behaviour', *London Journal*, 8, 1 (1982), 9.
46. *Jewish Chronicle*, 12 October 1900, p. 7, quoted J. Garrard, *The English and Immigration 1880–1910* (London, 1971), p. 118.
47. Garrard, *English and Immigration*, pp. 113–19: G. Alderman, *The Jewish Community in British Politics* (Oxford, 1983).
48. *East London Advertiser*, 14 August 1886, p. 5; *Eastern Post*, 20 July 1895, p. 5; *Jewish Chronicle*, 13 January 1905, p.10; *East London Advertiser*, 27 July 1889, p. 6; 12 March 1898, p. 8; D. Dainow, 'The Jewish Vote', *East London Advertiser*, 1 January 1910, p. 8.
49. *Eastern Post*, 6 October 1900, p. 4.
50. *Jewish Chronicle*, March 7, 1902, p. 6, letter.
51. D. Feldman, *Englishmen and Jews: Social Relations and Political Culture 1840–1914* (London, 1994), p. 386; Alderman, *Jewish Community*, p. 45.
52. *East London Advertiser*, 14 August 1886, p. 5.
53. H. McLeod, *Class and Religion in the Late Victorian City* (London, 1974), pp. 57–8.
54. *East London Advertiser*, 27 July 1895, p. 8.
55. Stedman Jones, *Outcast London*, pp. 184–5.
56. The Peabody Trust buildings in Shadwell: *Life*, 1st series, 3, pp. 49–50.
57. Booth MSS B350, p. 227.
58. New Tower and Old Tower Buildings, Wapping Polling District, St. George's-in-the-East Division Electoral Register 1892.
59. M. Brodie, 'Voting in the Victorian and Edwardian East End of London', *PH*, 23, 2 (2004), 238–40, 245–6.
60. Booth, *Life*, 1st series, 3, pp. 31–41, and ibid., p. 26; cf. M. Tebbutt, *Women's Talk?: A Social History of 'Gossip' in Working-class Neighbourhoods* (Aldershot, 1995), p. 59.
61. Quoted R. O'Day, 'Katherine Buildings', in R. Finnegan and M. Drake (eds) *From Family Tree to Family History* (Cambridge, 1994), p. 146.
62. See S. C. Williams, 'Religious Belief and Popular Culture: a Study of the South London Borough of Southwark c.1880–1939', unpublished D.Phil thesis, (University of Oxford, 1993), pp. 80–4.

63. J. E. Thorold Rogers, 'Confessions of a Metropolitan Member', *The Contemporary Review*, 51, May 1887, pp. 688–9.
64. Booth MSS B171, p. 20, Rev. W. Daniel, Coverdale Chapel, Limehouse; B223, p. 15, Rev. T. Sissons, Wycliffe Chapel, Commercial Road; B182, p. 45, Rev. A. E. Dalton, St. Dunstan's, Stepney; B169, p. 35, Rev. F. H. Dinnis, St. Peter's, Mile End; B182, p. 5, Rev. A. Chandler, Rector of Poplar; *London City Mission Magazine*, 51, June 1886, p. 105. M. Loane, *Neighbours and Friends* (London, 1910), p. 203.
65. Loane, *Neighbours*, p. 260.
66. *Biblewomen and Nurses*, 20 (November 1903), p. 226 and 6 (April 1889), p. 71.
67. Booth MSS B175, pp. 53–5, Rev. J. Parry, Rector of Bromley, Booth MSS B175, pp. 53–5.
68. Quoted Pugh, *The Tories*, p. 53.
69. A Working Man, 'A Week of Canvassing', *Daily News*, 29 September 1885, p. 3.
70. *North Eastern Leader*, 27 October 1894, p. 3.
71. P. Hollis, *Ladies Elect: Women in English Local Government, 1865–1914* (Oxford, 1987), p. 37.
72. For the role of women: Brodie, *Politics of the Poor*, ch. 3.
73. J. Vernon, *Politics and the People: A Study in English Political Culture, c.1815–1867* (Cambridge, 1993), p. 92.
74. *Daily News*, 29 July 1908.
75. Pugh, *The Tories*, p. 53.
76. *Oxford House Magazine*, II, 7 (July 1910), p. 34.
77. Interestingly, in both the South and Centre wards the major Nonconformist churches by the end of the century were dominated by local leaderships who had gradually shifted sides through the 1880s and 1890s from Liberal to Conservative, in line with the general drift outlined earlier.
78. *East London Advertiser*, 16 September 1899, p. 8.
79. J. Mogey, *Family and Neighbourhood* (1956), pp. 107–8, quoted in Tebbutt, *Women's Talk*, p. 63.
80. H. L. Smith and V. Nash, *The Story of the Dockers' Strike*, (London [1890]), p. 42; Brodie, *Politics of the Poor*, ch. 5.
81. *East London Advertiser*, 29 August 1891, p. 8; 24 October 1891, p. 8.
82. Rogers, 'Confessions', p. 691.
83. Ibid., p. 688.
84. *London Statistics*, 23, 1912–13, p. 32.
85. Booth MSS B169, pp. 5–9 and 177–9.
86. Savage, *The Dynamics of Working-Class Politics*, pp. 108, 117.
87. This assumes an average voter turnout of around 65 per cent in those parliamentary elections in which the Conservatives did best.
88. Bebbington, 'Nonconformity and Electoral Sociology', p. 645.

9
'In Darkest Lambeth': Henry Morton Stanley and the Imperial Politics of London Unionism

Alex Windscheffel

Imperial London

The culture of imperialism permeated late Victorian and Edwardian London. As the imperial capital, the 'heart of the empire', London was a cosmopolitan, international city, governing vast swathes of the globe. The imperial nature of the city clearly distinguished Londoners from the inhabitants of other English towns and cities.[1] As Jonathan Schneer has demonstrated in his pioneering study of the 'imperial metropolis', London – its public spaces, monuments and cultural preferences, as well as its inhabitants – was closely defined and reshaped by its imperial character.[2] Recent research has elaborated the extent to which metropolis and empire were mutually constitutive and intersecting sites. Michael Port has drawn attention to the imperial nature of the capital's architecture,[3] although some politicians complained that the capital lacked the imperial grandeur of Berlin and Paris.[4] Antoinette Burton has deployed postcolonial theory to scrutinize London as an unstable site for traffic, interaction and encounter between colonizer and colonial subject, with the potential to subvert imperial hierarchies.[5] Angela Woollacott has investigated how white Australian women travelled to and negotiated the public spaces of the imperial metropolis as part of a process of self-identification.[6] Yet, few historians have addressed the influence of imperialism upon the politics of late Victorian London.

Late Victorian metropolitan politics was suffused with imperial and racialized discourses and imagery.[7] The writer and intellectual Edward Dicey considered that 'Londoners are influenced by the *genus loci* of the city in which they dwell. In the very air they breathe there is a certain savour of imperialism'.[8] The use of the languages of imperialism, by Tories in particular, was commonplace. One Conservative candidate in 1885 urged Londoners to think of the 'native races who long and sigh in vain for the English flag and English trade and civilisation to come among them'.[9] Another candidate proclaimed confidently that 'no man can be a Radical who has travelled east of Aden'.[10] Ever since the resounding success of jingo demonstrations in the City of London in 1878, Conservatives had enjoyed political dividends in the metropolis by affirming the intersection of local and imperial interests.[11] For Conservatives, imperial pageants such as Queen Victoria's Golden Jubilee in 1887 celebrated the bonds between the metropolis and empire.[12] The *Morning Post* held that the Jubilee was less a national celebration than 'an imperial ceremony', demonstrating that 'London is not only the capital of Great Britain but is also the metropolis of an Empire which has its provinces in every part of the globe'.[13] In addition, in a leading article published in the triumphant aftermath of the 1900 'khaki' election, the *Daily Telegraph* exulted:

> The first city of the empire, London was the pioneer of the imperial sentiment in home politics. London was the earliest of the great civic communities ... to break away from the little Liberalism, and to set the example for what has been called the revolt of the boroughs. London, in perceiving the true spirit and tendency of Radical foreign policy from the outset, was not behind ... but was in front of the provinces.[14]

But this Conservative-voting imperial metropolis needed to be actively constructed and defended. The predominant Conservative vision of the imperial metropolis regularly emphasized the material and spiritual benefits that empire brought to London, celebrated the imperial birthrights and responsibilities of its inhabitants, and likened the city to the splendours of imperial Rome. In a widely circulated speech at St. James Hall in June 1892, Arthur Balfour delivered a calculated response to a speech given by Gladstone to the London Liberal and Radical Union the previous week. The Liberal leader had declared that 'London is justified in taking to some extent a London view of public affairs', and pledged his support for registration reform, the taxation of ground landlords, the unification of metropolitan government, and the satisfaction of labour questions.[15] Balfour, however, informed his audience that:

> If London is anything, it is an Imperial city, and it is bound to take an Imperial view – not a London view of London affairs, but an Imperial

view of Imperial affairs. London has its interests bound up with the prosperity and health of the whole of the Empire ... with the sanctity of contracts, in the security of trade, in the greatness of the Empire, in the strength of your foreign policy. Let [Londoners] recognise that important as these municipal affairs may be, there are yet affairs in which they are yet more closely concerned, and those affairs are the prosperity, the security and the greatness of the Empire of which London is the head.[16]

Balfour's response was, at least, a more positive valuation of London's role in the empire than that offered at a speech in Limehouse in July 1889 by Lord Salisbury, who implored his audience with characteristic optimism: 'Just conceive what London would be without the empire ... a collection of multitudes, without employment, without industrial life, sinking down into misery and decay.'[17]

Nonetheless, the languages of imperialism remained a contestable terrain in the late Victorian metropolis. One Liberal paper, for example, appealed to anti-imperialist sentiment in 1885 by complaining that Tory candidates 'care not what iniquities are perpetrated abroad in the British name', and were always 'ready to talk about imperial interests but fight shy of home questions'.[18] Likewise, on the eve of the inaugural metropolitan borough council elections in 1900, Lord Rosebery reminded voters that 'the Empire is not South Africa alone, or Canada alone, or Australia alone, or India alone. The heart of the empire is Britain, and the heart of Britain is London'.[19]

The ties between London Conservatism and empire were more than merely imaginative. A sizeable proportion of late Victorian Conservative MPs for London had experienced colonial administration or service, as the history of two seats exemplifies. The MP for Kensington North between 1885 and his defeat in 1892 was the oleaginous Roper Lethbridge, one-time Press Commissioner for India; the seat was regained for the party in 1895 by William Sharpe, a member of the Ceylon Legislative Council. In Hackney Central, Lewis Pelly, formerly Lieutenant-General of the Indian Staff Corps, was elected in 1886 and succeeded by Andrew Scoble, erstwhile Advocate-General for Bombay. However, the politician who most visibly and visually identified late Victorian Conservatism with empire was the Parsi barrister Sir Mancherjee Merwanjee Bhownaggree. A native of Bombay, a journalist, lawyer, and agent to the Thakore of Bhavnagar, Bhownaggree was selected as the Unionist candidate for Bethnal Green North-East in early 1895, and ousted the veteran radical George Howell in July. 'I was kicked out by a black man, by a stranger from India', complained an incredulous Howell.[20] Bhownaggree was to retain his seat five years later with an increased majority of 379 votes.[21] 'A sincere believer in Imperial unity',[22] Bhownaggree represented, for Unionists at least, the propitious embodiment of the essential unity of interests between India and Britain, between Bethnal Green and the Empire. 'I can assure you that my whole life and interest is bound up with the Empire', he reassured his electors.[23] Bhownaggree's candidacy also offered Londoners a more optimistic version of India's role within the Empire than that suggested by the veteran Indian nationalist Dadabhai Naoroji, who had been elected as a Liberal for the Clerkenwell division of Finsbury in 1892 by just five votes.[24] Both Bhownaggree and Naoroji are best viewed as hybrid subjects, holding intermeshing Indian and British identities, and claiming to speak simultaneously for their constituents and for India.

The most renowned of the Unionist metropolitan candidates to lay claim to the politics of imperialism was the journalist and explorer Henry Morton Stanley, who contested the constituency of Lambeth North in 1892 and 1895. A detailed consideration of Stanley's campaigns – previously overlooked[25] – provides us with the opportunity to interrogate the recycling of imperial discourses into the domesticated and localized contexts of the metropolis, and to revisit the controversies over the methods and purposes of late Victorian imperialism.

Henry Morton Stanley, William Booth and imperial London

Stanley's candidature represented a notable coup for the Unionist party. Stanley – as *Bula Matari*, or the 'breaker of rocks' – was one of the best known and certainly the most self-consciously 'modern' of the Victorian explorers of Africa. As Sidney Low wrote upon his death in 1904, 'the map of Africa is a monument to Stanley ... he is the great – we may say the final – systematiser of African geography'.[26] This is not the place to rehearse in detail the familiar biographical narrative of Stanley the explorer.[27] Suffice to say that Stanley's iconic status reached its apogee in 1890 upon his return from the controversial Emin Pasha Relief Expedition of 1887–89, the fourth of his major expeditions to the continent. His return was celebrated by the 'Stanley and Africa' Exhibition at the Victoria Gallery in Regent Street, and the publication in the same year of his best-selling account of his journey, *In Darkest Africa*.[28] This text provided a repertoire of imperial tropes and images that could subsequently be applied to the metropole. As Felix Driver has written, 'the language and politics of exploration abroad were recycled in the context of debates over social policy at home as the frontiers of geographical knowledge were mapped onto the heart of the empire'.[29] Stanley's title was in turn self-consciously appropriated by General William Booth of the Salvation Army, in his sensationalist book, also published in 1890, *In Darkest England and the Way Out*. Booth's work of purported social investigation into the degraded conditions of the metropolitan poor was divided into two parts: 'Darkness' and 'Deliverance'. The text began by recalling Stanley's desperate ordeals in the Ituri rain forests:

> But while brooding over the awful presentation of life as it exists in the vast African forest, it seemed to me only too vivid a picture of many parts of our own land. As there is a darkest Africa, is there not also a darkest England? Civilisation, which can breed its own barbarians, does it not also breed its own pygmies? May we not find a parallel at our own doors, and discover within a stone's throw of our cathedrals and palaces similar horrors to those which Stanley has found existing in the great Equatorial forest?

The indomitable methods of Stanley's expedition needed to be transferred to the evangelical domestic mission, for as Booth exclaimed: 'Talk about Stanley and Emin! There is not one of us but has an Emin somewhere or other in the heart of Darkest England, whom he ought to sally forth to rescue.'[30] This usage of sensationalist imperial imagery was hardly novel: in his *How the Poor Live* of 1883, for instance, George Sims ventured into 'a dark continent that is within easy walking distance of the General Post Office'; whilst upon arrival in the East End, the journalist Henry Mayhew had imagined himself 'in a new land and among another race'.[31] Nor was such imagery uncontested. The socialist leader Henry Hyndman, for instance, regretted Booth's connection with 'the canting and murderous filibuster Stanley' and ridiculed 'the grotesque fetishism of the Salvation Army, with its strange semi-barbarous songs and dances'.[32] Nonetheless, Booth's text helped to reiterate and reassert the familiar, symbiotic identification between the empire and the metropolis following Stanley's triumphant return to London in April 1890.

'In Darkest Lambeth'

Stanley came forward in June 1892 to contest Lambeth North as a Liberal Unionist. His opponent was an Alderman Coldwells, once a gardener and now an outfitter in Croydon, where he served on both the School Board and newly incorporated borough. North Lambeth was a decidedly working-class constituency, including, in the words of one Liberal newspaper, the 'least hopeful, least ambitious, and most depressed classes of London workers'.[33] On the surface, this was unpromising terrain for a celebrity candidate. Stanley was a last-minute replacement for the sitting Tory MP, General Charles Fraser, 'the representative', according to the radical *Star*, 'of half-pay army officers', the paper adding laconically that 'there are no half-pay army officers in North Lambeth'.[34] Fraser had been induced to retire in Stanley's favour largely at the instigation of Sir Henry Doulton, owner of the local pottery works and chairman of the Lambeth Conservative Association.[35]

Stanley's autobiography and journals shed little light upon the motivations behind his curious candidacy. It would appear that he stood largely at the behest of his new, younger wife, the artist Dorothy Tennant, whom he had married at the height of his renown in 1890, in the 'event of the season',[36] and who was anxious to prevent her husband's return to the Congo.[37] However, Stanley's avowed Liberal Unionism is an important marker. For Stanley, politics should concern itself primarily with the exegetic elaboration of the imperial ideal. His political role model, unsurprisingly given his antipathy to Home Rule, was Joseph Chamberlain, that archetypal political man of action.[38] It is also no coincidence that among the members of the Emin Pasha Relief committee, which had organized and financed Stanley's expedition, were the London Unionists Lewis Pelly and William Burdett-Coutts, MP for Westminster.

Stanley presented himself in his election address 'not as a partisan' but, as befitting his reputation for heroic exploits, as 'a man deeply, vitally concerned; a man who at least has based his opinions upon practical and personal conversance with great and difficult affairs'. He declared his 'one mastering desire' to be 'the maintenance, the spread, the dignity, the usefulness of the British Empire', and continued that 'in all my wanderings, I have seen no power so great and so beneficent as the British Empire ... I believe that we Englishmen are working out the greatest destiny which any race has ever fulfilled'.[39] Elsewhere, he argued that indigenous trades in North Lambeth – india-rubber, pottery and varnish – would benefit immeasurably from imperial expansion and exploitation.[40] Whilst Stanley did not ignore domestic issues or social reforms, his chosen palliative in fact has an echo of William Booth's ambitious schemes for state-aided emigration for the casualized poor. 'I cannot but feel that the destiny of the English working classes depends in the last resort ... on enterprises of a larger scope', he declared on one occasion, observing that in the Highlands of Africa 'there is room, and to spare, for some twenty millions of happy and prosperous people'.[41]

The campaign was accompanied by the heavily gendered discourses and metaphors of geography and exploration. Following the announcement of Fraser's usurpation, the *Star* newspaper gleefully remarked that 'the great explorer invaded the place'; later the paper sneered that, in English politics, the explorer was 'as ignorant as an African babe unborn'.[42] Stanley was accompanied throughout by placards proclaiming 'Mr Stanley the great African explorer'.[43] He advocated that all MPs should take a year's sabbatical to better acquaint themselves with the colonies; and when asked his opinion upon the eight-hour day, he reportedly retorted that 'if he had worked 8 hours a day he would never have been ahead of the Germans in Africa. He would never have added 200,000 square miles of territory to this country'.[44]

The short but tumultuous election campaign seems to have been an ordeal for Stanley, whose wife later admitted: 'We were quite ignorant of electioneering, and I must say had a dreadful ten days of it.'[45] At a meeting at Hawkeston Hall on 29 June, Stanley was shouted down, the platform was stormed in 'a dastardly attack', and the door on his getaway carriage torn off.[46] As his wife later commented: 'Stanley was much disgusted: African savages, he thought, would have behaved better.'[47] Dorothy Stanley was constantly by his side during the campaign. On one occasion she burst into tears, jumped onto the platform and yelled melodramatically: 'When all of you and I are dead and forgotten, the name of Stanley will live.'[48] However, Stanley's failure to face down, or even acknowledge, the tumultuous rituals of the politics of disruption, and his dependence upon the presence of his wife, were presented by his opponents as abandoning the codes of heroic, physical manliness that he had exhibited in Africa. As one Liberal paper remarked disparagingly: 'However used he may be to pacifying quarrelsome African chiefs and settling in a rough-and-ready, but scarcely diplomatic manner, differences of opinion with the natives along the Congo, [he] is certainly not accustomed to the "heckling" which obtains so largely in civilized communities on the eve of a general election.'[49]

For Unionists, Stanley was the subjugator of nature, the conqueror of Africa, the personification of the reciprocal nexus between metropolitan and imperial destinies. In a leader entitled 'Bravo Stanley', the Conservative *South London Mail* celebrated the explorer as the idealized imperial man,[50] possessing heroic, masculine, and resolutely martial qualities, declaring him a 'maker of history ... a child of Destiny ... and 'a modern Ulyssis [sic]'. Commending the 'statesman who has almost single-handedly built up and successfully governed a state' permitted a stark contrast with his opponent, 'a retired vendor of shoddy', who would 'make an incongruous figure in the Imperial Senate'.[51] Doulton lionized Stanley as 'the man who found Livingstone and enjoyed his friendship, who opened up the Congo river and laid the foundations of a great state ... [and] the man who has done more than anyone to destroy the accursed slave trade', a controversial claim in the light of revelations about Stanley's employment of Zanzibari slave labour during the Emin Pasha expedition.[52] In an editorial, the *Evening News* used Stanley's familiar life story to remind its readers that Irish Home Rule would be an inevitable precursor to the dissolution of the wider empire:

> Mr Stanley is a Unionist by training, by experience and even constitutional necessity. He has seen the benefit of Union in the American democracy. He has lived through the war of secession ... If Ulster's trust be misplaced, what of India's? What of Australia's? ... Mr Stanley is a Unionist because his travels over a large part of the surface of the planet have demonstrated to him beyond controversy that the greatness and permanence of the British Empire depend upon the unity and solidarity of the United Kingdom. We are an imperial community in which each depends upon all and all depend upon each.[53]

The benefits of imperialism, and its constitutive centrality to metropolitan power, were self-evident in these Unionist discourses, drawing upon binary racialized understandings of colonial difference, dominance and subordination. This is not to suggest, however, that the use of imperial discourses went unquestioned within Unionist ranks. One of Stanley's fiercest critics was Robert Fowler, a Quaker and leading figure in the humanitarian Aborigines Protection Society, who was also the senior Conservative MP for the City of London seat. In 1878, Fowler had claimed that Stanley's 'heartless butchery of unfortunate natives' had 'brought dishonour on the British flag';[54] and in December 1890 he chaired the large public meeting of the Society at the Westminster Palace Hotel, at which Stanley was roundly condemned. Likewise, the *Saturday Review* commented of African exploration in 1889 that 'it is pretty certain that things have been worse, not better, during the 30 or 40 years of exploration which have turned the old huge blank on the maps into a thickly occupied maze of tribes and rivers and lakes.'[55]

The Emin Pasha expedition and critiques of Stanley

As Felix Driver has demonstrated, Stanley had been a controversial figure since the 1870s. His journalistic despatches about the violent 'chastisement' of the natives of Bumbiri, leaving 42 natives dead in his wake, appeared in the *Daily Telegraph*, generating a protest by Colonel Henry Yule and Henry Hyndman at the Royal Geographical Society.[56] Stanley's candidature as a Liberal Unionist in 1892 served to re-open and politicize the bitter controversies that had accompanied Stanley's triumphant return from the Emin Pasha expedition in 1890, serving to indicate the ways in which prevailing Unionist notions of imperialism were in fact fiercely contested in London.[57] For its supporters, the Emin Pasha mission was, as Sir John Scott Keltie put it, 'the most remarkable expedition that ever entered Africa', bestowing an enduring greatness upon the explorer.[58] Comparing his achievements to those of Drake, Hawkins and Raleigh, the *Evening News* hailed Stanley as 'the man who has made it possible to establish an empire in the Africa he has traversed'.[59]

However, the publication later in 1890 of the posthumous diaries of the officers whom Stanley had left in charge of the ill-starred Rear-Column at Yambuya, James Jameson and Edmund Barttelot – son of the Conservative MP for Horsham – offered revelatory alternative narratives of the expedition to compete with the sanitized official version provided by *Darkest Africa*, irreparably damaging Stanley's reputation.[60] Critics, including prominent metropolitan radicals, now rushed into print to challenge the heroic self-presentation of the explorer. In a reversal of the language of darkness, one reviewer opined that 'Stanley has triumphed, but central Africa is darker than ever.'[61] Henry Fox Bourne, secretary of the Aborigines Protection Society, published a lengthy polemic, which decried the 'empire-making errand', detailed the 'morally indefensible' human cost of the expedition, and denounced Stanley's dependence upon the notorious Arab slave-trader Tippu Tib, thus implying his complicity in perpetuating the trade.[62] Sidney Webb published a small pamphlet entitled 'The Stanley craze', presenting the expedition as 'nothing more than a huge land-grabbing commercial speculation, utterly unredeemed by any humane purpose and philanthropic feelings',[63] whilst John Burns denounced Stanley at the London County Council as 'the buccaneer of the Congo'.[64] In similar vein, the Socialist D. J. Nicoll bitterly portrayed Stanley as a 'modern commercial hero', whose journeys across Africa 'can be traced ... by a blood-red trail strewn with corpses'. Nicoll disputed Stanley's 'gospel of enterprise' for Africa, pointing out that capitalism had been accompanied in Britain by unhealthy factories, degrading poverty, and low wages, warning that 'the beautiful land of Uganda will not be greatly improved by being turned into a manufacturing district after the model of our Black Country'.[65]

For his many opponents then, Henry Morton Stanley had become the personification of the self-promoting, selfish and violent tendencies of the 'new imperialism', based on conquest, appropriation and exploitation. During the electoral campaign, Stanley was characterized as 'the representative of African plunderers', and accused of seeking parliamentary representation 'to promote filibustering expeditions to Africa'.[66] To his opponents, he was a *conquistador*, 'a champion of raw jingoism',[67] who had, as Coldwells put it, 'subordinated humanity to commercial interests'.[68] The outraged Nonconformist conscience now rallied around a manifesto issued by Reverend Arthur Jephson, Burns and Fox-Bourne, which melodramatically accused Stanley of having his 'hands dyed in the blood of the African', and implored 'all those whose moral sensibility is keen, and whose intellect cannot be dazzled by the glare of swashbuckling adventure' to condemn his candidacy.[69] To cue, the Liberal press eagerly and feverishly rounded upon the explorer. The *South London Press* accused Stanley of 'ruthless disregard for the comfort and the lives of his white companions, his black assistants, and especially the natives of the lands through which he passed'.[70] Likewise, the *Daily Chronicle* castigated the terrible 'butcher's bill in black human flesh', vividly proclaiming that 'the crack of the rifle and the shriek of the dying native have been the music to which Mr Stanley's African fantasias have been set'.[71] In addition, the *Star* reminded its readers of the punitive incidents at Bumbiri in August 1875:

> We have from his own pen a record of slaughter and blood-guiltiness which may well give pause to the Christian electors of North Lambeth. These were murderous operations against unarmed savages ... Stanley is never tired of telling the doughty deeds of that elephant-rifle ... Brave Stanley! The explorer might as well have gone out with his elephant rifle against a flock of sheep.[72]

Stanley's critics occasionally attempted to draw parallels between their allegations and the quotidian concerns of the citizens of imperial London. Coldwells's agent cautioned Stanley that the men of North Lambeth 'could not be dealt with exactly in the way the blacks were treated on the banks of the Congo'.[73] Meanwhile, Henrietta Colenso, daughter of the outspoken former Bishop of Natal, warned her audience: 'Men who, believing in might rather than right, disregarded the rights of Africans would do the same, if they could, in the case of whites.'[74]

Although Stanley had recently taken an oath of allegiance and re-naturalized as a British citizen, Liberals argued that, with his 'Yankee bounce',[75] he was ignorant of the rituals of British civic life and culture; 'a stranger and a sojourner in our midst', as one paper opined.[76] Not only were Stanley's claims as an authentic British citizen questioned, but so too his credentials as a genuine explorer. The *Daily Chronicle* for instance declared that 'he is – *tout simplement* – a journalist who has taken the interior of Africa as a good subject for descriptive articles'.[77] To this end, the memory of David Livingstone was calculatingly evoked and foregrounded during the election campaign in order to discredit and denigrate Stanley. As Felix Driver has rightly observed of Stanley's critics within the Royal Geographical Society: 'to them ... Stanley was everything that Livingstone was not'.[78] Morally uplifting memorializations – largely imaginary, of course – of Livingstone's life as an African missionary, living in peaceful harmony with obedient, child-like natives, sought thereby to discredit Stanley's methods. Coldwells contrasted the 'intrepid spirit', the 'noblest motives' and the 'goodness' of Livingstone, with 'the man who had used deadly weapons against noble savages, not in the cause of civilization, but in the interests of trade'.[79] According to the *Daily Chronicle*, 'Livingstone lived and died in peace and friendship with the wild men whom he vainly sought to win to a higher civilization', whereas Stanley's expeditions heralded 'an evil and ominous departure in African exploration'. The paper added cuttingly that 'his voluminous books on Africa would be gladly exchanged for one fresh page from the wondrous record of Livingstone's lifelong martyrdom and splendid zeal for knowledge and truth'.[80] According to such accounts, Stanley had distorted and betrayed the legacy bequeathed by Livingstone, thus perverting the noble and legitimate – and implicitly liberal and civilizing – purposes of imperialism.[81]

In the event, Lambeth North was lost to the Unionist cause by 130 votes, prompting the *Star* to rejoice that 'the nigger-slayer has been knocked down by the Liberal ballot papers as surely as the exploring adventurer used to pot the natives of Africa with "elephant bullets" '.[82] The Conservative-leaning *South London Observer* felt that Stanley had suffered from 'overconfidence in his fame', and wryly observed that 'he must now realize that it is far easier to penetrate an African forest than the thick sconce of a London radical'.[83] Nonetheless, Stanley was persuaded by his wife to remain the Unionist candidate for Lambeth North, although with the proviso that he would never be expected to undertake what he described as 'silly personal canvassing' or to 'put myself in the position where I can be baited like a bull in the ring'.[84] Indeed, his autobiography relates only one public appearance in Lambeth before the next general election, at a smoking-concert in November 1893.[85]

Lambeth conquered: The 1895 election

The 1895 contest consisted largely of a reiteration of the same controversies concerning the legitimacy of Stanley's African journeys. Just as in 1892, when Stanley was represented as 'a British working man who has proved himself the equal of kings',[86] Stanley declared on the stump that 'I have earned my living' and was 'one of themselves, a man of their own ranks'.[87] This careful self-positioning as a humble populist, informed by first-hand experience, and practice of conducting himself in a 'frank, fearless and gentlemanly way', could additionally be contrasted with his young aristocratic opponent, Charles Trevelyan, 'who had never done a day's manual labour in his life'.[88]

This time, in his election address, Stanley placed greater emphasis upon the practical economic benefits conferred upon the metropolis by Africa, which he depicted as an 'unexhausted treasure house'; 'we should no longer shirk our duties towards our new African possessions', he continued, adding that Britain 'in the performance of her duties to virgin Africa' might find 'that the long day of her world-ingathering Empire has only just begun.'[89] The Conservative metropolitan press reiterated this appeal to economic self-interest, emphasizing the reciprocity between imperialism and metropolitan economic prosperity, jobs and higher wages. As the *South London Mail* declared: 'The man who finds new markets for our commerce will do more to solve the vexed question of the unemployed than all the socialistic proposals put together can ever achieve'.[90] Intriguingly, if rather tenuously, one editorial in the *News of the World* sought to shift the geography of Stanley's achievements away from King Leopold's Congo State, a site now witnessing the stirrings of philanthropic disquiet,[91] and towards the Cape Colony and Cecil Rhodes's Chartered Company:

> To Mr Stanley we owe probably the nation's wealthiest possession. To him we owe the power we hold in Africa; to him we owe millions of money that has flowed into London during the last two years; to him we owe the untold wealth that has risen to us out of the diamond mines of Kimberley; to him we owe the wealthy colony which will preserve England's vitality for generations to come; to him we owe

the reality which has been opened to us as the greatest romances of Rider Haggard. There is no denying that, but for the pluck, energy, endurance and indomitable courage of H. M. Stanley, England would not be the power that she is in South Africa.[92]

Stanley was also supported by the widely reported visit to the constituency of Joseph Chamberlain, who argued that Gladstone had betrayed the Liberal party's ancient attachment to empire. For Chamberlain, Stanley had 'done more for British trade, for the British workman, and therefore for the prosperity of the United Kingdom' than the entire outgoing Gladstonian administration; his name was a 'household word across the civilised world', to be celebrated as 'one of the greatest of our modern pioneers and explorers, which should commend him to any working-class constituency'.[93]

Once again, as in 1892, Stanley's opponents sought to combat him by articulating alternative, liberal narratives of empire. The *Star* countered Unionist rhetoric about the economic benefits of Africa to London by denouncing Stanley as the 'African freebooter' who had 'got a million pounds out of the country already, which is nice for his backers, but not very useful to North Lambeth'.[94] The *Daily Chronicle* challenged Stanley's claims for his contribution to geographical knowledge by declaring that 'his books are largely worthless as scientific documents; the volume of his actual discoveries is small'. The paper added that his explorations had brought 'no benefit to the English working man' as 'the part of it to which much material use attaches was devoted to the service of the Belgians and the Congo State'.[95] Trevelyan sought to subvert not only Stanley's claims to worldly experience, dismissing him as 'an old grey-haired man', but also the utility of African exploration to the citizens of the metropolis, telling his opponent: 'your life has been spent in Africa; your knowledge is of Africa, and not of England'.[96] None of this is to suggest that the furious moral critique of Stanley was absent from the 1895 campaign. Trevelyan implored the voters of Lambeth to 'avenge the wrongs done to poor Africans',[97] whilst the *Daily Chronicle* again denounced Stanley's 'cruelty and vindictiveness', concluding that 'there is no candidate ... who has less right to ask for the suffrages of those who love not only their native land, but their fellow men of all races, white or black'.[98] According to the *Star*, Stanley's expeditions 'illustrate the methods of the modern African explorers', adding that his 'reckless disregard for human life' rendered him a natural supporter of the ' "don't hesitate to shoot" policy for Ireland'.[99] But this time, Stanley's opponents could not prevent him from gaining Lambeth

North by a majority of 405 in the Unionist landslide of 1895, on a swing of some 5.1 per cent. Befitting his self-image as a man of action rather than of words, Stanley despised his five-year term in parliament. He spoke rarely, resented the regular demands of his Lambeth constituents, and deplored 'the criminal waste of precious time' and 'devotion to antique customs' of parliamentary life.[100]

Conclusions: Conservatism and imperial politics

The candidacy of Henry Morton Stanley highlights the complex imperial contexts of the political culture of late Victorian London. The political discourses of the city, just as much as its cultural preferences, its economic formations, or its built environment, were entwined with the cultures of imperialism. Issues of global, imperial reach could be mediated and articulated at the level of local politics. The emphasis by London Unionists, in particular, upon imperial messages, and upon the intersection of empire with the daily routines of Londoners, helps to explain the party's success in late Victorian parliamentary elections, culminating in the 1900 election, aptly described by one despairing Liberal as a 'festival of triumphant khaki'.[101]

This insistence upon the imperial nature of their cityscape became one means by which Conservatives sought to counter the increasingly vocal Liberal rhetoric for metropolitan self-government – or 'Home Rule for London' – in the early 1890s. As Henry Doulton argued: 'We wanted men such as Stanley in parliament to represent imperial interests ... local interests were important but imperial interests were vital.'[102] In a similar vein, when juxtaposed against Stanley's imperialist credentials, the *South London Mail* could remark that Alderman Coldwells, 'however fitted to adorn a local vestry, must make an incongruous figure in the Imperial Senate'.[103] We might also conclude that, paradoxically, the imperial dimensions of London Unionism help to explain the party's seeming inability to find a role in municipal and local politics following the creation of the London County Council in 1888.[104]

Yet, Stanley's 1892 defeat should serve as a reminder that the politics of imperialism could be a fiercely contested terrain. The languages of imperialism were not after all a Conservative monopoly, but could be challenged and undermined by liberal and radical opponents. Indeed, it is possible to trace the continuities between the languages of the 1890s and the anti-war movement which emerged after the outbreak of hostilities with the Boers in 1899. In the reactions of metropolitan radicals to Henry Morton Stanley discussed in this chapter, an additional argument about economic exploitation was bolted on to the traditional moral and humanitarian critique of Conservative imperialism – or 'Beaconsfieldism' – which had first been enunciated during Gladstone's Midlothian campaigns of the late 1870s. Liberal representations of Stanley as a buccaneering and exploitative freebooter anticipate the critiques of imperial adventurism articulated by the pro-Boers a decade later, especially in the writings of J. A. Hobson.[105] Nicoll's concluding plea, 'let us get our own house in order first before we talk of "civilising" others',[106] also significantly foreshadows the diagnoses of Edwardian New Liberal social reformers, who tended to depict imperialism as a demoralizing, primitive force that distracted attention from the urgent social and moral reforms required to improve the unknowable, physically degenerate metropolis.[107] As such, the Second Boer War may be less of a discontinuity in the politics of imperialism than is usually assumed.

The American political scientist, A. L. Lowell, in his *Government of England* (1908), concluded that 'the capital of an empire is naturally imperialistic'.[108] Yet, Stanley's contentious candidature demonstrates that this reading of London politics is too deterministic. The fashioning of a Conservative-voting imperial metropolis in the years after 1874 involved a complex process of mediation between politicians and electorate. As a result, the nature of both the empire, and London's role within it, needed to be continually interpreted, redefined and reworked. As Stanley's defeat in 1892 suggests, for all the electoral benefits that an association with imperialism could bring to the Conservative party, this was far from an unproblematic process.

Notes

1. London was thus closer to Glasgow and Belfast than provincial English cities: J. MacKenzie, ' "The Second City of the Empire": Glasgow – Imperial Municipality', in F. Driver and D. Gilbert (eds) *Imperial Cities: Landscape, Display and Identity* (Manchester, 1999), pp. 215–37; idem, 'Empire and National Identities: The Case of Scotland', *TRHS*, 6th series, VIII (1998), 221–7. For a provincial example (Birmingham): C. Hall, *Civilising Subjects: Metropole and Colony in the English Imagination 1830–1867* (Oxford, 2002), pp. 265–433.
2. J. Schneer, *London 1900: the Imperial Metropolis* (New Haven, 1999) esp. pp. 3–14, 93–115, 259–63: his definition of 'London' excludes suburban districts.
3. M. Port, *Imperial London: Civil Government Building in London, 1850–1915* (London, 1995); Schneer, *London 1900*, pp. 17–36.
4. *West London Observer*, 17 July 1896, William Bull.
5. A. Burton, *At the Heart of the Empire: Indians and the Colonial Encounter in Late-Victorian Britain* (Berkeley, 1998) esp. pp. 1–23; idem, 'Making a Spectacle of

Empire: Indian Travellers in *Fin-de-Siècle* London', *HWJ*, XLII (1996), 127–46. R. Visram, *Ayahs, Lascars and Princes: Indians in Britain 1700–1947* (London, 1986).
6. A. Woollacott, *To Try her Fortune in London: Australian Women, Colonialism and Modernity* (Oxford, 2001), esp. pp. 47–65.
7. J. Marriott, *Metropolis, India and Progress in the Colonial Imagination* (Manchester, 2003).
8. E. Dicey, 'The Triumph of Conservatism', *Quarterly Review*, 182, October (1895), 538–67.
9. *South London Press*, 5 September 1885 (Henry Kimber, Wandsworth).
10. *Eastern Post*, 22 September 1900 (T. R. Dewar, St George's East).
11. H. Cunningham, 'The Language of Patriotism, 1750–1914', in R. Samuel (ed.) *Patriotism: the Making and Unmaking of British National Identity*, vol. 1 (London, 1989); idem, 'The Conservative Party and Patriotism', in R. Colls and P. Dodd (eds) *Englishness: Politics and Culture, 1880–1920* (London 1986), pp. 283–307.
12. *Evening News*, 22 June 1887.
13. *Morning Post*, 20 June 1887.
14. *Daily Telegraph*, 2 October 1900.
15. *Star*, 1 June 1892.
16. *Standard*, 16 June 1892, reprinted as 'London Questions', 1892/119, NUCA Pamphlets 1867–1914, Conservative Party Archive, Bodleian Library, Oxford University (X Films 63/1).
17. *Times*, 17 July 1889.
18. *South London Press*, 18 July 1885.
19. *Star*, 27 October 1900. The phrase was famously used by Charles Masterman in *The Heart of the Empire* (London, 1901). Conservatives did not entirely deny this interpretation of imperial values: *Evening News*, 20 October 1900.
20. Cited in F. M. Leventhal, *Respectable Radical: George Howell and Victorian Working-Class Politics* (London, 1971), p. 212.
21. Born in Bombay in 1851, Bhownaggree moved to London to study law in 1882. He was made a CIE in 1887, and knighted in 1897. Ousted from parliament in 1906, he served as President of the Incorporated Parsi Association of Europe until his death in 1933. John Hinnells and Omar Ralph, *Bhownaggree: Member of Parliament, 1895–1906* (London, 1995); John Hinnells, *Zoroastrians in Britain* (Oxford 1996); Schneer, *London 1900*, pp. 240–8.
22. *Standard*, 17 July 1895.
23. *Eastern Argus*, 13 July 1895.
24. Naoroji, also a Parsi, has received far greater attention from historians than Bhownaggree. O. Ralph, *Naoroji: The First Asian MP. A Biography of Dadabhai Naoroji: India's Patriot and Britain's MP* (Hansib, 1997); Schneer, *London 1900*, ch. viii; Visram, *Ayahs*, pp. 78–92. Lalmohan Ghose stood unsuccessfully as a Liberal for Deptford in 1885 and 1886.
25. F. McLynn, *Stanley: Sorcerer's Apprentice* (London, 1991), p. 372; Obituary, *Standard*, 11 May 1904: 'In parliament, the part that Stanley played was inconspicuous'.
26. *Cornhill Magazine*, July 1904, cited in D. Stanley (ed.), *The Autobiography of Sir Henry Morton Stanley* (London, 1909), pp. 392, 394.

27. Born in 1841 in North Wales as John Rowlands, he adopted the name Stanley in 1858 upon emigration to America. His first three journeys involved his 'discovery' of Livingstone at Ujiji, Lake Tanganyika in 1871; his explorations of 1874–77 when he crossed Africa from east to west along the River Congo; and his work to establish King Leopold's Congo Free State between 1879–84. The Emin Pasha Relief Expedition of 1887–89 was the most controversial. For a sensitive account: J. L. Newman, *Imperial Footprints: Henry Morton Stanley's African Journeys* (Washington, 2004). F. McLynn, *Stanley: the Making of an African Explorer* (London, 1988); idem, *Sorcerer's Apprentice*; R. Hall, *Stanley: An Adventurer Explored* (London, 1974). Cf. J. Bierman, *Dark Safari: the Life behind the Legend of Sir Henry Morton Stanley* (New York, 1990).
28. H. M. Stanley, *In Darkest Africa – or the Quest, Rescue and Retreat of Emin, Governor of Equatoria*, 2 vols (London, 1890). T. Richards, *The Commodity Culture of Victorian England: Advertising and Spectacle, 1851–1914* (Stanford, 1990); A. Coombes, *Reinventing Africa: Museums, Material Culture, and Popular Imagination in Late Victorian and Edwardian England* (New Haven, 1994), ch. 4.
29. F. Driver, *Geography Militant: Cultures of Exploration and Empire* (Oxford, 2000), p. 23.
30. W. Booth, *In Darkest England and the Way Out* (London, 1890), pp. 11–12, 156.
31. G. Sims, *How the Poor Live*, cited P. Keating, *Into Unknown England, 1886–1913: Selections from the Social Explorers* (Glasgow, 1976); H. Mayhew, *London Labour and the London Poor*, 4 vols (London, 1861), iii, p. 233. Stanley made similar observations: *In Darkest Africa*, ii, p. 79.
32. H. M. Hyndman, *General Booth's Book Refuted*, (London, 1890) pp. 4, 11. For parallels between Stanley and Booth: Driver, *Geography Militant*, ch. 8. P. Walker, ' "I Live but not yet I for Christ Liveth in Me": Men and Masculinity in the Salvation Army, 1865–1890', in M. Roper and J. Tosh (eds) *Manful Assertions: Masculinities in Britain since 1800* (London, 1991), pp. 92–112.
33. *Daily Chronicle*, 14 June 1892.
34. *Star*, 14 June 1892.
35. *Times*, 19, 20 July 1892, for Fraser's claim he was deselected, and Doulton's refutation.
36. *Figaro*, 12 July 1890.
37. Stanley, *Autobiography*, p. 439. *Figaro*, 21 June 1890, reported Stanley would return to the Congo as Governor-General.
38. Stanley later admitted: 'I could die for Chamberlain. He says what he means to do – and why – and then he does it'. Quoted in Hall, *Stanley*, p. 377, and pp. 282–3 for Home Rule; Stanley, *Autobiography*, p. 479.
39. *Times*, 23 June 1892.
40. *Daily News*, 25 June 1892.
41. Stanley, 1892 election address, Bristol University Election Addresses Collection [BUC].
42. *Star*, 6, 19 July 1892.
43. *Daily News*, 25 June 1892.
44. *Daily Chronicle*, 28 June 1892.
45. Stanley, *Autobiography*, p. 439.
46. *Evening News*, 30 June 1892.
47. Stanley, *Autobiography*, p. 439; Hall, *Stanley*, p. 346.

48. Hall, *Stanley*, p. 346; *Daily News*, 25 June 1892.
49. *Daily News*, 30 June 1892: 'his traditional coolness and imperturbability deserted him', and mocked his 'bold buccaneer-like style of oratory'.
50. For 'imperial man': Hall, *Civilising Subjects*, pp. 23–65.
51. *South London Mail*, 25 June 1892.
52. *Daily Chronicle*, 2 July 1892.
53. 'Stanley for North Lambeth', *Evening News*, 23 June 1892.
54. Cited in H. L. Malchow, *Gentlemen Capitalists: the Social and Political World of the Victorian Businessman* (London, 1991), p. 240.
55. *Saturday Review*, 6 April 1889.
56. Driver, *Geography Militant*, pp. 131–8; H. Yule and H. M. Hyndman, *Mr Henry Stanley and the Royal Geographical Society: Being the Record of a Protest* (London, 1878); *Saturday Review*, 16 February 1878.
57. For reactions to the Emin Pasha expedition, Driver, *Geography Militant*, ch. 6; idem, 'Stanley and his Critics: Geography, Exploration and Empire', *P & P*, 133 (1991), 134–66. See also McLynn, *Stanley*, ch. 19.
58. J. S. Keltie, 'What Stanley has Done for the Map of Africa', *Contemporary Review* 57 (January 1890), 130.
59. *Evening News*, 26 April 1890.
60. Sir W. Barttelot (ed.), *The Life of Edmund Musgrave Barttelot from his Letters and Diaries* (London, 1890); J. S. Jameson, *Story of the Rear Column of the Emin Pasha Relief Expedition, Edited by Mrs J. S. Jameson* (London, 1890). For other participants: A. J. Mounteney Jephson, *Emin Pasha and Rebellion at the Equator* (London, 1890); R. Troup, 'Mr Stanley's Rear-Guard', *Fortnightly Review* 48, December (1890), 817–29; H. Ward, *My Life with Stanley's Rear-Guard* (London, 1891); J. M. Konczacki (ed.), *Victorian Explorer: the African Diaries of Captain William G. Stairs, 1887–92* (Halifax 1994). C. Peters, *New Light on Dark Africa: Being the Narrative of the German Emin Pasha Expedition* (London, 1891). For a brilliant satire: F. C. Burnand, *A New Light Thrown Across (the Keep-it-Quiet) Darkest Africa* (London, 1890). *Star*, 'The Stanley Boom and Bubble', 8 November 1890.
61. Anon., 'Stanley's Expedition: a Retrospect', *Fortnightly Review*, 47 (January 1890), 96. See also E. L. Godkin, 'Was the Emin Expedition Piratical?', *Forum* 10 (1890), 633–44.
62. H. R. Fox Bourne, *The Other Side of the Emin Pasha Relief Expedition* (London, 1891), pp. 195, 196, 200.
63. S. Webb, *The Stanley Craze: or the True Story of the Quest and Rescue of Emin Pasha* (London, n.d.).
64. *Evening News*, 15 January 1890. George Bernard Shaw denounced Stanley: *Captain Brassbound's Conversion* (London, 1899).
65. D. J. Nicoll, *Stanley's Exploits: or Civilising Africa* (Aberdeen, 1891), pp. 3, 13, 21–2.
66. *Star*, 6 July, 25 June 1892.
67. *South London Press*, 2 July 1892.
68. Ibid., 25 June 1892. cf. Driver, *Geography Militant*, pp. 138–43.
69. For the full manifesto: *Daily News*, 5 July 1892.
70. *South London Press*, 9 July 1892.
71. *Daily Chronicle*, 30 June 92.
72. 'Out Stanley, Out'; *Star*, 2 July 1892.

73. *South London Press*, 25 June 1892. Cf. a poem in *Star*, 11 July 1895: 'Chaps that make black slaves o' niggers / Want to make white slaves of you'.
74. *South London Press*, 2 July 1892. For the controversies involving Bishop Colenso in the 1860s, see D. Lorimer, *Colour, Class and the Victorians* (Leicester, 1978).
75. *Star*, 6 July 1892.
76. *Daily Chronicle*, 30 June 1892 – a familiar theme in representations of Stanley; cf. Driver, *Geography Militant*, pp. 121, 127–31; cf. also J. Conrad, 'Geography and Some Explorers', *National Geographic Magazine* 45, March (1924), 237–74.
77. *Daily Chronicle*, 30 June 1892.
78. Driver, *Geography Militant*, 143.
79. *South London Press*, 25 June 1892.
80. *Daily Chronicle*, 30 June 1892.
81. For Stanley's defence, Yule and Hyndman, *Stanley*, pp. 38–9.
82. *Star*, 6 July 1895.
83. *South London Observer*, 9 July 1892.
84. Stanley, *Autobiography*, 403.
85. Ibid., pp. 445, 455.
86. *South London Mail*, 25 June 1892.
87. *South London Press*, 13 July 1895; Stanley, 1892 election address, BUC.
88. *South London Mail*, 13 July 1895.
89. Stanley, 1895 election address, BUC.
90. *South London Mail*, 20 July 1895.
91. A. Hochschild, *King Leopold's Ghost: a Story of Greed, Terror, and Heroism in Colonial Africa* (Basingstoke, 1999); W. Samarin, *The Black Man's Burden: African Colonial Labour on the Congo and Ubangi River*s (Boulder, 1989).
92. *News of the World*, 14 July 1895.
93. *Standard*, 8 July 1895.
94. *Star*, 11 July 1895.
95. *Daily Chronicle*, 8 July 1895.
96. *South London Mail*, 6 July 1895.
97. *Daily Chronicle*, 15 July 1895; 10 July 1895, and letter of Dorothy Stanley.
98. Ibid., 8 July 1895.
99. *Star*, 15 July 1895. Stanley, *Autobiography*, p. 466. Liberal newspapers alleged that Stanley 'nightly slept on a pillow steeped in blood' during his African journeys.
100. Stanley, *Autobiography*, pp. 476, 502.
101. J. A. Spender, 'The Patriotic Election – and After', *Contemporary Review*, LXXVIII (November 1900), 752; P. Readman, 'The Conservative Party, Patriotism, and British Politics: The Case of the General Election of 1900', *JBS*, 40 (2001), 107–45.
102. Lambeth Archives, Minet Library, I/15919/4, Miscellaneous papers about Henry Doulton.
103. *South London Mail*, 25 June 1892.
104. J. Davis, *Reforming London: the London Government Problem, 1855–1900* (Oxford, 1988); idem, 'The Progressive Council, 1889–1907', in A. Saint (ed.) *Politics and the People of London* (London, 1989), pp. 27–48.

105. J. A. Hobson, *The Psychology of Imperialism* (London, 1901); idem, *Imperialism: A Study* (London, 1902); P. Cain, *Hobson and Imperialism: Radicalism, New Liberalism and Finance* (Oxford, 2002).
106. Nicoll, *Stanley's Exploits*, p. 29.
107. C. Masterman, 'Realities at Home', in Masterman (ed.) *Heart of Empire* (London, 1901). See also idem, *From the Abyss* (London, 1902).
108. A. L. Lowell, *The Government of England*, 2 vols (New York, 1908), ii, p. 232.

10
London-over-the-border: Politics in Suburban Walthamstow, 1870–1914

Timothy Cooper

> The greatest advance in the decade is shown not in the cities themselves but in the ring of suburbs which spread into the country about them. If this process goes on unchecked the Englishman of the future will be of the city but not in it. The son and grandson of the man from the fields will neither be a dweller in the country nor a dweller in the town. He will be a suburb dweller. The majority of the people of this island will live in the suburbs; and the suburban type will be the most widespread and characteristic of them all, as the rural has been in the past, and as the urban may perhaps be said to be in the present.
>
> Sidney Low, *Contemporary Review*, October 1891

We now know that Sidney Low's words were prophetic. There was indeed a remarkable transformation in the shape and function of the Victorian city occurring by the end of the nineteenth century, caused by the geographical dispersal of metropolitan populations. This 'rise of suburbia' affected most late Victorian and Edwardian cities and London most extensively of all.[1] In some respects the phenomenon was not new: London had experienced the expansion of its suburban districts since at least the sixteenth century. However, the speed, extent and nature of suburbanisation changed dramatically from the 1870s with the emergence of efficient suburban railway services and cheaper fares which pushed suburbia deeper into the villages and towns surrounding London, making formerly rural villages like Walthamstow into suburbs of the imperial metropolis. It has long been recognised that this process had important implications for London politics. On the one hand it has been identified as a factor helping to institutionalise Conservative majorities in the new single-member suburban constituencies created by the Third Reform Act in 1885. On the other, it has been blamed for the de-radicalisation of London's working class since it removed the skilled, affluent, artisanate which had provided its core political leadership in much of the century before 1870. This chapter sets out to challenge these conclusions by analysing the political impact of suburbanisation on one working-class suburb.

Historiography

Previous historical writing on the Victorian suburb has tended to concentrate on its social and economic aspects. The most famous, and still definitive, work is H. J. Dyos's *Victorian Suburb*. In this vastly impressive study the author neatly dissected the many inputs which contributed to the building of a suburb and showed that, for all the appearance of uniformity, in spatial terms there was considerable variety in the style and aims of suburban development over time. He also revealed the role played by the speculative builder as a provider of suburban housing, and the influence of the law in defining the nature and quality of house construction. This undoubtedly brilliant work set the agenda for a generation of urban historians, and in many ways it still outshines them in its innovative methodology, the range of sources it employs, and the range of issues it addresses (which included the role of local government and politics and the culture which created the suburban impulse). Dyos's work was followed by numerous, largely imitative, contributions studying different suburbs at different times which confirmed and extended his basic findings.[2] As a result we have a detailed understanding of suburban building processes and morphology but, as Dyos himself also came to note, the history of suburban culture and politics have consequently been largely neglected. Another criticism is that much of the research following the agenda Dyos set has studied the suburb in its bourgeois form; the impact of working-class suburban migrations has remained a marginal concern.[3] There are very few extended studies of the working-class suburb. Urban and social historians have largely studied the suburb in search of an explanation of social cleavages within the city. Suburbia has thus come to be seen as a place with largely middle-class social characteristics and is associated with the process of residential segregation thought to have created slums of the poor and suburbs of the affluent.[4]

Politically middle-class suburbanisation has long been associated with the success of the Conservative Party. As early as the 1900s suburbia had come to be seen as inherently Conservative. For instance, Charles Masterman found in the character of suburbia an explanation for the crushing defeat suffered by Progressivism in the London County Council election of 1907.[5] He complained that, 'suburban life has little or no conception of social services, no tradition of disinterested public duty, but a limited outlook beyond personal ambition'.[6] The suburbans were activated only by detestation of the working class, and, tired of 'working-class legislation' and complaints of unemployment and poverty, 'the suburbans swarm to the polling booths to vote against a truculent proletariat'.[7] What remained was a kind of anti-social Conservatism:

> A public spirit in local affairs which is deplorably low, which sends a minute percentage of voters to Council or Guardian Elections, and accompanies a perpetual contempt for the present municipal mismanagement with a refusal of the personal effort to make that management clean and efficient. An outlook upon imperial affairs which is less a conception of politics than the acceptance of social tradition: which leaves suburbia securely Conservative because Conservatism is supposed to be the party favoured by Court, Society and the wealthy and fashionable classes.[8]

This image of the Conservative suburb attained historical respectability through James Cornford's seminal article on the transformation of late Victorian Conservatism. Cornford argued, in a manner reminiscent of Masterman, that the growth of suburban commuting had steadily changed the 'tone and politics' of London's rural fringe particularly in those outer suburbs that 'were the exclusive preserve of middle-class commuters'.[9]

> The growth of the Metropolis and the great towns, destroying any sense of community, separating population by class particularly in the third quarter of the century, when the middle-classes were enabled to leave the towns for peripheral suburbs but the working-classes could not afford the fares. Not only was class separated from class, but in large enough groups to make separate constituencies.[10]

The image of the bourgeois Conservative suburb has subsequently exercised a powerful influence upon interpretations of suburban politics.[11] Savage and Miles, for example, have recently restated the argument that 'suburbanisation had a widespread impact', arguing that 'it created generally middle-class areas which formed an increasingly solid bedrock of Tory support'.[12]

However, the view that the suburb is an inherently Conservative political territory has recently been challenged from a variety of perspectives. In part this arises from a loss of confidence in social explanations for political affiliations.[13] Historians like Jon Lawrence have claimed that, down to 1914, the residential districts of most cities actually remained socially mixed and that suburbs were not therefore primarily, inhabited by the middle class.[14] Complementing their work are the insights of scholars such as Mark Clapson, who, inspired by controversy among American academics over the character of suburbia, have recently challenged the characterisation of the suburb as culturally dull, socially bourgeois or politically Conservative.[15] These insights have in turn shaped a third strand, which is the emergence of a broadly 'revisionist' approach to suburban politics that rejects the notion of the Conservative suburb, preferring to argue that suburban Conservatism was unstable, subject to challenge, and constantly seeking to create new political alliances in order to sustain majorities in suburban constituencies.

This approach was first outlined in an article by Frans Coetzee in which he attacked the notion that there was any 'innate Conservatism' in suburbia, claiming that Conservative voter loyalties were more 'a function of local organisation, local notables, local concerns and their integration in the institutional role of the party'.[16] He shows that in Croydon the strong position of the Conservative party by the 1890s was the consequence of a series of electoral battles that were far from foregone conclusions and that there was some expectation in the years after 1885 that the seat might be captured for Liberalism.[17] Conservative success, Coetzee argues, was initially based on the exploitation of a 'suburban sensibility' and a 'sense of place', which enabled Conservatives to forge a claim to represent the residential elite.[18] The identity of the suburb as a place was thus of considerable importance to political parties who might contest the claim to represent the suburb. This implies that the political and place identities of a suburb are not static but dynamic and that no political party or ideology can assume that its claim to represent a particular place will remain permanently valid. It was the ability of Conservatives to adapt to the changing nature of place that brought about their success in the late nineteenth century. To illustrate this Coetzee shows that, by the 1900s, it was Croydon's role and identity within the nation as a whole that Conservatives were able to exploit for their own success.

Coetzee's approach has received support and elaboration from a number of younger scholars. Alex Windscheffel has recently rejected the idea that suburbia was innately Conservative.[19] He recognises that the social heterogeneity of the suburb poses problems for explanations of suburban politics which rely upon its middle-class character. Windscheffel argues that it is 'impossible therefore to sustain the view either that London's social and cultural structures permitted a class-based political system, or that a latent "Villa Toryism" achieved political expression after the creation of single member, socially exclusive suburban seats in 1885'.[20] In addition Matthew Roberts and James Moore have provided detailed studies of the politics of particular suburbs. Roberts has looked at the formation of political languages in suburban constituencies around Victorian Leeds and has attacked the idea that there was a 'transformation of Conservatism' that was the inevitable result of residential segregation.[21] Roberts believes that many of the cultural and religious divisions of the suburban middle class continued down to the twentieth century, and that there was a widespread survival of what he terms 'Villa Liberalism'. This is an analysis that finds support in James Moore's article on Liberalism in suburban South Manchester.[22] Moore shows that progressive Liberalism was able to establish itself in suburban Manchester by exploiting suburban aspirations for a healthy environment against the self-interest of suburban landlords who opposed projects of municipal improvement.

It will be obvious that there has been a considerable transformation in recent studies of suburban politics. The image of the middle-class suburban trooping to the polls in order to mechanically return large Tory majorities is no longer sufficient; the historian must take account of the variety of political alternatives in the suburb which were also struggling for success. Similarly he must be more aware of the local peculiarities of suburban places and how they could be exploited for political ends. The suburb was no mere appendage to the city but was a functioning community in its own right. If Conservatism was more successful in suburbia then the question is whether this was because suburbs were inhabited by the middle class or because Conservatives were simply better at exploiting the politics of locality and community? Yet, while recent work recognises the fact that suburbs were not simply dominated by middle-class Conservatism, none of the studies noted earlier has taken the role of the *working-class* suburb into serious consideration.[23] This matter is potentially of considerable interest: by the 1890s the fastest growing areas of the country were actually outer-ring working-class suburbs of London such as East Ham, West Ham, Leyton, Tottenham and

Walthamstow.[24] Much of 'London-over-the-border' was, therefore, working class. It is this problem that the rest of this chapter will analyse.

Walthamstow and the sense of place

In the final decades of the nineteenth century Walthamstow was one of the fastest growing suburbs of London (in 1850 it had been little more than a village of 5000 but by 1914 it had a population of 120,000).[25] Before the beginning of its rapid development Walthamstow was home to wealthy merchants, gentlemen, their families, and their servants, tradesmen, and farmers, along with the rural poor and a number of suburban artisans.[26] Those references made to Walthamstow in the 1870s and early 1880s invariably used the vocabulary of the 'parish' or 'village', rather than of the 'town', to describe the area. Such terminology reflected the close identity between Walthamstow's rurality, the legitimacy of parochial government, and the continuing dominance of both the Church and the elite in local affairs. Autobiography illuminates the centrality of rural identity to the image of Walthamstow at this time. Gilbert Houghton, Clerk to the Local Board until 1895, recollected the Wood Street area before suburbanisation, remembering that it was 'just a village street with large houses at both ends and cottages and small shops on the west side. Pamplin's nursery and green fields occupied the greater part of the east side'.[27] He also recalled the close associational life of the elite down to the 1880s, when there remained a strong attachment to the traditions and rituals of the manorial courts and the rogationtide ceremonies, which he tells us 'waned with the building over of the manors'.[28] Houghton thus reveals something of the image of pre-suburban Walthamstow, structured through rurality, the elite's *esprit de corps*, and the ancient rituals of parochial life, modes of reference which helped to construct the elite sense of place.

It is in this context that we can understand elite ideas of the most suitable form for suburban development to follow. House building in Walthamstow from the 1850s to the 1870s was largely based upon the production of freehold cottages for respectable artisans. Freehold Land and Building Societies, which have often been seen as generally speculative ventures by the 1870s, were, in Walthamstow, still seeking to promote social, temperance and suffrage causes.[29] In his *History of Walthamstow* the developer Ebenezer Clarke defended freehold development for having 'brought many persons with their wives and families from the fog and smoke of London into a clearer atmosphere, and enabled others to purchase land and build their own houses. There are many who can date their first practical effort to provide for their future independence to these societies'.[30] Clarke asserted that, in 1861, 203 of 402 county electors in Walthamstow claimed the vote because of their possession of freehold property.[31] The ideals of freeholding were shared widely among the elite of rural Walthamstow. David Morgan, the Chairman of the Local Board in 1877, stated that, 'For myself, I should like to see the lodger converted into a tenant and the tenant into a freeholder. Temperance, with hard work, self denial, and forethought, are in God's providence, the means to this end.'[32] The development of freehold housing for respectable artisans was, therefore, believed to encourage the sort of development likely to promote self-help and temperance among working-class residents, something that sat comfortably with elite images of Walthamstow as a cohesive paternalist community.

The mid-1880s were the point when these images began to break down. The construction of a mass of small dwellings by speculative developers suggested that the future would be an urban working-class transformation of the town. This prompted a response in defence of the quality of local community which centred on maintaining the rurality of Walthamstow. In 1877 David Morgan was urged by one local resident 'to be very careful of the ratepayers' money, and not to indulge in large works [of sewerage and road laying], but to keep Walthamstow a country parish as long as possible'.[33] Writing in the 1890s for the *Life and Labour* series, Jesse Argylle reveals the effects that working-class suburbanisation subsequently had on the elite's relationship with the town: 'Walthamstow was until recent years little more than a large country village, as genuinely rural in character as if situated a hundred miles away.'[34] However, he recounts that after the movement of London workers to the suburb had begun, 'the older residents looked askance upon this invasion, destroying as it did the rural quiet and selectness of the locality, and many of the wealthier families gave up their homes and retreated further afield'. Argylle gives us an idea of how the breakdown of elite landholding began in the 1870s. While the Warner family were the owners of an extensive estate, which was later developed on a large scale, it was the tendency of smaller landowners to sell up and move deeper into rural Essex which provided the first opportunities to speculative builders. No doubt the incentive to sell-out was increased by the intensity of the agricultural depression in rural Essex.

As Walthamstow developed ideas about its true identity became increasingly contested. Indications of divergent attitudes can be found in the response of the religious denominations. Suburbanisation undermined the dominance of the Anglican Church in Walthamstow because, from the 1880s, Nonconformist congregations were growing more quickly. The Anglican denominations responded with ill-disguised disgust. In 1882 the Reverend Grantham Robinson showed his lack of enthusiasm for the changing nature of the district based upon an idealised sense of Walthamstow's past rurality:

> It would be impossible to understand the change that had taken place during the past seventeen years. Then the aspect of Walthamstow was beautiful with beech, elm and oak trees, pretty walks, and everything that could make it a charming place of residence. This, however, was not destined to last for at length the spoilers came ... Then the penny trains brought the workmen.[35]

The churchyard of the parish church of St Mary the Virgin was itself fenced in to keep out undesirables in 1884, the Reverend Thomas Parry complaining that:

> Since our quiet village has been transformed into a busy town, our churchyard has suffered in the general decadence from rural simplicity, and it must grieve many to observe the irreverence of wayfarers and loiterers. We might have hoped that the surrounding memorials of the dead would have been considered as warnings against such behaviour.[36]

In stark contrast was the enthusiastic embracing of a working-class identity for Walthamstow by a plebeian and Radical church like the United Methodist Free Church. The 'Lighthouse' (as it termed itself) and its preachers enthused about the nature of social change in Walthamstow and played on the divisions between elite residents and the incoming commuting working class. Lighthouse preachers employed language that underscored their enthusiasm for the changes that had taken place in the nature of the town's community. In the *Free Methodist* in 1890, Walter Mines spoke to the emerging sense of the suburban working-class commuter identity and what he saw as its implications for the transformation of the town's social and political life:

> In a word the whole Bible thrilled with the cry *'third class in front'* ... the third class people were urged to be to the front in Walthamstow in demanding and securing for themselves a better representation on the Local Board and other governing bodies of the town, the kind of men who were needed were Godly democratic

men, representatives in touch with the spirit of Christianity and in touch also with the wants and needs of the working classes.[37]

Far from being a cause of deterioration in the quality of the community working-class suburbanisation would, with the right degree of Christian application, transform Walthamstow into a democratic space.

The few elements of the changing sense of Walthamstow outlined here indicate that the sense of place was increasingly contested on a social and cultural level. The elite vision of Walthamstow was gradually being challenged by a more democratic image of the suburb's future. The emergence of Radical politics in the 1890s owed much to the development of Nonconformity and drew strength from the ongoing contest over Walthamstow's identity as it forsook its isolated rural past and donned its new guise as a 'suburb' of London. It is to the politics born of these changes that I will now turn.

The rise of Radicalism

Before 1885 the elite's sense of place found political expression in an exclusive and localist politics. The Vestry and, after 1873, the Local Board of Health helped to sustain this by basing representation upon property qualifications and plural voting.[38] This made it remarkably difficult for newly arrived residents to gain representation. In the 1870s local representation was still widely constructed as the preserve of those with local connections and knowledge. In 1875, an attempt by some 'new men' to be elected to the Local Board was rejected by the editor of the elite newspaper the *Walthamstow Chronicle*, who denigrated the new candidates as 'strangers' compared to the 'widely known and respected' members of the existing Board.[39] '[I]s it fair to men who have a stake in the parish, and have resided here a lifetime, to supersede them by those, who may after all be "birds of passage"?', he went on. This localist discourse, which privileged long-term residents over newcomers, remained strong until the mid-1880s when the influx of new residents, and the exodus of the old, began to undermine it.

It was this exclusive localism that an emerging Radicalism sought to challenge after 1885, in what was increasingly perceived as an urban and working-class suburb. The emergent Radicalism in Walthamstow was of a complex character, a mix of 'Radicalisms' which reflected the indeterminate borderland status of Walthamstow during its most dynamic period of growth. It is clear, for example, that Radicalism must have derived much, probably the majority, of its support from migrant Radicals from

London. However, their most vocal leader, James Joseph McSheedy was a Radical Irish Nationalist, and it is clear that some aspects of local Radicalism must have had rural origins, as there were always a considerable number of migrants from Essex to Walthamstow. Indeed this latter factor may partly explain why in its early stages Radicals focused their efforts on reforming the Vestry. For Radicals the Vestry, and especially its administration of the charities, seemed to represent all that was wrong with the corrupt, paternalist social order of the old 'rural' Walthamstow, making it a natural target for their hostility. Looking back in 1898, James McSheedy, the leading light of Walthamstow Radicals, remembered that:

> The Vestry elected the burial board, charity governors, churchwardens. Monoux School Governors, Overseers, Allotment Wardens and fixed the poor rate. The mode of election was by show of hands, and if a poll was demanded, by open and plural voting. Each man had from 1 to 12 votes. Little or no public interest was shown in the meetings. About a dozen persons, pecuniarily or socially interested, met in a small room at the back of the town hall (laughter).[40]

Radicals had no real chance of gaining ground under the restrictive franchise and plural voting system for the Local Board; however, the system of open Vestry meetings and the show of hands at elections presented the best opportunity for a public challenge to the local elite. Consequently, the Easter vestries of the late 1880s and early 1890s were characterised by a series of, largely unsuccessful, Radical efforts to elect a 'people's' churchwarden to 'represent' the new suburban working class. Despite their lack of material success these occasions provided an opportunity for the airing of critical views. Radical arguments presented the Vestry, and its administration of the charities, as old-fashioned Tory corruption. In 1889 McSheedy complained about the administration of the charities, claiming its revenues were 'expended by the church party, and the church party were Conservative, and the poor people thought that because they got the charities from the Church party they were bound to support it'.[41] Radicalism was presented as an innovative force for renewal and modernisation. McSheedy, 'hoped the Conservatives of Walthamstow would continue to attend the Vestry meetings in good numbers, and thus come into contact with the Radical and Democratic element and by doing so promote their political regeneration and emancipation'. McSheedy's own role within this narrative is of some note. He was a peculiarly charismatic and theatrical figure, who had a particular taste for the grand gesture of defiance.

The following example is typical of the form of theatre politics practised by McSheedy. Having been thwarted in August 1896 in an effort to get the Vestry's Charities Board to admit the public to its meetings:

> Mr McSheedy rapidly advanced towards the doors of the Committee Room, flung them open, and invited in the parishioners, who were packed outside. They pressed forward with a rush and filled the room, amid ringing cheers for Mr McSheedy and loud hisses for the Rev Langhorne.
> Rev Langhorne and his Tory colleagues hastily rose ... As the clerical tyrant, pale and trembling slunk away the people displayed a threatening mien, and Mr McSheedy had to beg that he should not be molested.[42]

The introduction of such divisive political techniques into the traditionally apolitical world of local government dramatised the notion that Walthamstow was no longer the idealised deferential community of the 1870s. In its place, Radicals had supplied a dramatic narrative of contest and discontent, of heroic struggle by the democracy and inspired leaders against 'clerical tyranny'.

Within this context the role of 'place' was accentuated by the fact that the Radical campaign for greater working-class representation drew most of its support from the suburbanising St James's district. Suburbanisation had created a social divide in the town between the eastern and western halves of Walthamstow by suddenly implanting a working-class commuting community in St James's. Radicals were able to exploit the increasing consciousness of this divide in sustaining their demands for fair representation. This was the context to the campaign from 1887 for a ward system for Local Board elections. One Radical wrote to the *Walthamstow Guardian* in January 1887, 'Who are the Local Board?':

> He could only reply, a few respectable gentlemen living near the Town Hall, which perhaps accounted for the streets being better paved and lighted in that locality. This was one of the reasons why it was so very desirable that the parish be divided into wards, as the requirements of each part of the parish would receive its due share of attention. James Street district (the most populous part of the parish) was practically unrepresented, both upon the School and Local Boards.[43]

Agitation for improved representation thus carried a meaning not only in terms of class but also in terms of the developing geography of the suburb. As far as the Radicals' mental map of Walthamstow was concerned, power lay in the east of the district whereas population and political legitimacy lay in the west. This was underlined in 1896 by the submission made by McSheedy to the Essex County Council for a redistribution of ward seats, in which he argued that the redistribution should be based upon 'the population of the districts' because: 'This was a more equitable basis of representation than either property or mere electoral strength', and because, 'the St James and High Street Wards contained a population of 30,000, or nearly half of the entire population'.[44] The issue of working-class representation reached a peak with the introduction of Urban District Councils in 1894. This reform encouraged Radicals, who saw it as giving them the means not simply to challenge, but to finally *eliminate* elite control of Walthamstow. Looking to the forthcoming election McSheedy felt:

> There is no doubt that the privileged classes of Walthamstow will make a big fight for their happily vanishing authority. It is hard for them to realise that the ruling of their fellows will no longer be the mere perquisite of social position ... They have had a good run for their money. Unquestioned authority, social supremacy, personal insolence of bearing towards the working classes, these they have exercised so long that they have come to think them the natural order of things.[45]

The new Councils, McSheedy went on, 'would bring to the fore the local Hampdens, who could now struggle more successfully for the rights of the people against mere privilege and wealth'. It was a vision tied explicitly to the identification of Walthamstow as what McSheedy described as 'a working-class locality': let once 'the working-classes unite and act', he concluded, '... all the troubles and difficulties which have blocked the march of progress in this town will disappear as the mists in the morning sun'.

The electoral success of the Radicals after 1894 reinforced this tendency to identify the suburbanisation of the working class with the social and political transformation of Walthamstow. The Radical paper, the *Walthamstow Whip*, argued in May 1897 that:

> Before Walthamstow became a town it consisted of three items: the parson, the squire and some other people. The old inhabitants represented by the parson, and the 'squire' really formed the town between them, and mostly owned it too, but in their generosity and

leniency, and goodness of their hearts they graciously condescended to allow a few poor wretched beings to live, or rather exist in it.[46]

The process of becoming a town was thus used both to explain and to justify the purpose of Radicalism in Walthamstow. It suggested that a Radical political identity was the only real choice for a working-class suburb. Commuting was particularly central to the development of this discourse of place. The railway had broken the shackles of a backward looking rurality, and was a harbinger of modernity and democracy. For instance, the *Walthamstow Whip* recounted successful Radical efforts to eject the parish clerk, Gilbert Houghton, here the notorious 'Fatman' of local Radical demonology, from his position in 1895. In doing so it connected Radical politics, commuting and the transformation of place: 'During the past ten years or more, in fact, since the running of workmen's trains rendered it possible for working people who were not related to Fatman to live here, local politics has represented one continual struggle to grab Fatman, bit by bit, and boost him out of his multitudinous offices into the nether darkness where he belongs.'[47] Radicals thus constructed the process of suburbanisation as a democratising and radicalising process, a discourse which was present down to the end of the period. In 1913, Radicals took up the defence of Walthamstow's recently completed but costly tram system because trams were 'open to the richest and the poorest, the ill-dressed, the magnificently garbed. If democrats have ever a banner, the tramcar must be represented in golden threads upon the bellying brocade. The tramcar is to democracy exactly what the square is to freemasonry.'[48]

Such images of working-class suburbanity could also be found at the constituency level, especially after 1885 when the new constituency of South West Essex, or Walthamstow, replaced the previous two-member division for South Essex. The Liberal candidate for the Walthamstow division in 1892, Walter Basden Whittingham, himself no friend of McSheedy, was nonetheless optimistic about Liberal chances believing that suburbanisation was, in fact, a process that would make Walthamstow a safe Liberal constituency. During one election meeting Whittingham expressed the belief that it was suburban workingmen who 'had the providence and forethought to live a few miles out of London' that 'were the best class of workingmen'.[49] Walthamstow was a 'constituency that was growing at an extraordinary rate' and therefore ought to be 'a progressive constituency'. 'They generally found', he continued, 'that a constituency in which such rapid and important changes were taking place was a progressive constituency.' Whittingham looked to the 'great and populous districts around Hoe Street Wood Street and St James' Street' which he felt sure would 'be the backbone of [his] support in Walthamstow'.

Suburbanisation could thus be interpreted as a progressive process. Walthamstow, by attracting the most respectable, politically active, workers possessing 'providence and forethought' would make a safe Liberal constituency. Such attitudes were not surprising when one considers that Liberals and Radicals were closely connected to the physical process of suburbanisation. Whittingham's own brother was secretary of the National Freehold Land Society, which through the British Land Company, was involved in housing development in Walthamstow.[50] Similarly, the prominent Liberal MP and local Radical hero, Courtenay Warner, was a local landowner and developer. Their activities were not just about profit, for, as we have seen, the tradition of suburban freehold development had promoted both enfranchisement and individual economic independence. Later speculative development also had an element of idealism about it. The better housing conditions of suburbia were, after all, visible evidence of artisanal self-help and advancement on the part of working-class suburbans. The emergent Liberal and Radical constituency in Walthamstow, therefore, had close links to the transformative process of development itself.

Challenging Radicalism

Although Radicalism exploited the tensions suburbanisation created and gave to the process a language of democratisation, there remained an ambiguity in its attitude: an ambiguity that is illustrated by Radicals' inability to create a hegemonic position in the suburb. Despite the overwhelming proportion of workers in the district by the 1890s, the constituency division remained Conservative-dominated until 1897, suggesting the limits to notions that a working-class suburb would also inevitably be Radical. There was also the constant difficulty for Radicals of the great number of voters who did not participate in local politics or elections at all. Such problems were also attributed to the nature of Walthamstow's suburbanity. In July 1897, the *Walthamstow Whip* complained of the 'suburban instinct' in Walthamstow, which it felt stood in the way of establishing a proper working-class identity in the town.

> In places like Walthamstow where the suburban instinct is strong, a man might almost as well hang himself as acknowledge that he works. He may do anything he likes so long as no one sees him, but if he happens to be called out in a hurry and appears on the streets in

his working clothes his reputation is gone forever. Even the men of the District Council ... are not exempt. It is known by their description on their nomination papers that some of them work for a living, and the 'respectable' portion of the town hold up its hand in holy horror at their daring to take such a position.'[51]

Continuing, the *Whip* wistfully hoped that this 'humbug' of respectability would be broken down. As the editor put it, 'It is the man himself, and no matter whether he works with his hands or his brains, so long as he works and does his duty in the world he is entitled to our respect.' The nature of the commuting lifestyle was also a potential obstacle to Radicalism, which, during elections, had to appeal to the civic instincts of its constituency against the obvious attractions of dinner and rest. The *Walthamstow Reporter* before the general election of 1895 made the following 'Appeal to the toilers of Walthamstow': 'Every working man of Walthamstow who is an elector is earnestly requested when he arrives at the railway station in the town not to put off going to the polling station until he has had his tea and a wash, but to go at once and record his vote. If he puts off going it may be too late.'[52] Thus Radical thinking about suburbia was double edged. On the one hand working-class suburbanisation was imagined as a progressive force; on the other, Radicals feared that working-class politics could be stymied by a residual suburban respectability. These fears may be explained by the persistence of those who did not share the Radical sense of Walthamstow as a purely working-class place, and whose most important political representation down to 1914 came from the local Moderate party, an alliance of Tories and disaffected local Liberals, which fought local elections in one form or another after 1894.

In May 1901 the Radicals suffered a severe defeat in the Urban District Council (UDC) election and they were replaced by a Moderate administration which persisted until 1904. Throughout the remainder of the 1900s Radicals faced severe competition from the Moderate party. The disappointed McSheedyite organ, the *Walthamstow Reporter*, complained that, 'It is no use closing our eyes to the patent and lamentable fact that in the elections of last Saturday nearly double the number of electors voted against local progress as voted for it – and this in a town where nearly 80 per cent of the population are of the working-classes.'[53] McSheedy himself knew where to pin the blame: 'the snobbish gentry' and their allies the 'shabby gentility class', the 'respectable' and the 'clerks'.[54] The Progressive-Radicals' defeat was indicative of the latent fragility of their position and, consequently, also of their social and political image of Walthamstow. A divide, as identified by McSheedy, continued to exist between the commuting working class and the remnants of the residential elite, tradesmen, clerks, and those residents with local employment, many of whom inhabited the parts of the town east of Hoe Street. Thus it is important to remember that the identity of Walthamstow as a purely working-class suburb was not universally acknowledged. For non-commuting inhabitants, working-class suburbanisation was an increasingly costly burden. The increasing population was not matched by a proportionate growth in rateable value; and this left the costs of suburbanisation to be picked up by local traders and residents. The sensitivity of these groups to the costs of suburbanisation underpinned the emergence of a language which increasingly sought to re-assert the local role and legitimacy of the permanent resident and those of higher social class.

Moderates employed this language to challenge the Radical claim that the working-class population was representative of Walthamstow's community *as a whole*. An article of February 1907, in the Conservative and Moderate *District Times*, attacked the 1894 Parish Councils Act, claiming that, 'The monstrous oppressiveness of the Act comes in where it permits a handful of "councillors" nominally but not necessarily representative of the ratepayers to initiate ... scheme[s] ... against the will of the ratepayers.' 'Another gross scandal' the *District Times* raged:

> Is that it should be possible for the irresponsible adventurer with nothing but what he stands up in and a plausible tongue to get elected, and assist in increasing a town's liabilities, whilst a responsible townsman is outvoted, and why? Simply because he is a responsible man, with something to lose, and who would carefully shun increasing debts recklessly, and which would fall as heavily upon himself as upon other ratepayers.[55]

The paper went on to complain that it was the rent-paying worker who was really duped by this system of local government: 'he is told by election seekers that local expenditure comes chiefly out of the pockets of the landlord or capitalist, so he votes in a body for the man who is not a capitalist but who, he thinks, will make the capitalist spend his money, little thinking that his smiling friend is the cause of his rent being so high – for as rates rise, so must rents'. Moderate language argued that democratic representation had merely allowed political adventurers, such as McSheedy, to triumph over the local man. Moderates thus shared a continuity of rhetoric with the paternalist elite of the 1870s, when they had abhorred seeing 'new men' and 'birds of passage' standing for local office against local representatives. These themes were also present in the language of 'ratepayer interest', direct ratepayers being contrasted with compounding ratepayers for their superior knowledge and interest in local conditions. In 1900 a debate over abolition of the position of Vestry Clerk led the Moderate, Councillor Wilkinson, to demand that: 'the direct ratepayers ought to be consulted in the matter'.[56]

Moderates also challenged the Radicals' claim to represent Walthamstow, arguing instead that their primacy rested only on their dominance of the working-class suburban wards. In 1896, during discussions with the Essex County Council over the redistribution of council seats and wards, Councillor Finch argued that Moderates sought representation 'for the parish in general, not for one ward against another' and, referring to the high turnover of population among working-class residents, he asked 'Do we represent the shifting population or the electorate?', 'The electorate', rather than population, he concluded was 'a fair and equitable basis' on which to base representation.[57] Similarly, in 1908, when conflict erupted between the Progressive UDC and the Essex County Council over the appointment of representatives to joint conferences of the two bodies, Moderates deprecated the impact of such argument on the ground that 'unfortunately outside the district it is not the reputation of individuals that suffers but that of the community'.[58] The *District Times* stated:

> Surely the day is not distant when the ratepayers of this important district shall rouse themselves into a fuller realisation of the injuries inflicted upon them as a community by the demonstrated incapacity and lack of judgement shown in certain quarters, and take, if necessary, drastic remedies against those who thus drag the name of the town in the dust.'[59]

Moderates thus opposed the divisiveness of local democracy because it reduced the importance of attachment to the interests of the locality as a collective identity. One element of this position saw the nature of suburbanisation itself as the key cause of Walthamstow's problems because of the social costs it imposed upon the community. As the *District Times* observed in 1908, Walthamstow 'rests under enormous penalties as the dormitory, the nursery and the Poor Law Union of a vast industrial population whose burden should be shared by the metropolis'.[60] The solution envisaged by Moderates was the improvement of the social quality of the population of the suburb. J. W. Dunford made use of the familiar figure of the commuter when he argued in February 1905 that:

> If Walthamstow was to remain a prosperous community the second class passengers, must have more consideration. (Applause) The amount obtained from houses rated at £16 and under was not sufficient to cover the cost of administration. For the year 1901-2 the returns showed that 62 per cent of the houses in Walthamstow were rated at £16 and under ... It was not in the interest of the working classes that any railway company should neglect to provide proper facilities for a sprinkling of other classes coming down at the same time. There was an urgent and pressing necessity for a second railway.[61]

Moderates desired to reverse, or at least limit, the trend towards working-class suburbanisation in order to re-establish a kind of mixed community. After 1910, when the UDC sought powers to establish a town plan for Walthamstow, the *District Times* took it as an opportunity to press the cause of the ratepayer, and to attempt to reverse the decline in Walthamstow's social status. The *Times* argued that something ought to be done to 'arrest the continual growth of th[e] tenement class of property which is such a drain on the district' because 'the public services performed for the inhabitants are not nearly met out of the rates raised from the properties'. Confronting the Radical image of a plebeian and democratic Walthamstow, the *Times* continued:

> It is very nice to be proud of the fact that Walthamstow is the dormitory for London workers, but we can easily foresee the time when residents will be driven from the more highly rated properties to seek less rated districts if the wholesale catering for democracy goes unchecked. Some misguided folk look upon the providers of tenement property as public benefactors in the development of the district, but ... a most cursory investigation will easily disclose the fact that every artisan family of five or more souls that comes into the district is a distinct burden to the more highly rated property of the town.[62]

Town planning could be utilised to halt working-class suburbanisation, or at least to limit it, and to privilege the better class of resident who might more readily subsidise the rates. Moderates thus harked back to a more integrated sense of suburban civil society; one they felt to be more sustainable and which would require a more vigorous control of the qualities of the suburban community in order to retain wealthier suburbans. In its submission to the Local Government Board in 1912 the UDC argued that town planning 'cannot be otherwise than beneficial not only to the district, but in the interests of the ratepayers, rentpayers, and owners themselves'.[63] In contrast therefore to Radical images of Walthamstow as an exclusively Radical and working-class suburb, Moderates presented a powerful discourse of community, and the common interest of ratepayers and rentpayers in limiting or reversing the impact of working-class commuting and with it the cost of suburbanisation.

It is important to note, however, that Moderates were not the only threat to Progressive-Radicalism. From 1900 Progressive-Radicals also faced a more and more well-organised socialist and labour challenge. The year 1900 saw the first attempt by an SDF candidate, George Hewitt, to be elected to the UDC. Socialist language sought to contrast itself with Radicalism's vision of Walthamstow, as the Moderates had done. In particular, it sought to underline Radicalism's connections to capitalist house production. 'We have pointed out many times', Hewitt pointed out again in October 1900, 'that the Walthamstow Progressives' "progress" is specially designed for the benefit of the landlord class. Is this to be wondered at considering that so many of the Progressives are interested in land and house jobbery?'[64] Hewitt believed that the worker of Walthamstow languished in badly built homes whilst 'Sam Woods the "labour representative" and Courtenay Warner, the rack-renter and capitalist-landlord-exploiter, work harmoniously together for "the benefit of the worker!" So we're told.'[65] Unsurprisingly, the foremost issue of Hewitt's campaign was the Housing Question. In contrast to both Progressive and Moderate policies he saw no solution to the housing of the working-classes in improving commuting facilities because 'Any increase of wages, betterment or improvement of a neighbourhood, cheaper train or tram service, or whatever advance is made, is at once taken advantage of by the landlord in raising the rents.' Instead, Hewitt combined arguments about the quality of housing with the question of rateable values. He argued for a municipal house-building programme to 'compete with the landlord companies that are exploiting Walthamstow at the present time, and whose property is a loss and a financial burden to our town'. Thus by emphasising the demand for municipal housing Hewitt was able to play off the connection of Progressivism and landlordism, and undermine its claim to represent Walthamstow's working-class residents' interests. It is worth pointing out, however, that both socialism, and independent labour remained very weak before 1914.

Conclusion

From the end of the 1880s Radicals successfully participated in a remaking of politics in Walthamstow, temporarily sweeping away the elite dominated rural village and, they believed, creating a working class and Radical town. Radicals thus showed an ability to appropriate suburbanisation in order to challenge the rural image of Walthamstow and the political legitimacy of its elite. However, the appearance of a Radical triumph should not obscure the limited nature of their achievement. The nature of Walthamstow's suburbanity remained contested, particularly in the east of the district where development was less exclusively working class. Radicalism's achievement was not, therefore, secure from counter claims to the representation of suburban interests. In this respect the politics of working-class Walthamstow mirror the politics found in Croydon by Coetzee, although with a quite different political outcome. What does this indicate more generally? Certainly suburban politics were dynamic and contested. This reflected the essential instability of the identity of place in a suburb. Unlike most city centres, which were more socially stable by the late nineteenth century, suburbs stood at the frontier of social and political change. It was there that historic communities faced the enormous challenges of rapid urbanisation and where the politics associated with these changes were most intense. Rather than being uniquely de-politicised by the late-nineteenth century suburbs may well have been uniquely politicised compared to the city precisely because the social and political identity of place was unsettled. It may also be the case that in working-class suburbs the politics of mid-Victorian artisan London were able to survive into the late-nineteenth century. It was here that working-class Radicalism was able to adapt a politics of class that in urban centres was becoming increasingly disputed after the 1870s. If this was so then the effect, as we have seen, was probably temporary. Nonetheless, it would still require an important revision of our picture of working-class suburbia, which has so far emphasised its role in diminishing rather than sustaining the politics of class.

Notes

1. H. Perkin, *Rise of Professional Society: England since 1880* (London, 1989), p. 100; P. J. Waller, *Town, City and Nation* (Oxford, 1999), p. 30.
2. F. M. L. Thompson, *The Rise of Suburbia* (Leicester, 1982).
3. H. J. Dyos 'Workmen's Fares in South London, 1860–1914', *Journal of Transport History*, 1 (1953), 3–19; 'Railways and housing in Victorian London: II. Rustic townsmen', *Journal of Transport History*, 2, 2 (1955), 90–100.

4. C. G. Pooley 'Residential Differentiation in Victorian Cities', *Transactions of the Institute of British Geographers* 9, 2 (1984), 131–44; M. Savage, *The Dynamics of Working-class Politics* (Cambridge, 1987), pp. 101–33.
5. C. F. G. Masterman, *The Condition of England* (London, 1909), p. 80.
6. Ibid., p. 80.
7. Ibid., p. 71.
8. Ibid., p. 80.
9. J. Cornford, 'The Transformation of Conservatism in the Nineteenth Century', *VS*, 7, (1963), 35–66.
10. Ibid., 65.
11. M. Fforde, *Conservatism and Collectivism, 1886–1914* (Edinburgh, 1990), pp. 66–7; E. H. H. Green, *The Crisis of Conservatism: the Politics, Economics and Ideology of the British Conservative Party, 1880–1914* (London, 1995); P. Marsh, *The Discipline of Popular Government. Lord Salisbury's Statecraft* (Hassocks, 1978), p. 36; H. Perkin, *Rise of Professional Society*, p. 45; D. Steele, *Lord Salisbury: A Political Biography* (London, 1999), p. 160; Waller, *Town, City and Nation*, p. 152.
12. M. Savage and A. Miles, *The Remaking of the British Working Class, 1840–1940* (London, 1994), p. 63.
13. P. F. Clarke, 'Electoral Sociology of Modern Britain', *History*, 47 (1972); J. Lawrence, *Speaking for the People* (Cambridge, 1998), pp. 21–4.
14. Ibid., pp. 26–40; G. Stedman Jones, 'Working-class Culture and Working-class Politics in London, 1870–1900', in idem, *Languages of Class: Studies in English Working Class History* (Cambridge, 1993), p. 218.
15. A. Wieze, 'Stubborn Diversity: A Commentary on Middle-class Influence in Working-class Suburbs, 1900–1940', *Journal of Urban History*, 27, 3 (2001), 347–54. M. Corbin Sies, 'North American Suburbs, 1880–1950: Cultural and Social Reconsiderations', *Journal of Urban History*, 27, 3 (2001), 313–46.
16. F. Coetzee, 'Villa Toryism reconsidered: Conservatism and Suburban Sensibilities in late-Victorian Croydon', *Parliamentary History*, 16 (1997), 29–47.
17. Ibid., pp. 33, 39–41.
18. Ibid., p. 45.
19. A. Windscheffel, 'Villa Toryism? The Making of London Conservatism', unpublished PhD thesis (University of London, 2000), p. 27.
20. Windscheffel, 'Villa Toryism?', p. 30.
21. I am grateful to Matthew Roberts for sight of his forthcoming article 'Leeds Conservatism and the insecure world of Villa Toryism, 1885–1902'.
22. J. R. Moore, 'Liberalism and the Politics of Suburbia: Electoral Dynamics in Late Nineteenth-century South Manchester', *Urban History* 20 (2003), 225–50.
23. In a paper entitled 'Socialism and suburbia' presented to the London Socialist Historians Group (12 March 2005) David Young suggested that SDF clubs sustained the political traditions of metropolitan radicalism.
24. *Report of the Board of Trade into the cost of living of the working classes* (Parl. Papers, 1908, CVII).
25. The population of Walthamstow grew from 21, 697 in 1881, to 124, 580 in 1911. P. P., 1871–72, XVI, p. 317; P. P., 1912–13, 111, p. 134.
26. R. Wall, 'A History of the Development of Walthamstow, 1850–1900', unpublished M Phil thesis (University of London, 1969).

27. G. Houghton, *Walthamstow Past and Present. Some Random Recollections* (Walthamstow, 1929), p. 21.
28. Ibid., p. 14.
29. E. Clarke, *The Hovel and the Home. Improved Dwellings for the Labouring Classes and How to Obtain Them* (London, 1870), p. 5; M. Chase, 'Out of Radicalism: The mid-Victorian Freehold Land Movement', *EHR*, 106, 419 (1991), 343.
30. E. Clarke, *History of Walthamstow* (Walthamstow, 1862), p. vii.
31. Ibid., p. 46.
32. *Walthamstow Guardian*, 14 April 1877.
33. *Stratford Express*, 31 March 1877.
34. J. Argylle, 'Walthamstow', in C. Booth (ed.) *Life and Labour of the People in London*, 17 vols (London, 1902–03) Poverty Series, I, pp. 254–5.
35. *Walthamstow Guardian*, 12 August 1882.
36. Vestry House Museum, London [VHM], Rev. T. Parry, April 1894, *St Mary's Parish Magazine*, W.83/1.
37. VHM, *The Free Methodist*, 13 November 1890, Lighthouse Chapel, W.85/14/4690.
38. A Local Board of Health took over responsibility for roads and sanitary affairs from *ad hoc* Vestry Committees in 1873.
39. *Walthamstow Chronicle*, 10 April 1875.
40. VHM, McSheedy, 1898; *Ten years of local government in Walthamstow*, W.32/6, p. 2.
41. *Walthamstow Guardian*, 27 April 1889.
42. *Walthamstow Reporter*, 3 January 1896.
43. *Walthamstow Guardian*, 15 January 1887.
44. *Walthamstow Reporter*, 10 January 1896.
45. Ibid., 26 October 1894.
46. *Walthamstow Whip*, 15 May 1897.
47. Ibid., 15 May 1897.
48. *District Times*, 25 April 1911.
49. *Walthamstow Guardian*, 9 April 1892.
50. P. P. 1871, XXV, *Royal Commission to inquire into friendly and benefit societies*, q. 7431.
51. *Walthamstow Whip*, 17 July 1897.
52. *Walthamstow Reporter*, 19 July 1895.
53. *Walthamstow Reporter*, 29 March 1901.
54. Ibid.
55. *District Times*, 8 February 1907.
56. *Walthamstow and Leyton Herald*, 19 January 1900.
57. Ibid.
58. *District Times*, 3 January 1908.
59. Ibid., 10 January 1908.
60. Ibid., 21 February 1908.
61. Ibid., 24 February 1905.
62. Ibid., 6 September 1912.
63. National Archives, Kew [N. A.], HLG 4/2413, Walthamstow Urban District Council Town Planning Scheme, 1912.
64. *Socialist Critic*, 27 October 1900.
65. The remainder of this paragraph is based on ibid., 25 August 1900.

Conclusion
Matthew Cragoe and Antony Taylor

It is a curiosity of British political history that nineteenth-century London lacks an overall political narrative. The issue of mobilising London was always central to the effectiveness of political groupings that hoped to project a national image. In the nineteenth century, London still represented the political nation to a much greater degree than did the regions. Its centrality made it a major arena of conflict between central and local government, established party politicians and street-level orators, patriots and radicals, and politicians of the centre and the periphery. It has been the aim of this volume to offer some initial forays into this unknown dimension of the capital's past; in this final chapter, we aim to draw together some lines of this research and suggest directions in which future investigation might profitably be pursued.

The wider cultural climate affecting the political history of nineteenth-century London bears restatement. In the first place, as the new wave of cultural histories of the Victorian capital have amply demonstrated, London was a place of danger. In contrast to the regions, London consumed, rather than produced. London was J. A. Hobson's 'mighty vampire', or William Morris's 'grim net ... stark with the greed of the ages' that drew in willing victims and spat out their withered husks.[1] These images of the capital had important consequences for interpretations of its contemporary political character. From John Gay's eighteenth-century 'Barnstaple values' onwards, a perception gained ground that the true spirit of Liberalism resided in the regions. In Gladstone's Midlothian Speeches, it was here that the true vigour, virtue, industry and commerce of Britain was to be found: London, by contrast, was home to effete sybarites living off their unearned increment.[2] Liberalism established a view of a 'provincial purity' informed by the Nonconformist puritan ethic versus 'corrupt metropolitan superficiality' that was later taken up by the Labour Party. Yet, as was noted in the introduction, suspicion of Londoners' integrity was not confined to Liberals and Radicals: Conservatives, too, shared the prevailing hostility to all attempts to give London its just weight in the affairs of the nation, and fought to limit the direct representation of the capital in parliament, citing the degraded nature of the existing representatives as sufficient cause. For contemporaries, therefore, London was clearly a difficult place to 'imagine' in positive political terms, and the contemporary political narratives into which it fitted were not progressive. As a consequence it can seem 'untypical' of its age.

A second source of uncertainty regarding London politics was the problem of its precise extent. Boundaries and peripheries were, and are, important in any consideration of the capital yet here, once again, London eludes classification: the 'edge' remains difficult to locate. Some nineteenth-century authors, noting the remorseless expanding churn of inner London, saw the city as 'illimitable' and were moved to define 'the metropolitan' in psychological, rather than geographical terms.[3] A shifting penumbra of suburban sprawl pushed 'London' outwards from the mid-eighteenth century onwards. The capital gradually subsumed the garland of dormitory towns and villages around it, providing substance for the *cliché* that London comprised a collection of villages or 'a hundred townlets amalgamated'.[4] From the apocalyptic predictions of Mark Rutherford, watching from Stoke Newington the ominous light of London encroaching 'like some unnatural dawn', to the complaints of green-belt preservationists, London has been seen as a remorseless maw that afflicts, torments, and finally engulfs its neighbours.[5]

This process had enormous contemporary political implications, which have barely been addressed in the recent historiography of the capital. In particular, the differential rates of growth within the capital had very important consequences for political life; in effect some parts of London's boundary expanded faster than others. For the purposes of this study we adhered to a view of London proper as bounded by Hendon and Highgate in the north, the Isle of Dogs in the East, Blackheath in the south and Hammersmith to the west – an area that accords roughly with the nineteenth-century metropolitan police boundaries expanding outwards in a 12-mile radius from Charing Cross. The importance of this boundary for Londoners is emphasised by David Campion in his chapter on metropolitan policing; it should be noted that outlying parishes often sought refuge from the problems of criminality by integration into the inner London belt to take advantage of the police protection it provided. However, within this boundary there was another 'edge' that provoked constant problems: the moving frontier of suburban development. From the 1820s onwards, an increased local 'particularism' was evident in the surrounding villages threatened with relegation to dormitory-suburb status. Trespass by the city on communal village land led to a revival of the custom of 'beating the parish boundaries' in threatened areas like Chelsea and Hammersmith in a literal attempt to beat back the city and resist the 'encroachments made by the National Cemetery at Kensal Green, the Hippodrome, or new racecourse at Notting Hill, or by various private individuals on the ancient footpaths or Church Ways that have from time immemorial existed in these portions of the extensive parish of Kensington'.[6] And later in the century, very similar fears underpinned the politics of towns like Walthamstow, which, as Tim Cooper's chapter shows, far from remaining passive in the face of expanding 'Greater London', demonstrated a thriving civic culture, and a vibrant politics. At stake in the battles that engulfed Walthamstow were issues that went to the core of the inhabitants' identities: the politics of 'London over the border' is clearly an area which merits much greater attention than it has hitherto received.

Untypical and indefinable, it might be, yet historiographical neglect has rendered London curiously 'weightless' in comparison with the regional political cultures of the nineteenth century. It has been the purpose of this book to add a new substance to the political history of the capital, and, while relating it to the wider political narrative of the period, to draw out the elements that render it distinctive. Thus Matthew McCormack's re-interpretation of Wilkes and Burdett in terms of widely available discourses concerning electoral independence in no way diminishes the metropolitan flavour of the agitations which grew up around them. And the fact that London remained essentially non-industrialised, with a social hierarchy reflective of eighteenth-, rather than of nineteenth-century commercial society, ensured that this would remain a constant throughout the remainder of the period covered here. As Ben Weinstein demonstrates, Londoners remained profoundly susceptible to the lure of an urban Whiggery already failing in the regions. This accords with Roy Porter's vision of the city as an embodiment of the virtues of aristocratic rule, in which the construction of the West End by titled entrepreneurs entrenched the verities of the Whig tradition of liberty at the heart of London politics.[7] The enemy was not the aristocrat, it was the City financier or stock-jobber. In the manner of the Wilkites, metropolitan radicalism continued to target the financiers and joint stock companies of the City who supported government and opposed Wilkes. As late as the 1870s in the eyes of radicals, the City elite and aristocracy of London were still tainted by their proximity to the financial institutions and centres of power in London. These were the 'Lombard Street Usurers' who were at the heart of Ernest Jones's 'Shoddyocracy'.[8]

The London crowd retained its traditional place at the centre of the metropolitan political drama long after it had been cowed by respectability, rational recreation and the provincial police in the provinces, as numerous observers noted. As late as 1910 Ford Madox Ford could write in his modernist fable, the *Soul of London*:

> On successive days it will welcome its king going to be crowned, its general who has given it a province, its enemies who have fought against it for years, its potentate guest from Teheran – it will welcome each with identically rapturous cheers. This is not so much because of a fickle-mindedness, but because since it is so vast it has audiences for all players. It forgets very soon, because it knows so well that, in the scale of things, any human achievement bulks small.[9]

The chapters by Matthew McCormack, Detlev Mares and Antony Taylor all consider the 'continuities' within metropolitan radicalism dictated by the toxic nature of crowd politics (see Figures 2, 7 and 8). Emphasising the 'outdoor' nature of metropolitan politics, the street level of political activity, the characterisation of public space as uncontrolled and uncontrollable and the colonisation of the public arena, both by reformers and by the authorities, these chapters demonstrate the pressures on London's open areas, and locate their ideas strongly in the context of traditional metropolitan social inquiry. Moreover, in their re-examination of the political figures that appealed most strongly to the crowd, they detect definable 'metropolitan' types like Wilkes and Burdett (or *pace* Nash, Charles Bradlaugh) who connected with the folklore and popular tempo of the capital. More work needs to be done to bring such issues into clearer focus, and to unify the different arguments about the social geography of space and its impact on crowd politics in the capital.

Yet the capital, irredeemably associated in the popular imagination with dirt, riot and disorder, was also home to the great national monuments and treasures, the royal palaces, grand ceremonial boulevards, and the government offices at Whitehall. After the construction of Trafalgar Square in the 1840s, London became a showcase for empire and overseas conquest. In a London redefined in imperial terms, public monuments and street furniture evolved to mirror these preoccupations at the Victoria Memorial and elsewhere.[10] As Alex Windscheffel has demonstrated in this volume, against this backdrop, the politics of

London might be interpreted in loyalist and patriotic ways. Patrick Wright agrees, seeing the capital as lending itself to loyalist, and often, royalist appropriations.[11] Lacking a grand civic vision of London and entering the debates leading to the foundation of the LCC reluctantly and late in the process, in the 1890s the Tories monopolised the notion of London as the capital of empire. In proffering the explorer Henry Morton Stanley to the electorate of Lambeth in 1895, they sought to harness the politics of London to the politics of empire. Recent research on the capital has demonstrated the ways in which Conservatives trawled metropolitan culture in a search for patriotic and nationalist manifestations that could work to their advantage.[12] The Tories mined these patriotic inflections and placed them at the heart of their platform. By 1892 they had paved the way for a Conservative recovery in the capital. As Marc Baer suggests, the presence of the entrepreneur and churchman W. H. Smith on the Conservative platform in London in 1868 demonstrates the swing away from the Liberals and towards the Tories by Liberal Conservatives and the metropolitan middle classes. In the 1860s this trend converted Westminster from a bastion of radicalism into a Conservative stronghold. The Tory vision of London drew on memories of the central role played by aristocratic entrepreneurs in the construction of the West End. It was also a confection of royal palaces, national monuments and religious architecture.[13] This was a defiantly anti-modernist vision, rooted in aesthetic visions of London as the 'New Rome', that emphasised the charm and mythic style of Augustan London, and cemented the position of the cheerful, deferential and patriotic 'cockney' in the mainstream of London life.[14] Much remains to be discovered about the process whereby the lower class Londoner was transformed from the inhabitant of a capital of crime and disorder, into a stalwart of patriotic values and royalist fervour.[15]

This collection has also reconsidered the relationship between the franchise, poverty and political action in the capital. Many studies of London begin and end with poverty. Through the Boothite social surveys of the 1880s and 1890s London was irredeemably tarnished by its association with slum life. This contrasts markedly with the eighteenth-century image of London as a palace of wonders offering a menu of social and sexual pleasures. Many nineteenth-century metropolitan historians, however, find it difficult to see beyond the powerful images of poverty evoked by the late Victorians. By the 1900s contemporary fears of poverty as a destroyer of the metropolis had fused with conceptions of the 'aberrant individual'. Defined as cancer, canker and disease, poverty was depicted as an expression of the impure. Alfred White represented poverty as a creeping murrain that threatened to overwhelm the cityscape of London in the later part of the nineteenth century.[16] Thriving on rejection and social isolation, it was itself an embodiment of social decay and dissolution. Impelled by the 1880s debate about the social fragmentation and polarisation of London, the image of the poor thrived on the revelations of Alfred Mearns, Charles Booth and Charles Masterman. Analysis of the *bilsdungsroman* literature produced by Arthur Morrison and others connects up with these contemporary fears about an aimless, rootless, feral proletariat. In their work, poverty promoted the disintegration of group loyalties, community life and the family.[17] These images of a passive and frequently inebriated poor now seem excessively reliant on the observations of a few key figures. Politics, if it is considered at all in the traditional accounts, focuses around riot and social disorder, evoking images of the churning rookeries and warrens of the East End of London, where anger and dispossession readily turned to violence. Articles in this volume provide a corrective to these traditional accounts. The images of a debilitating poverty, accentuating apathy and political disengagement, and at the same time removing East End communities from all electoral processes are disputed by Marc Brodie. He maps out an analysis of poverty that re-imagines the fallen state of the poor. For him, the East End was a place of contest and compromise in which the poor navigated the different pressures of landlord, rent-man, and the police in their incarnation as 'domestic missionaries'.[18] We still know very little about the ways in which possibilities of resistance were opened up amongst the poor, but Brodie challenges traditional narratives in which poverty both deactivated and immiserated. Following Brodie's lead, there are now new possibilities for re-visiting deeply ingrained images of the East End.

Moreover, as this collection has demonstrated, there are myriad 'dogs that do not bark' in the history of London. One such is religion. London was never a great Protestant city in the manner of Geneva or Amsterdam. A city dominated by religious monuments like Westminster Abbey and St. Paul's, London, nevertheless, had a hollow religious centre. In marked contrast to the regions, the capital's political history appears remarkably free of the religious and denominational concerns that characterised the Liberal, Tory and even radical platforms of Wales, the North-West and the English Midlands. London embodied the 'Old Corruption' at the heart of the Anglican Church. As the population expanded beyond the old city walls, so too the Anglican Church was left, in Roy Porter's words, with an 'embarrassment of riches' within the City and elsewhere.[19] The Anglican monopoly in London had collapsed by the end of the eighteenth century, creating a vacuum and allowing a proliferation of eccentric sects like the 'Plumstead Peculiars' and 'Walworth Road Jumpers'.[20] Crumbling, semi-derelict and unused religious accommodation provided a metaphor for the decline of Anglicanism itself in London. As Antony Taylor establishes in his chapter on radical continuities, the absence of strong religious identities in the capital sets metropolitan politics apart from the politics of the regions, where religious divisions promoted the emergence of parties defined by conflicting religious adherences. From the 1850s, the nineteenth-century rage of party was, in part, a conflict of different faiths. London remained apart from this. As Ben Weinstein demonstrates, Whiggery continued to flourish in London when it was superseded or by-passed altogether in the regions. Partly its longevity in the capital was assured by the absence of those denominational issues surrounding Anglicanism in the 1850s that tested Whig loyalties in relation to the Anglican hierarchy. These imperilled its position in the regions, damaging its relationship with Nonconformity; in contrast Anglicanism in the capital had much less purchase on the emotions of the electors and the crowd. The decline of Anglicanism in London also provided an opportunity for secularist and free thought lecturers, as David Nash demonstrates in this volume. Against the background of the vacant and unoccupied religious buildings of London, freethinkers railed against the wealth and injustices of a state church the metropolitan population barely attended. In the years from the 1820s onwards they were a regular sight on the open land and brown-field assembly places of the capital. Here, they emphasised the metropolis as a space and phenomenon where difference and dissidence flourished. Their capital provided a place of freedom from all religious constraints. Taking account of such perspectives, Marc Brodie has attempted to reassess the relationship between politics and religion in the capital. The East End he revisits was a place of defiant and pervasive religious faith missed altogether by the social investigators of the 1880s. Brodie has tried to recover the essence of a religion that was non-institutionalised, devolved and undemanding. Much work remains to be done to catalogue the profoundly urban set of religious dogmas within the capital that defy categorisation within conventional doctrinal definitions.

In the late eighteenth century, and throughout the nineteenth century, London posed significant problems for its politicians. Managing the electorate against the background of the turbulent, unruly and feckless crowd politics of London proved challenging and demoralising in equal measure. Broad-based movements reliant on popular support often suffered at the hands of Londoners. In addition, the reputations of some

London politicians were tarnished through their association with shambolic and unruly party organisation. Herbert Morrison wrote in 1924 that 'London was the despair of the Labour movement'. He painted a picture of metropolitan Labourites as a 'gassy, protesting, quarrelsome, cantankerous, crowd, very good at cursing the enemy and cursing ourselves, but no good at effective fighting against the well-organised political parties'.[21] The everyday fare of regional small town politics, including employer paternalism and coercion, and the influence of strike action are also conspicuous by their absence in the capital. Strikes in London were generally short in duration and, in the absence of a homogenous economic activity that coloured all the industries of the metropolis, seldom acted as a spur to any broader, more sustained programme of rights as they did in the single-industry towns.[22] The significant barriers to the effective organisation of London politics and metropolitan political parties barely figure in recent treatments of the capital. Too much has been overlooked through the concerns of urban and cultural historians to identify and define the unique and different character of London. Patrick Joyce in particular sees the nineteenth-century city as a modernist phenomenon paving the way for sanitation reform, and good local government. Presented here is an essentially 'liberal' vision of social progress.[23] London fits into this conception, uneasily, if at all. Far from acting as the model for a 'liberal' city, London provided a distillation of all the social fears of the nineteenth century. Moreover, despite the capital's democratic impulses, by 1900 the Tories were a significant presence on the LCC, and provided 80 per cent of all London's MPs. Often labelled as 'pre-industrial', London navigated a space between liberalism and conservatism, backwardness and modernity. We remain profoundly ignorant about the methods employed by political parties to bring London to heel. As a consequence, metropolitan techniques of political mobilisation, and the methods employed to quell dissent and overcome political opponents remain ambiguous and opaque. Nevertheless, the scale and liveliness of London's political responses are undoubted and were frequently noted by contemporaries in the nineteenth century. Paul Thompson makes this point well, suggesting that in an environment in which communities were absent or had broken-down, and where there were few, if any, of the large urban employers whose interventions frequently dictated the course of elections in the northern mill-towns: 'here, rather than in the provinces, can be seen the political setting of the future'.[24] Questions remain, however, about how this electorate was contained, controlled and curbed.

A collection of essays can only do so much: its most efficient purpose is to act as a 'ginger group', stimulating interest in an issue and raising its profile within the scholarly community, providing a base-line from which further research can take place and setting out markers as to the paths along which that effort might fruitfully be pursued. We hope that this volume will provoke a new interest not only in the politics of the metropolis itself, but in the relationship of metropolitan to national narratives of British political history in the nineteenth century. Popular politics was invented in London, and Chartism and other movements of political radicalism survived in London whilst declining in the regions; yet London politics was seldom about religion, had little or nothing to do with free trade, and involved a systematic appeal to crowd politics when that was a dying art in the regions. How this mass of excitement and opinion was informed, directed and ultimately brought under the control of the great political parties by the century's end is a story that deserves to be told.

Notes

1. J. A. Hobson, *Problems of Poverty: An Inquiry into the Industrial Conditions of the Poor* (London, 1891), p. 57; *Commonwealth*, 1 April 1885, p. 20.
2. C. Hill, *Liberty Against the Law: Some Seventeenth Century Controversies* (London, 1996), ch. 1; H. C. G. Matthew, *Gladstone 1875–1898* (Oxford, 1995), pp. 43–60.
3. Ford Madox Ford, *The Soul of London* (ed.) A. G. Hill (London, 1995), ch. 2.
4. E. T. Cook, *Highways and Byways of London* (London, 1902), p. 17.
5. W. H. White (ed.) *The Autobiography of Mark Rutherford* (Oxford, 1990), p. xv.
6. *Gentleman's Magazine*, 12 April 1837, quoted in *Journal of the Commons, Open Spaces and Footpaths Preservation Society*, 4 (1935), pp. 202–5.
7. Porter, *London: a Social History* (London, 1994), ch. 5 and *Lansbury's Labour Weekly*, 30 January 1926, p. 1, for the greed of London's aristocratic landlords.
8. *People's Paper*, 24 March 1855, p. 4; J. E. Thorold Rogers, 'British Finance: Its Present and Future', *Contemporary Review*, 34 (1879), 303; C. Murray, *A Letter to Mr George Jacob Holyoake* (London, 1854), p. 16.
9. Ford, *The Soul of London*, p. 12.
10. T. Smith, ' "A Grand Work of Noble Conception": The Victoria Memorial and Imperial London', in F. Driver and D. Gilbert (eds) *Imperial Cities* (Manchester, 1999), pp. 21–39.
11. P. Wright, *A Journey through Ruins: The Last Days of London* (London, 1991), pp. 232–62.
12. J. Schneer, *London 1900: The Imperial Metropolis* (Yale, 1999), chs 1–3.
13. Not all were impressed: Hippolyte Taine famously described Nelson's Column as resembling 'a rat impaled on the top of a pole': Cook, *Highways and Byways of London*, p. 451.

14. A. J. Weitzman, 'Eighteenth-Century London: Urban Paradise or Fallen City', *Journal of the History of Ideas*, 36 (1975), 469–80.
15. K. Beckson, *London in the 1890s: A Cultural History* (New York, 1992), pp. 344–78; G. Stedman Jones, 'The Cockney and the Nation 1780–1988', in D. Feldman and G. Stedman Jones (eds) *Metropolis-London: Histories and Representations since 1800* (London, 1989), pp. 272–324.
16. A. White, *The Problems of a Great City* (London, 1886), pp. 179–240.
17. W. Fishman, *East End: 1888* (London, 1987), chs 4, 6; M. Freeman, 'Journeys into Poverty Kingdom: Complete Participation and the English Vagrant 1866–1914', *HWJ*, 52 (2001), 99–121, P. J. Keating, *The Working Classes in Victorian Fiction* (London, 1971), ch. 7; A. Morrison, *Tales of Mean Streets* (London, 1894), pp. 7–25; A. Palmer, *The East End: Four Centuries in the Making of London Life* (London, 1999), chs 5–8.
18. M. Brodie, *The Politics of the Poor: The East End of London, 1885–1914* (Oxford, 2004).
19. Porter, *London*, pp. 199–200.
20. C. M. Davies, *Unorthodox London: Phases of Religious Life in the Metropolis* (London, 1873), pp. 89–108, 293–301.
21. Quoted in J. Marriott, *The Culture of Labourism: The East End Between the Wars* (Edinburgh, 1991), p. 278.
22. Strikes were deemed ineffective in London: *The Leader*, 29 December 1855, p. 1248. For a rare metropolitan complaint about 'the screw', *East London Observer*, 19 September 1868, p. 4.
23. P. Joyce, *The Rule of Freedom: Liberalism and the Modern City* (London, 2003); T. Hunt, *Building Jerusalem: The Rise and Fall of the Victorian City* (London, 2003), ch. 11.
24. P. Thompson, 'Liberals, Radicals and Labour in London 1880–1900', *P & P*, 27 (1964), 73–101.

Index

Aborigines Protection Society 198–9
Addison, Joseph 59–60, 72n14
Africa 194–205
Aikin, Lucy 59
Aldersgate School 68
America 30
  policing in 40
Anarchists 114, Figure 3, Figure 4
Anglicanism 173–90, 217–19
Annet, Peter 101
Anticlericalism 102, 221
Anti Corn Law League 14, 77, 82–3, 85, 91, 92, 124, 127
Arch, Jospeh 135
Argylle, Jesse 217
August, Andrew 170
Austin, Henry 65, 68
Aylesbury 27
Ayrton, A. S. 125–6

Baer, Marc 12, 13, 237
Baker, H. Barton 89
Balfour, Arthur 192–3
Ball, Michael 123, 171
Barttelot 199
Bastille, the 32, 99
Beaconsfieldism 205
Beal, James 152–3
Beales, Edmond 132
Bebbington, David 174
Bedford, Duke of 61–2
Bee-Hive, The 78–9
Beesly, E. S. 158, 160
Belchem, John 31
Bentham, Jeremy 31, 68, 74n66, 160
Bermondsey, St Mary Magdalen 5
Bernal Osborne, Ralph, MP 58
Bernard, Sir John 24
Bhownaggree, Sir Mancherjee Merwanjee, MP 193–4, 206n21

Birmingham 2, 11, 127, 130, 131, 134, 170
  policing in 40
  BPU 132
Bishop Bonner's Fields 86, 102
Blackheath 124
Blake, William 99
Bloomsbury 61
Boer War 174, 204–5
Booth, Charles 89, 170–4, 178, 237–8
Booth, General William 81, 195, 196
Boroughbridge 31
Boughton, John 170
Bourne, Henry Fox 199, 200
Bow 185
Boyd, Revd W. G. 175
Bradlaugh, Charles 8, 78, 89, 102–3, 107–17, 130, 132–3, 154, 236
Brassey, Thomas 125
Brecon 124
Brentford 5, 108
Briggs, Asa 121
Bright, John 92, 127
Brodie, Marc 12–13, 238, 239
Bromley 5, 182, 185
Brooks's Club 58
Brothers, Richard 99
Brougham, William 64
Burdett, Sir Francis 4, 12, 19–22, 30–33, 70, 72n38, 79, 83, 144, 145–51, 155–6, 160–1, 235, 236
Burdett-Coutts, William 158–9, 196
Burns, John 199, 200
Byng, Commissioner 51
Byng, George, MP 32, 64

Cabinet Newspaper 85
Campion, David 6, 234

Index

Carlile, Richard 102, 105, 106, 107, 113
Caroline, Queen 20, 63
Cartwright, Major John 26, 148
Catholics 3
Cattell, Charles Christopher 130
Centralisation, fear of 41–2, 58, 69
Chadwick, Edwin 64, 69
Chamberlain, Joseph 11, 127, 196, 203, 207n38
Chambers, T. Marylebone, MP 9
Chartism 7–8, 21, 52, 75–96, 108, 114, 122, 127–8, 131–2, 140n36, 159, 241
Chelsea 10, 11, 12, 89, 108, 235
Church of England 173–87, 217–18, 220–1, 238–9
Clapham 5, 10
Clapson, Mark 214
Clark, Sir James 66
Clarke Ebenezer 216–17
Clay, William 58, 80
Clerkenwell 6, 81, 194
Clerkenwell Green 86, 87
Club Autonomie Figure 3, Figure 4
Cobbett, William 23
Cobden, Richard 14, 92, 127
Cochrane, Charles 152
Cochrane, Lord 146–9, 152
Coetzee, Frank 214, 230
Cogers Club 89
Cold Bath Fields, Clerkenwell 6, 32, 46–8, 52
Cold Bath Fields Prison 31
Coldwells, Alderman 195–9, 204
Colenso, Henrietta 13, 200–1
Collinson, Patrick 97
Comte, Auguste 114
  and the Positivists 91
Coningham, William 153
Conservative Party 148, 151–2, 234
  Mid-century struggles 5–6, 57, 81–2, 84
  Late century regeneration 145, 154–61, 166–87, 191–205, 211–16
Cooper, Thomas 89
Cooper, Timothy 13, 235
Copenhagen Fields 86

Cornford, James 213
Corn Laws 152
Coutts family 31, 146
Covent Garden 147, Figure 9
Crowds 2–3, 19–20, 46–8, 78–9, 84–7, 92–3, 236, 239–40
Crown and Anchor 19
Croydon 214, 230
Culley, Robert 46–7, 55n37, 55n40

Daily Chronicle 200, 201, 203
Daily Telegraph 153, 192, 199
Dainow, David 176
Davies, Charles Maurice 110–13
Davin, Anna 102
Deptford 6, 206n24
Desmond, Adrian 66, 68
Devonshire, Duchess of 4
Dewar, T R 176–7
Dickens, Charles 58, 111
Diggers, the 98
Dilke, Sir Charles 11, 12, 89, 125
Disraeli, Benjamin 64, 73n42
District Times (Walthamstow) 226–8
Divey, Edward 191–2
Dorest 62
Doutlon, Sir Henry 196, 204
Driver, Felix 194–5, 201
Duncombe, Thomas Slingsby 83, 85
Dunfor, J. W. 228
Dyos, H. J. 212

Earle, Peter 66
East Ham 13, 215
East London Advertiser 177
Eats London Observer 172
Ebrington, Viscount 70
Edinburgh Review 59
Egan, Pierce 111
Electioneering 22–34, 83–5, 145–60, 182–3, 197, 202–3
Elliott, Jane 169
Eluisis Club, Paddington 89
Emin Pasha 194, 198, 199–202
Engels, Friedrich 38, 50, 52
Epstein, James 31
Essex 217, 222, 223, 227
Evans, George DeLacy 150–3

Evans, Howard   129, 135
Evans-Gordon, Major William   175–6
Evening News, The   198, 199

Fawcett, Henry   125
Federation of Synagogues   177
Feldman, David   177
Fifth Monarchy Men   98
Finsbury   11, 63, 82, 83, 85, 194
　Finsbury, St Luke's   85
Finsbury Park   110
Ford, Ford Maddox   236
Foretescue, Hugh   58, 70, 74n70
Fowler, Robert, MP   198
Fox, Charles James   4, 12, 22, 24–5, 60, 144, 145
Fox, C. R.   58, 60–1, 70
France, Revolution in   100, 101
Fraser, General Charles, MP   196, 207n35
Freedom   86
Freethinker   113
Freethought   97–120, 239
Fulham   10

Gardener, Sir Alan   25
Gavin, Hector   66
Gay, John   233
Ghose, Lalmohan   206
Gladstone, William Ewart   80, 85, 192, 233
Gott, J. W.   114
Graham, John   25
Grainger, R. A.   66, 68, 69
Grant, Robert MP   63–4
Green, Ewen   173
Green Dragon, Fleet St.   89
Greenwich   6, 7, 73n43
Greenwood, James   89
Grey, Earl   63
Griffiths, Trevor   169
Grosvenor, Lord Robert   58, 64, 69–70, 153–4
Grosvenor family   61, 62

Hackney   5, 10, 11, 193
Haggard, H. Rider   203
Hales, John   132

Hammersmith   10, 235
Hampstead   10
Hampstead Heath   88
Harman, Moses   114
Harrington, Edward   87
Harrison, Frederick   160
Harrison, Sir Brian   90
Hawes, Benjamin   58, 64
Health of London Association   67–70
Health of Towns Association   7, 64–70
Hennock, Peter   170
Henriette, Peter   78
Hetherington, Henry   104, 105
Hewitt, George   229
Highgate   10
Hill, Octavia   180
Hobhouse, John Cam   26, 60, 148–51, 160–1
Hobson, J. A.   205, 233
Holborn   81, 128
Holland, Lord   60
Holland House   58, 60
Holland Park   61
Hollis, Patricia   182
Holyoake, Goerge Jacob   103, 105, 107, 109–10, 114–15
Horne, William   63, 64
Hornsey   10
Houghton, Gilbert   216, 223
House of Commons   29, 38, 148
Howell, George   78, 89, 125, 132, 193–4
Hume, Joseph   63
Hunt, Henry   19, 89, 148
Hunt, Leigh   58
Hyndman, Henry   92, 199

Ilive, Jacob   101
Imperialism   13, 26–7, 82, 191–205, 236–7
In Darkest Africa   199
In Darkest England and the Way Out   195
Inns of Court   66
International Herald   137
International Working Men's Association   122, 130, 131, 136–7
Islington   5, 10

James, W. A., agent   84
Jameson, James   199
Jenks, Timothy   25
Jephson, Henry   75
Jephson, Revd Arthur   200
Jerrold, Douglas   58
Jewish Chronicle   175, 176
Jews, disabilities of   63
Jingoism   82
John of Gaunt   87
Jones, Ernest   91, 236
Jones, Gareth Stedman   12, 66, 166–7, 170–2, 178
Joyce, Patrick   13, 57, 75, 116–17, 169, 240

Keltie, Sir John Scott   199
Kensal Green   235
Kensington   10, 193, 235
Kent   6
Kilburn   10
Kingston   98, 108
Kirkwood, David   134
Koss, Stephen   174
Kropotkin, Peter   114
Kynaston, David   4

Labourism   21
Labour Party   234
Labour Representation League   122, 126, 134–5, 157
Lamb, George   148
Lambeth   10, 11, 63, 79, 83, 194–210
Lambeth Conservative Association   196
Lancashire   2, 81, 90, 107, 128, 168
Land and Labour League   135
Land Tenure Reform Association   135
Langhorne, Revd   221
Lansbury's Labour Weekly   87
Lawrence, Jon   13, 169, 214
Le Bon, Gustave   93
Leeds   2, 9, 11, 80, 81, 215
Lethbridge, Roper, MP   193
Leyton   13, 215
Liberalism   21
Liberty of the Tower   5

Limehouse   167, 172–90, 193
Lion   102
Liverpool   11
  policing in   40
Livingstone, David   198, 201
Lloyd, Trevor   11
London (*and see individual constituency entries*)
  Aristocracy, and   60–2, 145–6, 153, 158–9, 237
  City of   6, 18–19, 81, 97, 113, 235–6
  Clubs   88–91, 103, 108–10, 123, 158, 183–4
  Elections in   22–3
  Expansion of   13–14, 100, 211–30, 234–5
  Historians, and   1–4, 9, 12–13, 14, 19–22, 75–7, 166–87, 191, 214–15
  Jewish population   3, 174–7
  Liberalism in   82–6, 107, 152–8, 160–1, 183–5, 190–205
  MPs, character of   9, 21–2, 24–34, 57–8, 60, 63–4, 70, 144–65, 182, 193–4
  Open Spaces   86–7, 102, 106, 125–6
  Parliamentary Reform and   3
  Policing of   6, 38–56, 101
  Political character   14, 18, 34, 78–86, 122–6, 138, 168–70, 187, 192–3, 233, 239–40
  Politics of the poor   12, 81, 166–87, 195
  Provincial agitations, and   1–2, 75–86, 107–8, 121–38
  Radicals and   7–9, 12, 14, 18–34, 75–117, 123–38, 145–54, 219–30, 236
  Religious character   81–2, 97–120, 173–87, 238–9
  Social and economic character   7–8, 11, 66–9, 76–7, 91–2, 100–1, 170–3, 226, 235–6, 240
  Vestry Politics   62, 70, 204, 220–1, 227

London, City of (parliamentary seat) 3, 4, 5, 7, 10, 11, 19, 22, 28, 70, 82, 198
London and Westminster Working Men's Constitutional Association 156
London Atheistical Society 105
London Corresponding Society 19, 25, 146
London County Council 81, 187n6, 204, 237, 240
London Tavern, The 85
London Working Men's Association 9
Low, Sidney 194, 211
Lowell, A. L. 205
Lucraft, Benjamin 128
Lushington, Charles 58, 64

McCalman, Iain 19, 88, 104
Macaulay, Thomas Babington 59, 60
McCormack, Matthew 4, 83, 235, 236
McDonnell, J. P. 126
McLean, Andrew 44
McLeod, Hugh 177–8
McSheedy, James Joseph 220–30
Mainwaring, William, MP 31–2, 35n24
Mall, The 88
Manchester 2, 7, 9, 11, 14, 40, 78, 80, 81, 82, 83, 90, 124, 131, 138, 215
Manners, Lord John 64
Mares, Detlev 8–9, 236
Marx, Karl 130
Marylebone 5, 7, 9–10, 11, 62, 63, 70, 82, 84
area 61
Masterman, Charles 92, 206n19, 213, 238
Mayhew, Henry 58, 92, 111, 195
Mays, Superintendent 46–8
Maxse, Capt Frederick, land reformer 79
Mearns, Alfred 111, 238
Melbourne, Viscount 148
Merchant of Venice 109

Methodism 218–19
Metropolitan Association for the Improvement of the Dwellings of the Industrious Classes 67
Metropolitan Board of Works 7
Metropolitan Commission of Sewers 69
Metropolitan Police 38–57, Figure 3, Figure 4
Metropolitan Sanitary Association 7, 64–70
Middlesex 3, 4, 5, 7, 11, 22, 25, 27–34, 63, 64, 65, 69, 146
Mile End 3, 167, 172–90
Mill, John Stuart 130, 152–5, 160–1
Mitchell, Leslie 60
Montagu, Samuel 177
Moore, James 215
More, Hannah 101
Morgan, David 217
Morgan, John de 126, 130
Morgan, William, reformer 91
Morley, John 160
Morning Chronicle 62, 92
Morning Post 192
Morpeth 64–70
Morris, William 233
Morrison, Herbert 240
Muggletonians, the 98, 99
Mundella, Anthony 125
Murphy, Thomas 62

Naorojim Dadabhai MP 194, 206n24
Nash, David 8, 239
National Agricultural Labourers' Union 135–6
National and Constitutional Association 85
National Association of United Trades 78
National Charter Association 77
National Freehold Land Society 224
National Organisation of United Trades 78
National Reformer, The 111, 133
National Republican Brotherhood 130–1
National Secular Society 108

National Union of the Working Classes 6, 43–8, 52
Nelson, Sir Thomas 113
Newcastle 128
Newgate Prison 99
News of the World 202–3
Newton, William 78, 85, 91
New York 2
Nicoll, D. J. 199–200, 205
Nonconformity 173–90, 218–19
Northumberland, Duke of 145
Nottingham 132
Notting Hill 235

O'Brien, Bronterre 89, 123
Odger, George 78, 125–6, 130, 134–6
O'Gorman, Frank 23
Old Corruption 149, 158, 238
Owen, Robert 104, 105, 109, 114

Pack, Ernest 114
Paddington parish 5
Paine, Thomas 100, 102, 113, 115, 160
Paris Commune 130
Parks
  Hyde 86, 89, 95, 106n46, 124
  Regent's 86, Figure 6
  Victoria 86, 102, 106 (*see also* Bp Bonner's Fields)
Parliamentary and Financial Reform Association 85
Parry, Jonathan 9
Parry, Revd Thomas 218
Paull, James 25–6
Peckham Rye 86
Peel, Sir Robert 3, 4–5, 6, 38, 39, 40–3, 51, 151
Pelling, Henry 12, 81, 166–7
Pelly, Lewis 193, 196
Percy, Earl 145–6
Pere Lachaise Cemetry 88
Peto, Sir Samuel Moreton 85
Place, Francis 14, 19, 20, 36n29, 60, 62, 77,148, 150, 160
Police Reform Act (1839) 51–2
Poor Man's Guardian 104
Popay, Sergeant 43–5, 55n20
Poplar 185

Port, Michael 191
Porter, Roy 238
Portman, Edward Berkeley 62, 63
Potter, Beatrice 180
Potter, George 9
Powell, Thomas 105
Preston 185
Priestley, Joseph 99
Primrose Hill 86
Primrose League 182–3
Prompter, The 102
Prout, Thomas 150
Public houses 83–4, 88–9, 173, 180
Pugh, Martin 168

Quakers 98
Quelch, Harry 88

Railways 211, 213, 218–19, 223, 226, 228
Ranters, the 97
Rational Society 104
Reddalls, G. H. 130
Redfern, Percy 90
Reform Act (1832) 4–6, 51, 57, 62, 79, 132, 145, 150, 161
Reform Act (1867) 9–10, 122, 133, 145, 154, 159
Reform Act (1884–85) 11, 145, 157, 212
Reform League 128–30, 132–4
Reform Union (Manchester) 9, 128–30
Religious Census, 1851 110
Report on the Sanitary Condition of the Labouring Population of Great Britain 64, 65
Republican 102, 134
Republicanism 89–90, 102, 130–4
Reynolds's Newspaper 57, 89
Riots
  Anti Dilke republican riots 1871 89
  Church and King mobs 99
  Gordon Riots 99
  Murphy 168
  Sunday Trading (1855) 92
  West End Riots 1886 Figure 1, Figure 7
Ritchie, Mr 176–7

Roberts, Matthew   215
Robinson, Revd Grantham   218
Rockingham, Marquis of   144
Rogers, J. E. Thorold   180–1, 184
Rogers, Nicholas   24
Romilly   62, 147
Roseberry, Lord   193
Rotherhithe, St Mary   5
Rothschild, Lord   177
Rotunda, the   106
Rous, Henry   151–2, 160–1
Rowan, Sir Charles   44–5
Rowe D. J.   77
Rowntree, Seebohm   171
Royal College   66
Royal College of Surgeons   66
Royal Geographical Society   199, 201
Royle, Edward   108
Rudé, George   30
Russell Lord John   7, 9, 60–74
   followers of   57–74
Russell family   61
Rutherford, Mark   234

St George's in the East   167, 172–90
St Pancras parish   5
Salisbury, Lord   11, 193
Salvation Army   107, 195
Saturday Review   198
Savage, Mike   169, 185, 213–14
Schneer, Jonathan   191
Scoble, Andrew MP   193
Scotland   107, 127
Secularism   8, 97–120, 177–8, 239
Seklew, Melfew   114
Shadwell   178–9
Sharpe, William MP   193
Sharples, Eliza   103
Sheffield   130, 134
Shelley, Sir John Villiers   152–3
Silk weavers   91–2
Sims, George R.   195
Six Acts, The   148
Slavery   63
Smith, J. P., critic of police   42
Smith, Sydney   159
Smith, Thomas Southwood   65–70, 74n66
Smith, W. H.   12, 153–61, 237

Smithfield   87
Social Democratic Federation   92, 231n23
Society for Improving the Conditions of the labouring Classes   66
Society for the Suppression of Vice   101
Somers, Lord   61
Southampton, Earl of   61
Southcott, Joanna   99
Southgate, Donald   7
South London Mail   197–8, 202, 204
South London Observer   201
South London Press   200
South Place Ethical Society   111–12
Southwark   3, 5, 10, 11, 22, 23, 26, 79, 134
Spectator, The   144
Stanhope, Lincoln   72n33
Stanley, Henry Morton   13, 191–210, 237
Star, The   197, 201, 203
Starr, Mark   87
Stepney   167, 172–90
Stepniak [Sergius Mikhailovich Kravchinsky]   114
Stewart, William   114
Stoke Newington   10, 234
Storch, R. D.   50
Strand   Figure 1
Stratford le Bow   5
Streatham   5, 10
Suburbanisation   13–14, 114, 211–30
Sullivan, T. D.   87
Sunderland, David   123, 171
Surrey   5

Tanner, Duncan   12, 167, 173
Taylor, Antony   7–8, 108–9, 236, 239
Taylor, Miles   6
Temperance   90–1, 174–5
Thompson, Dorothy   91
Thompson, E. P.   99
Thompson, F. M. L.   168
Thompson, Paul   173
Thorne, Roland G.   32–3
Tippu Tibb   199
Tillett, Ben   184
Times, The   11, 46

Tooke, John Horne 19, 22, 25, 31
Torrens, W. A., MP 83
Tottenham 13, 215
Tottenham and Hampstead Railway 10
Tower Hamlets 5, 10, 11, 61, 75, 82, 83, 171
Toynbee, Joseph 66, 67
Trafalgar Square 88, 124, 236
Trevelyan, Charles 202, 203
TUC 127
Twelvetrees, Harper 84
Tyler, Wat 87, Figure 5

Unitarians 111

Vernon, James 75, 183
Victoria, Queen 192
Voltaire 113

Wakely, Thomas, MP 83, 85
Wales 127, 238
Walthamstow 13–14, 211–32, 235
Walthamstow Chronicle 219
Walthamstow Guardian 221
Walthamstow Reporter 225
Walthamstow Whip 222, 223, 224–5
Walton, J. K. 90
Wapping 178–9
Warner, Courtenay MP 224, 229
Watts, Charles 130, 133
Webb, Sidney 199
Webb Street School 68
Wedderburn, Robert 106
Weinstein, Ben 7, 239

Wellesley, Marquess of 25
Wellington, Duke of 41
Westerton, Charles 152
West Ham 13, 215
Westminster, Borough of 3, 4, 5, 10, 11, 12, 20, 22–34, 30–3, 64, 79, 82, 144–65, 237, Figure 9
Westminster, Duke of 61, 153
Westminster Conservative Association 156
Whig Party 42, 57–74, 83
White, Alfred 237–8
Whittingham, Walter Basden 223–4
Wilkes, John 4, 22, 24, 27–30, 34, 79, 83, 89, 235, 236
Wilkinson, W. A., MP 83
Willesden 13
Williams, Sarah 180
Wilson, Sir Robert 26
Wimbledon Common 88
Windscheffel, Alex 13, 215, 236–7
Winstanley, Gerrard 98, 118n4
Women and politics 181–5
Wood, Sir Thomas 5
Woods, Sam 229
Woollacott, Angela 191
Woolwich 6
Wright, Patrick 237
Wynn, Charles, MP for Montgomeryshire 5

Yorkshire 22, 75, 77, 81, 90, 107, 128, 130, 131
Young, David 231n23
Yule, Col. Henry 199